Freedom and Its Conditions

Freedom
and Its Conditions
Discipline, Autonomy, and Resistance

Richard E. Flathman

ROUTLEDGE
NEW YORK AND LONDON

Published in 2003 by
Routledge
29 West 35th Street
New York, NY 10001
www.routledge-ny.com

Published in Great Britain by
Routledge
11 New Fetter Lane
London EC4P 4EE
www.routledge.co.uk

Routledge is an imprint of the Taylor and Francis Group.

Printed in the United States of America on acid-free paper.

10   9   8   7   6   5   4   3   2   1

Library of Congress Cataloging-in-Publication Data

Flathman, Richard E.
  Freedom and its conditions : discipline, autonomy, and resistance /
Richard E. Flathman.
      p. cm.
Includes bibliographical references and index.
  ISBN 0–415–94561–5 (cloth : alk. paper) — ISBN 0–415–94562–3 (pbk. :
alk. paper)
  1. Liberty. 2. Liberty—Philosophy. I. Title.
  JC585.F553 2003
  320′.01′1—dc21

                                                      2003006789

For Nancy, love of my life

Contents

Acknowledgments ix

Chapter 1 Introduction 1

Chapter 2 Discipline, Freedom, and Resistance 11
Preliminary Reflections by Way of an Engagement with Foucault

Chapter 3 The Self Against and for Itself: I 37
Montaigne on Freedom, Discipline, and Resistance

Chapter 4 The Self Against and for Itself: II 65
Nietzsche as Theorist of Disciplined Freedom of Action and Free-Spiritedness

Chapter 5 Stuart Hampshire on Freedoms and Unfreedoms of Mind and of Action 101

Chapter 6 Stuart Hampshire on Freedoms and Unfreedoms of Action 125
Freedom, Discipline, and Resistance

Conclusion 163

Notes 171

Bibliography of Works Cited 187

Index 189

Acknowledgments

It is a pleasure to express my thanks to the numerous colleagues, students, and friends who have given me valuable assistance in writing this book. Jane Bennett, Bill Connolly, Sean Greenberg, John Marshall, Jerry Schneewind, John Tambornino, Peter Digeser, and Matt Scherer all read and commented helpfully on one or more of the chapters. At John Marshall's kind invitation, Chapters One to Three were presented to the Seminar in Moral and Political Thought at Johns Hopkins, and discussions on those three occasions, which were attended by students and faculty from several departments, were lively and provocative. At David Weinstein's invitation parts of the manuscript were presented as the Steintrager Lecture at Wake Forest University. My thanks to David and his colleagues and students for an agreeable and stimulating two days. The chapter on Foucault was presented to the Department of Political Science at the Australian National University where I was privileged to spend several months as a Visiting Research Professor. Many thanks to John Hart, David West, Barry Hindess, and Bob Goodin for much enjoyable conversation and superb hospitality. It was also read and helpfully discussed by my long-time friend Paul Brass. Two of the chapters were presented at the Annual Meetings of the American Political Science Association, and Chapter Three has been published in revised form in *The Monist*, volume 83, no. 4, pp. 491–521. The issues explored and thinkers engaged in the book have been prominent in graduate and undergraduate seminars and classes at Johns Hopkins. I continue to be deeply indebted to the superb Hopkins students. It would not be possible adequately to convey the pleasures I have enjoyed in working with them now more than twenty years. Thanks also to the several anonymous referees who critiqued the manuscript for presses to which it was submitted. In revising the work, I have done my best to respond to their often trenchant but always instructive assessments of it.

Special thanks to Lisa Williams. Without her expert and always good-natured help this work would remain lost somewhere in the, to me, impenetrable maze of a succession of computers.

Complete references to all works cited are given in the Bibliography.

As always, my greatest debt is to the wonderful person to whom the book is dedicated and to our three amazing daughters, Kris, Karen, and Jen.

Si l'on peut-être fier de quelque chose, n'est-ce pas d'un pouvoir acquis par soi-même dont nous sommes à la fois la cause, l'effet, le principe et le resultat.

Balzac, *La Fille aux Yeux d'Or*

—

CHAPTER 1

Introduction

How should we understand the relationship between discipline and freedom? What do either or both have to do with the idea of resistance to others and/or to culturally, socially, or politically established norms and expectations, authorities, and powers? These are the questions explored in this work.

On the views that I have previously accepted and advanced, basically the promotion of the fullest possible freedom "negatively" understood (in the tradition of Hobbes, Constant, and Berlin), it is not easy to resist the thought that discipline and freedom stand in a relationship of antagonism if not mutual incompatibility. If freedom is the absence of impediments or obstacles to movement and to action, and if discipline is constraint, restriction, control, and the like, then the one would appear to exclude, deflect, or at least diminish the other.[1] On this view, it follows that resistance to attempts at discipline and control will very often be necessary to achieving and maintaining freedom of movement and action.

Notions such as autonomy, independence, and authenticity, and also concepts prominent here such as self-overcoming and self-enactment, are often and cogently used to qualify the understanding just sketched. If I discipline myself, if the constraints on me (for example, constraints I myself place on my own "first-order" desires and especially "first-order" volitions) are self-imposed, then the fact that I myself have chosen—willed—the restraints seems to take from the latter the quality of eliminating or diminishing my freedom.[2] We are familiar with the doctrine that freedom consists in obeying a "law" that the self legislates to itself. Of course, from Kant and Rousseau forward, this line of thinking has been put to repugnant uses by impersonalist, agent neutral, and other true or higher self theorists who claim, all appearances to the contrary notwithstanding, that constraints or disciplines that in fact are imposed by law, by parents, teachers, social workers, therapists, and the like somehow originate with or at least are legitimated by me.

At the level of the conceptualization of freedom, I have little to add to what I have previously said about these absurdities.

But there are numerous complications and complexities that require further attention. Some of these are signaled by deployments of the notion of situatedness that is less patently moraline than that of—for example— Charles Taylor and Taylor's Hegel. Assume that we begin our reflections on these matters with a Wittgensteinian theory of meaning as use and with a Wittgensteinian/Davidsonian theory of action as consisting of desires, beliefs, intentions, purposes, and movements or utterances. If we do so, we will realize that the meaning of what I do will be partly due to, that is partly dependent on, the rules, conventions, and so forth of the language-games and forms of life in which I do X. To this extent, the argument that action is always "situated" requires our endorsement.

There are, however, well-trodden paths that one can take in order to reconcile, at least conceptually, the freedom of agents and the various forms of other-imposed disciplines that come along with situatedness. Following these paths allows us to recognize the situated character of action but also to hold open the possibility that individuals both can and may act in ways that are influenced but neither fully determined nor morally or jurally required by social, moral, or political norms and rules. Why do I perform *this* speech- or other act? The Wittgensteinian/Davidsonian conditions are enabling, but the very moves that they open up—for example, moves that foreground the ineliminable indeterminacy of all norms, rules, and even commands— leave unsettled whether I do *this* or *that* among the numerous possibilities that are, so to speak, made available to me by my linguistic and more generally cultural, social, and political surroundings.[3]

Some further considerations relevant here are provided by the Benn-Weinstein[4] (but more generally Austinian) argument that significant or felicitous (as Austin liked to say) talks about freedom ordinarily takes place (jokes, play-acting, and the like aside) in settings in which something is at issue, in which some form of action or some achievement or accomplishment matters to me but is not assured to me. On this cogent view, we don't worry/talk about freedom in respect to actions or types of action about which we are indifferent or to which we can think of no practicable alternatives. But there is another and less explored side to this understanding. It seems to be equally the case that we would not think or talk about freedom—however much the action mattered to us—if no other persons were threatening to interfere with our actions and/or nothing in our moral and political circumstances constrained or inhibited us from taking those actions. [5] It is the presence of attempts to constrain me—or the existence of forces constraining me—from doing that which I want to do, preventing me from accomplishing the purposes that I have set for myself, that, existentially and perhaps semantically, perhaps phenomenologically, perhaps ontologically, are necessary to the question of freedom arising and hence being answered negatively or positively.

On this latter view, strongly suggested by Nietzsche and Foucault, and earlier by thinkers explored here, namely Sextus Empiricus and especially Montaigne, discipline and freedom, so far from being antithetical, are not only imbricated but mutually dependent. Or rather, attempts by other persons or by society more generally to impose discipline on me are necessary conditions of questions about freedom arising in a meaningful way, but—with the possible exception of self-discipline—the at least (possible?) partial failure of those attempts is a necessary condition of saying that this or that act was done freely or done in freedom. To take an example from a leading formulation in the "negative" freedom tradition, when Hobbes talks about inanimate objects moving freely, he is implicitly saying that the movements have overcome the resistance created by other forces, for example, inertia and gravity. Hobbes's attribution of freedom to inanimate objects is conceptually inappropriate and is rejected below. But his more general point that a world of conflicting forces is the conceptual and indeed the ontological condition of a world in which "freedom" has meaningful uses deserves acceptance.

I conclude this introduction by anticipating a few of the arguments that are developed in the body of the work. First, however, a word concerning the selections I have made of thinkers to be engaged in addressing the issues sketched above. These remarks are followed by a brief comment concerning a secondary objective that is in my mind as I explore and respond to the four theorists primarily addressed.

Why Foucault, Montaigne, Nietzsche, and Hampshire? And why proceed ahistorically and perhaps anachronistically by beginning with Foucault and then turning to Montaigne, Nietzsche, and Hampshire? As to the first question, critical reflection concerning freedom and unfreedom has been pervasive in philosophy, political theory, and other domains of thought from the Greeks to the present. Accordingly, there are any number of thinkers whose works would repay close attention and there is no right or best choice or choices to be made among them. In returning to issues that I had discussed in previous publications, I wanted to enlarge the scope of my reflections by taking up formulations that I had considered, if at all, only in passing in previous works. More particularly, I wanted to address thinkers who had an abiding concern with freedom but also with ideas concerning discipline and resistance, ideas which I had come to think vital to the theory of freedom. Because previous reading and teaching had intensified my awareness that the four thinkers I have chosen satisfied this criterion especially well, I elected to focus my attentions on their writings. The justification for these choices, which of course is not an argument against numerous eligible alternatives, must primarily be provided by the detailed explorations presented in the chapters that follow.

I begin with Foucault primarily because it was by reading and teaching his works that I came to realize that he repeatedly speaks directly and provocatively to questions that I had previously neglected. Issues concerning discipline and resistance are at the center of much of his work, and they are very often addressed with more or less specific reference to their bearing on freedom and unfreedom. Accordingly, there are important respects in which my engagements with the other three thinkers were inflected and in part framed by understandings arrived at in attempting to understand and assess his formulations. Readers of an historical bent more decided than my own may think that it would have been better to subordinate this anecdotal fact and present the materials in the order in which they became available to students of these subjects. I considered but rejected this option primarily because I found that my discussions of Montaigne and Nietzsche were difficult to articulate without frequent references to Foucault. Once again, the merits of this procedure must be shown by the results achieved by following it.

Those familiar with Foucault's extensive debts to Nietzsche, and, in part, through the latter to Montaigne, may be untroubled by my considering them together and by the sequences in which I do so. It may be objected, however, that Hampshire does not belong in this company, a view expressed by more than one of the early readers of the manuscript. It is not difficult to understand the objection. As I note at the beginning of the first of the two Hampshire chapters, the British philosopher makes no references to Foucault and only a few references or allusions to Montaigne and Nietzsche. Certainly his intellectual formation and much of his stylistics are importantly different from theirs. Hence engaging his thinking in company with the three other thinkers considered requires some adjustments or adaptations in the stance taken or protocols followed by readers. Recognizing this, I have compressed somewhat my original responses to Hampshire and have altered the presentation to make it more readily accessible to readers largely unfamiliar with his writings. I have also inserted, at the beginning of each of the chapters, outlines of topics and sub-topics by which the discussions are organized.

I remain convinced, however, that engaging Hampshire not only enlarges but in important respects deepens the reflections stimulated by the other three thinkers. To begin with, there is no denying that his interest in questions about freedom is as continuous and intense as that of the other three thinkers discussed. More important, his thinking about freedom is repeatedly interwoven with reflections concerning various modes of discipline. In the earliest of his writings questions about discipline and resistance are discussed primarily with reference to forms of discipline that individual persons exercise over themselves and ways in which concern for their freedoms of thought and action require them to resist impulses and dispositions that work against attaining and sustaining such freedoms. Discipline and resistance in any robust sense of the qualifier "political," as well as recognizably political questions generally, figure primarily in his later writings, but when they make their appearances they are addressed with vigor and in my estimation with considerable originality. With something of an exception for Nietzsche (especially the Nietzsche of substantial stretches of the collection *Will to Power*), Hampshire gives closer attention to issues in epistemology and the philosophy of mind than the other three, and he convinces me that numerous such issues are highly pertinent to thinking about freedom and unfreedom. These issues are of course highly complex and cannot be usefully discussed in a few paragraphs or pages.

The secondary objective mentioned above concerns my continuing attempt to broaden and enrich the theoretical resources available to thinking under the ideological rubric of liberalism. There was no such thing as liberalism in Montaigne's time and he of course does not refer to it or identify with it. Primarily because of his robust promotion of a broad religious tolerance, he has occasionally been characterized as a "proto-liberal," as a thinker who not only anticipated but provided powerful support for views that soon became a main feature of liberal ideology. Together with, or rather strongly augmented by, his distinctive championing of self-made or self-enacted individualities, these features of his thinking are reason both for characterizing him as a precursor of liberalism and for appropriating his thoughts in the continuing attempt to strengthen, deepen, and perhaps toughen liberal thinking.

Nietzsche, Foucault, and Hampshire are of course familiar with various of the formulations of liberal ideology. Nietzsche makes not more than a few references to them, most of which are dismissive and sometimes openly disdainful. As with the other three, my argument is not that Nietzsche should be classified as a liberal, but rather that elements of his thinking, especially his strong voluntarism and his closely related enthusiasm for the ideal of individual free-spiritedness, can strengthen features always present in but too often recessive components of liberal thinking and practicing. Foucault is sometimes friendly toward recognizably liberal views. To my knowledge he nowhere identifies himself as a liberal but, in part for reasons similar to those mentioned concerning Montaigne and Nietzsche, his abiding concern for freedom and his view that discipline and resistance are often essential to its realization, contribute strongly to liberal thinking. Finally, Hampshire is unequivocal in his admiration for leading features of liberal societies and polities. If it would be misleading and perhaps simply wrong to treat him *as* a liberal, I argue that liberalism would be enriched if self-designated liberals and their critics were receptive and responsive to his nuanced reflections. As with Montaigne and Nietzsche, the strongest case for this judgment resides in his dispositional skepticism and his enthusiasm for a pluralism sufficiently robust to embrace notions of individuality reaching to what he calls singularity.

The detailed conclusions of these engagements are developed in the course of the several chapters and gathered in the Conclusion. To briefly reiterate and anticipate, in the terms in which I have posed the issues primarily discussed, perhaps the most general result of these reflections is that there is no general, certainly no categorical, incompatibility between freedom on the one hand and discipline and resistance on the other. The least controversial of these conclusions is the view that resistance to forces seeking to destroy or limit freedom of action is very often if not always necessary to achieving and maintaining the latter. The most general argument for this conclusion is the one sketched above, namely that the presence of forces preventing or impeding freedom is a usual if not an invariable condition of significant thinking and acting that employs or involves the concepts freedom and unfreedom. If or to the extent that this conceptual or linguistic thesis is true, it also follows that freedom can be achieved and sustained only if the person or persons seeking it discipline themselves sufficiently to be able to resist the forces opposing their attempts to do so.

There are, however, qualifications that need to be entered to both the conceptual and the descriptive or existential claims just stated. On the conceptual point, at least two qualifications must be made. First, the acting agent's awareness of the presence of actually or potentially restricting forces varies from person to person and case to case. If, as is often the case with, say, a person ordering a meal, the awareness diminishes to the vanishing point, the agent will simply take the action and the question of freedom or unfreedom to do so will not arise. To repeat, as the agent's awareness of obstacles and impediments increases, the likelihood that these concepts will come into play increases with it. A related point applies to the descriptions given by others of an agent's actions, and especially of generalizing characterizations of the extent to which freedom or unfreedom obtain in a society or polity. As to characterizations of the actions of individuals, even if you do not do so, I may say of you that it was welcome or regrettable that you encountered no resistance to your attempts to X. As to generalizations concerning a society or polity, I may express similar judgments concerning the conditions that generally obtain in it, for example, that it is a free society, one worthy of respect because it is distinguished by the presence in it of a large number of freedoms of thought and action.

Related observations apply to the existential thesis. In a more or less stable and orderly society, what Hampshire calls a minimally decent society, large numbers of persons may quite often encounter little or no constraints on or obstacles to numerous of their day-to-day activities and hence may experience little or no need to discipline themselves to resist conflicting forces. To the extent that this is reliably the case, they may feel little or no need to sustain and keep at the ready the resources necessary to effective resistance. Of course there is a normative issue lurking here. Those who think that such conditions obtain may welcome them and may resent the suggestion that they or their society should not be described as free. Social and political theorists who champion a highly stable and integrated society, for example, some communitarian thinkers, are disposed to this view and hence oppose the argument that the capacity for and a readiness to engage in resistance to social and political institutions and arrangements is, or frequently is, a condition of freedom. Indeed, those who frequently disobey or otherwise resist laws and other norms will be disapproved of and often punished. Against this view, and together with the thinkers engaged here, I argue that competition and conflict, and hence the capacity and willingness to engage effectively in them, are marks of a free society and for that reason worthy of approval and other forms of encouragement.

In part because I think of freedom and unfreedom as first and foremost conditions of individual persons, much of the argument for these conclusions concerns the thinking and acting of such individuals or individual "selves." In the titles of the chapters engaging with Montaigne and Nietzsche, and at intervals throughout the essays, I write of the "self for and against itself."

The basic thought here is that selves are complex entities some of the features of which contribute to the possibility and likelihood of their freedom, others of which diminish that possibility. Insofar as the individual seeks freedom, she must discipline herself to control those features of herself that operate against her freedom, and to develop those that work for it. In Montaigne's language, the self must "make" or "enact" itself so as to achieve and sustain the capacities and other characteristics that enable and otherwise contribute to her freedom. In Nietzsche's parlance, the self must "overcome" those inclinations and dispositions that work against her freedom, and develop what he calls "free-spiritedness," a state of being that enhances the self's courage, inventiveness, and related characteristics that enable spirited action.

Readers familiar with controversies concerning freedom will recognize that arguments of the kinds just sketched are most commonly advanced by theorists of what has come to be called "positive" rather than "negative" freedom. This is primarily because the arguments advance distinctions, prominent in theories of positive freedom, that distinguish between "higher" and "lower, "better" and "worse" selves and that tie, conceptually and otherwise, the attribution of freedom to actions taken by the higher or better self. Following the thinkers with whom I primarily engage, I move in this direction in that I partly endorse notions of autonomy, authenticity, independence, and the like, and I recognize that forms or regimens of discipline and the capacity for resistance that they enable are widely and on the whole correctly taken to be necessary to autonomous or independent action and hence strongly contributive to freedom in one important sense of the term. But I argue that what I call freedoms of action, when the actions in question manifest only minimal elements of autonomy, are legitimate and worthy instances of freedom. (In terminology I earlier used and that I introduce in later chapters, I call freedoms in this sense "freedoms2.")

There are two related aspects or dimensions to this argument. The first is that theories that foreground a distinction between action and autonomous action (below denominated "freedoms3") exaggerate the differences between them. To characterize an attempted mode of conduct as an action is ordinarily to attribute to the actor an element or component of thinking. Actions—as distinct from movements or behaviors—include elements such as beliefs, desires, intentions, and purposes, all of which may be influenced in various ways by other agents and by social and political arrangements and forces but none of which can be entirely reduced to the effects on the actor of considerations or forces external to her own thinking. On this view, all attempts at actions are the agent's own; if or to the extent that she is successful in taking them, she acts in freedom. We may say that autonomous actions are more entirely or completely the agent's own and there is an understandable temptation to say that they represent fuller and more estimable examples of freedom than freedoms of action. In addition to the first point just mentioned, however, this is not a convincing reason for the judgment that actions which display no more than the minimal characteristics necessary to calling them actions are unfree. In company with numerous theorists of negative freedom, I argue that such judgments are both unwarranted and dangerous. They are unwarranted for reasons already mentioned and developed more fully below, and they are dangerous to freedom because they license other agents to intervene in the actor's thinking and acting, often in the name of her freedom, so as to elevate her to autonomy.

Secondly, I argue that autonomy should be construed, primarily, in what can be called formal rather than substantive terms. Autonomy requires that the agent think critically about her beliefs, desires, and so forth; that she subject them to critical assessment before or while attempting to take them. But it does not require that she reach conclusions concerning them that meet already established or envisioned criteria of correctness, truth, or other epistemological or normative standards. I may think that the agent's assessments of her beliefs and values are mistaken or otherwise indefensible by standards that I endorse, but thinking this does not warrant the conclusion that they are not her own or that she is unfree because she is mistaken. If I am convinced that she is mistaken, in particular if I think that, if not prevented, her actions will be seriously harmful to me, to others, or to the society or polity, I may think that there is justification for trying to dissuade her from her views and, if this attempt is unsuccessful, to try to prevent her—perhaps forcibly—from attempting to act on them. But those who do so, in particular those who use force against her, must recognize that in doing so they act to restrict or diminish her freedom. They must defend their interventions in the face of this recognition. In short, while I do not deny that knowing the truth can contribute to one's freedom (just assuming that there is a knowable truth in the relevant respects), I reject what seems to be the biblical view (see John 8:32) that knowing the truth is a necessary or at least a sufficient condition of freedom. These and a number of related arguments are developed in greater detail in the chapters that follow and are gathered and extended somewhat in the Conclusion.

CHAPTER 2

Discipline, Freedom, and Resistance

Preliminary Reflections by Way of an Engagement with Foucault

I begin this engagement with Foucault by reworking his most famous title, that is, *Discipline and Punish*.[1] What if we write "Discipline and Freedom" rather than "Discipline and Punish"? To sharpen the question, what if we take something like the retributivist line about punishment and say that punishment is warranted only in regard to those of my actions that are an at least partially successful resistance to the attempts of others to direct, control, or constrain me? Punishment can be jurally warranted only where there is criminality or delinquency (*nulla poena sine lege* and *nulla poena sine crimen*), that is, only when controlling or disciplining conventions, rules, or directives are in place. But the mere fact that authoritative norms or commands have been established is only a necessary not a sufficient condition of those further forms of disciplining that are the infliction or attempted infliction of punishments. The latter are warranted if and only if I have succeeded in at least partially resisting the first form of disciplining, that is, if I have succeeded in acting in a fashion that contravenes the established or authoritative norms. On this view, perhaps encouraged by Foucault's various discussions of "local resistance" and more generally of the ways in which the attempts of others to discipline me often incite resistance on my part, disciplinary archipelagos or carcereal societies are at once the dearest friends and the most implacable enemies of freedom.[2]

As a first step toward an extended reflection concerning these issues and questions, toward what Foucault likes to call a "problematization" of these pervasive features of human interactions, I here engage a selection of Foucault's diverse, internally conflicted, and often ambiguous formulations.

I

In an interview published under the title "The Social Triumph of the Sexual Will,"[3] Foucault remarks that in *Discipline and Punish* and other previous works he "perhaps [had] insisted too much on the techniques of domination. What we call 'discipline' is something really important in this kind of institution [that is, institutions such as clinics and schools, asylums and prisons, and so on]; but it is only one aspect of the art of governing people in our societies. Having studied the field of power relations taking techniques of domination as a point of departure, I would like, in the years to come, to study power relations starting from the techniques of the self. [4] In every culture, I think, this self technology implies a set of truth obligations: discovering the truth, being enlightened by the truth, telling the truth. And all these are considered important either for the constitution of, or the transformation of, the self" (177–78). [5]

As indicated by Foucault's remarks about "truth," this shift of focus or emphasis should not be construed as an abandonment of his previous concern to identify the "epistemes" and to unearth the genealogical developments of truth/power constellations; constellations that "subject" individuals to various and typically insidious forms of domination as well as lesser forms of control by practices of "micro" or "pastoral" power. But even the forms of domination that had previously been his focus "subject" their addressees in both of the senses of "*assujettissement*" that Foucault repeatedly uses. The various processes of subjecting individuals and groups to domination "produce" "subjects" in the sense of agents or agencies that can be identified—differentiated—as capable of various forms of thought and action. They become subjects in the grammatical sense of a "who" or a "what" of whom or of which thoughts and actions can be predicated. Indeed, in *Discipline and Punish* and the other earlier works to which he refers in the interview in question, he had already placed very considerable emphasis on this aspect of the "productive" character of disciplining and even dominating power. It may not be too much to say that, for him, if (contrary to fact) we could imagine a human situation entirely without disciplining powers, we would thereby have banished from that situation any intelligible uses of the notions of agents and agency, actors and acting.[6] And we might thereby have rendered irrelevant the notion of freedom.[7]

These issues and themes are more fully explored in Foucault's subsequent work on techniques of the self. Accordingly, the latter writings are the primary focus of this chapter. Before turning to them, however, two points should be underlined. First the transition in question consists of changes in emphasis, not a radical departure from Foucault's earlier concerns. If he writes and speaks less often and less centrally of "domination," concern with the latter by no means disappears from his investigations. In his studies of ancient Greek thinking and practicing, for example, he repeatedly observes that women, slaves, and metics were routinely subjected to forms of domination so entire that the persons who were their objects could scarcely, if at all, be said to have had the status of "subjects" in the second of the two senses just noted. (These formulations represent what are arguably his most radical formulations of the notion of domination, a formulation that construes it as entire, or close to entire, determination.) Again, in his various remarks about Christianity, especially those concerning its monastic practices, he underlines the thoroughly, pervasively, subordinated position of the great preponderance of monks and nuns. Second and more important, for present purposes questions about "domination" are of great significance. If or insofar as practices of discipline and disciplining involve domination that removes, partly or entirely, those subjected to it from the category of subjects or agents, Foucault himself shows that we can speak of the freedom of the latter only in narrowly circumscribed ways. Those subjected to such domination achieve and sustain freedom only to the extent that they succeed, always with great difficulty in these circumstances, in resisting the disciplines that other agents and agencies seek to impose upon them. Foucault has great admiration for those who accomplish, however intermittently or narrowly, this difficult feat and there are moments in his earlier writings when it appears that freedom obtains in various carcereal archipelagos only to the extent that such "local resistance" is mounted with some degree of success.

In turning to the study of "techniques of the self" in the Greco-Roman world, he examines practices of discipline that involve important respects in which the subjects of the various disciplining techniques subject themselves to them. It is not always easy to discern exactly how Foucault evaluates disciplining practices of these kinds; whether, for example, he regards them as consistent with, contributive to, or destructive of the freedoms of those who subject themselves to them. But it is clear that he regards this as a more difficult issue than the question of whether or to what extent "dominating" forms of discipline allow of freedoms. In this regard, the concept of dominating disciplines provides a contrasting term or concept essential to the identification and assessment of techniques of the self that involve self-discipline but not domination by others.

II

As we might infer from the very terminology "techniques" or "technologies of the self," the forms of discipline that Foucault studied under these rubrics[8] are importantly applied or administered on or to the self by the self itself. He emphasizes, however, that the techniques, and more important their standing as culturally, socially, and politically appropriate forms of self-discipline, do not originate, or do not originate exclusively, from the individuals who adopt them and apply them to their own thinkings and doings. "If I am now interested in how the subject constitutes itself in an active fashion through practices of the self, those practices are nevertheless not something invented by the individual himself. They are models that he finds in his culture and are proposed, suggested, imposed upon him by his culture, his society, and his social group (1997, 291).[9]

These last remarks, in particular the reference to "imposition," will come as no surprise to those familiar with Foucault the theorist of "micro" powers and governmentalities that "produce" subjects whose characteristics are suited to the values and expectations (including, often, their own values and expectations as they have come to conceive of them) of the groups and societies, polities, and cultures in and from which their being is formed and enacted. If we found Foucault saying that individual Greeks and Romans invented and employed techniques of the self that owed nothing to relations of power or governmentality, we would have to classify him as an exceptionally, perhaps a uniquely, radical theorist of the distinction between ancients and moderns. But the tensions internal to the passage just quoted also signal, equally signal, other presently pertinent continuities between "early" and "late" Foucault. As part of sustaining his distinction between the two senses of *assujettissement*, even the most dispiriting of Foucault's analyses of capillary power emphasized the ways in which power relations not only allowed of or rather incited resistance on the part of subjects, but imposed on subjects the necessity of interpreting and applying social, cultural, and political norms and commands in their own thinking and acting. However effective micro powers and governmentalities have succeeded in making themselves, however much their subjects have internalized the requirements and expectations of those who oversee them from the tower of the cultural Panopticon, there is always room for those subjected to power to interpret the norms and commands of the power holders or wielders. And there are always possibilities for the former to resist the disciplines that the latter attempt to impose on them.[10] Regarding himself as an ethicist (as the champion of an ethos) for whom "ethics . . . is the practice of freedom," indeed for whom "Freedom is the ontological condition of ethics" (1997, 284), these beliefs are at the core of Foucault's thinking/being.

For purposes of this exploration, however, it is equally vital to note the qualifiers that Foucault attached to the remarks just quoted. "[F]or what is ethics, if not the practice of freedom, *the conscious [réfléchie] practice of freedom?* [E]thics *is the considered form that freedom takes when it is informed by reflection*" (Ibid., italics mine).

Whence the "consciousness," the reflection or reflexivity, that gives the distinctive freedom to the *tehknes* or *askeses* that constitute the techniques of the self. What does this consciousness free the self from? What does it free the self to do or to become? Perhaps more fundamentally, who or what are these selves who or which practice these disciplinary techniques on themselves? What characteristics, if any, differentiate them one from the others and how do these differentiations affect their interactions as they mutually and severally discipline themselves and seek to develop and sustain an ethos of freedom?

III

Foucault's answers to these questions change importantly as he moves from Greek to Roman materials and as he sketches the contrasts (which are evidently very important to him) between both Greek and Roman practices and those that became prevalent with the rise of Christianity. I begin with his sparse but strategic remarks concerning Christianity and its confessional and monastic institutions and practices.

As he reads the Christian record, Christianity does give great prominence to concern with the self, doing so in ways that, at the level of what he calls form or code, are often strongly reminiscent of Greek and Hellenistic doctrines. As regards substance or practice, however, Christianity is distinctive and distinctively objectionable in that the hermeneutics of the self that its confessional requirements imposed were for the sake of, had as their dominant objective, the renunciation or at least the strict subordination of the worldly or material self. There was a *souci de soi* and rigorous disciplines by and through which that concern was to be exercised, but its purposes were to convey to the self the truth or understanding that the self was definitively fallen, corrupt, and hence to be renounced. The Christian, in particular the monastic Christian, cared for, took concern with the worldly self, but only or primarily in order to rid herself of this very form or object of caring. *Souci de soi* had as its objective the improvement of the worldly self only in the sense of the self's bringing itself to a condition in which it ceased to care about itself, which led it to renounce such caring. Thus Christian discipline pursued *a kind* of reflective or conscious freedom. To the extent that the discipline was successful, it freed the self from care of or for its worldly or material condition and thereby freed itself to attend to its spiritual or otherworldly being. The *askesis* or *enkrateia* that the Christian self was urged/required to practice is a form of asceticism that is radical to the point of abnegation of the corporeal self. Although Foucault's account is written in a surprisingly antiseptic, non-judgmental prose,[11] it would be a naive or at least an undiscerning reader who construed these as evaluatively neutral. If by discipline we understand the self-renunciatory practices of Christian confessionalism and monasticism, discipline is indeed antithetical to *human* freedom. Because it aims to destroy or at least to renounce the material, worldly self, the self that is the subject of the quotidian predications of freedom and unfreedom, its objective is to annul, to obviate the possibility of, thinking, discourse, interaction concerning freedom.[12] Taken as worldly, the Christian self is resolutely against itself.

As noted, Foucault thought that forms of care of the self that may be contributive to human, terrestrial freedom became and importantly remain suspect in the modern world. And there are respects in which his discussions of the Greeks identify sources, independent of Christianity, of this anti-human (or inhuman) tendency. It will emerge, but only later in the present discussion, that some of his remarks along this line are pertinent to specifically political controversies presently being conducted under rubrics such as republicanism, communitarianism, and participatory or deliberative democracy. But it is clear that his archeological and genealogical investigations of the Greeks as well as the Romans were inspired primarily by the desire to unearth and make available conceptions of care of the self more friendly than Christianity and modernity to an ethos of terrestrial freedom.

The Greek thinking and practicing that drew Foucault's attentions certainly could not be accused of otherworldliness or of renunciation of the corporeal self. As he read the distinctive set of sources on which he concentrated, Greek thinkers and actors thought of ethics as the formulation and especially the enactment of an ethos understood as a way of being and hence of acting. As with the Romans who come after them in Foucault's narratives, the ethos that they cultivated gave pride of place to freedom. The freedom they sought, however, was the freedom of the self, the material or corporeal self, *to* become a something that it was not yet by thinking and acting in more reflective or more consciously self-controlled ways. By contrast with Christianity, the objective was not to escape, to achieve freedom *from* one's body, one's desires, and one's engagements with other selves, but rather to form, by self- and mutual-discipline, one's self, so as to enhance its being and its doings. Of course this disciplining required achieving freedom *from* the domination of impulses, desires, and inclinations, coming both from within and from without the self, that operated—as it were—of their own as distinct from the self's will; but the objective of this *askesis*, of these *tehknes*, was not purgation, renunciation, or even subordination, but rather achieving the mastery, by the several selves themselves, of their various qualities, characteristics, and relationships.

Reading between the lines, the foregoing would seem to be the elements or features of Greek thinking and practice that Foucault found most congenial. If this assessment is correct, it is neither easy nor impossible to question it. From what assumptions, perspective, or stance could a lover of freedom and individuality object to efforts by individuals to "overcome," to achieve and maintain control over, inclinations, dispositions, or tendencies in themselves of which they become aware in themselves but concerning which they are uncomfortable or dissatisfied? Let us assume, provisionally, that the self who is caring for itself experiences these tendencies as genuinely her own, as not imposed upon or insidiously instilled in her by social, political, or other forces or pressures that she regards as alien or antagonistic. At the same time, she assesses some among them as unwelcome, as in conflict or competition with other of her characteristics, objectives and ideals that she values highly and wants to cultivate and enact. By disciplining herself, by herself "saying no" to impulses and inclinations that she recognizes, acknowledges, are in a significant sense her own, "she," that is the person, self, ego that "she" would like to be, frees herself from qualities of herself that she regrets and at least to that extent frees herself to be or to become the self she has (now) imagined and wished for.

The experience of dissonance internal to the self, and the sometime gratifications of effecting, willfully as one might say, control over the contending forces, is not only a familiar but also a storied feature of lives in our societies. And Foucault's Greco-Roman studies (among many other such studies) make it difficult to deny that these experiences were also salient features of thinking and acting in societies prominent in the lineages of our own. On this or something akin to this understanding, the techniques, the disciplines, that the individual employs to care for her self are unobjectionable from the standpoint of freedom and individuality.

The question whether, when, or to what extent the assumption I provisionally made is justified is raised with some force by Foucault's more detailed examination of Greek thinking and practice. I turn to it just below. But a prior or at least a further question concerns what should be said regarding individuals who, whether knowingly or insouciantly, do not avail themselves of the technologies of self that are employed by other more self-disciplined members of the societies or cultures they inhabit. Such persons may or may not be notably aware of the conflicts and dissonances among their "first-order" desires and volitions, but in either case they "go with the flow" of their impulses as they experience them, acting on those that, here and now, strike them as the strongest, the most immediate, urgent, resonant, and so forth. We can readily imagine that such persons— let's call them, following Frankfurt, "wantons"—will from time to time experience regret concerning the choices they have made and the actions they have taken. Having taken action A in order to satisfy desire X, they later realize that they therefore or thereby forwent, at least temporarily and perhaps permanently, action B and hence the satisfaction of desire Y. Even if pleased to have satisfied or at least done what they could in the attempt to satisfy desire X, it becomes evident to them that Y is also genuinely, authentically, among their desires and that by doing A they have postponed and perhaps forgone the possibility of doing B to satisfy Y. Nor is it implausible to think that, even on the assumptions I am now making, they might formulate this assessment as regret over having deprived themselves, at least for the moment and perhaps permanently, of the freedom to do B in order to satisfy Y.

Given the logical inevitability that doing A will <u>sometimes</u> preclude doing B, and given the high probability that, existentially, doing A will very often preclude doing B, regrets of the kind just outlined are of course not only prominent but pervasive features of worldly thinking and acting (perhaps it will be different in heaven!?). And if we think of unfreedom as being in a condition such that it is impossible for me to take actions that I desire or am otherwise disposed to take, it may be cogent to express these regrets in the language of unfreedom.

The distinction (or one plausible version of it) between regret and remorse may be helpful here. It would be an extremely fortunate person, a person with a lot of moral and other kinds of luck, who never had occasion to experience regret concerning her choices and actions. The most obvious respect in which fortune would have to have smiled on such a person is that her actions always or at least quite regularly achieved the objectives to which she had directed them. Cultivating *savoir-faire* and various other *virtus* (itself a form of self-discipline, albeit one that is not prominent in Foucault's discussions) can diminish this dependence on *fortuna*, but as Hannah Arendt and numerous others in the Machiavellian tradition have insisted, it can never eliminate it. For present purposes, however, the more salient question concerns whether, or rather the frequency with which, A finds that doing X to achieve Y itself prevents her from doing W to achieve Z. Continuing to assume that X and Y are, in her own mind, among her clear preferences, if she is also attracted to doing W and to achieving Z, she is likely to regret the fact that she could not do both X and W, could not satisfy her desire for both Y and Z. On this scenario, A does not regret doing X. She regrets, rather, the circumstantial fact that she could not do both X and W.

By contrast, we feel remorse when we become convinced that it was wrong—prudentially, morally, religiously, aesthetically—for us to choose action X and objective Y, having realized that doing so prevented us from doing W to achieve Z. On this construal of regret versus remorse, regret is directed outward; it concerns the circumstances or limiting conditions under which we must act. Remorse is reflexive; it is directed at ourselves for failing to make the right or the best choice between or among alternatives both or all of which genuinely attract or appeal to us.

A stringent construal of *epimelia houtou*, that is, disciplined care of the self, would be that its objective was/should be to eliminate regret from the life of the person who cares for herself by exercising self-discipline. The freedom resulting from *enkrateia* can be construed as freedom from regret concerning one's choices and actions. Yet more expansively interpreted, those who adequately, appropriately, care for themselves would thereby achieve and sustain what Hobbes called felicity, that is, a condition in which they had been, now are, and have good reason to expect to continue to be successful in acting to achieve all of the objectives that were and are genuinely their own, were and are authentic to them. In this case, the agent or subject would experience neither regret nor remorse. As suggested, there are lots of reasons for thinking that both of these related understandings, taken as the goals or objectives of a life, are recipes for frustration, for both regret and remorse. The first, more restricted conception, however, was seriously entertained and pursued by Stoic thinkers and receives apparently sympathetic consideration from Foucault. A version of the more grandiose second conception can be discerned in Foucault's readings of some of the "practical" Greek thinkers that he examines. I start with the latter.

On Foucault's reading of his Greek sources, *enkrateia* and the other modes of self-discipline that he studied (for example, *aphrodism, chresis, erotics*) were of course directed to achieving "mastery" of the self. The objective of these techniques was not purification, was not to rid the self of sexual and other desires, but to achieve control over them, to assure that they operated in the service or to the advantage of considered (*réfléchi*) objectives and purposes, above all the objective of living or manifesting in one's life an ethos of freedom. The concept opposed to or most sharply contrasted with *enkrateia* was *akrasia*, a kind of weakness in the face of or submissiveness to forces that worked against this highest objective. As Foucault construes it, however, for the Greeks *enkrateia* was importantly other-directed or directed outward as well as or even more importantly than it was aimed at the undesirable characteristics or tendencies that one became aware of in oneself. Or rather, one cultivated mastery of oneself in order to eliminate or reduce to the practical minimum the likelihood that one would have to submit to the control or domination of others. Those—women, slaves, metics—who are incapable of self-mastery, not only must but ought to submit to the rule of those who effectively discipline themselves.[13] Yet more strongly stated, achieving self-mastery had as one of its objectives preparation for ruling, properly, over others.[14] In this respect, self-discipline had a decidedly political character, although Foucault insists that it was regarded as essential to ruling in the household as well as the city (thereby rejecting or at least qualifying the Constantian and Arendtian view that Greek thinking about freedom focused exclusively on the city or polis).[15] Effectively deployed, technologies of the self instilled "moderation" in the sense of controlling tendencies to various excesses generated by passions, desires, and untutored dispositions. But it was a "virile" moderation that enabled rule over other persons as well as rule over oneself.[16]

On this understanding, discipline stands in a complex, even an intricate, relationship with freedom. The self, the ego, the *moi*, that disciplines itself thereby frees itself from the control of passions and desires—forces—that are part of it but that a something in itself regards as alien or antagonistic to itself. "It" thereby frees itself to do, be, and become a self, a *moi*, that it itself, it *lui-même*, aspires to become. The unfreedoms deliberately brought about by these technologies, that is, firstly, the suppression, repression, oppression, of desires and inclinations that the self itself (as it were) recognizes as elements in or of itself but regards as unwelcome, alien, or antagonistic are either not viewed as unfreedoms or perhaps are regarded as an exchange of bad for good freedoms. And, secondly, the unfreedoms imposed upon those other persons who have shown themselves to be (or are assumed to be) incapable of self-mastery, are regarded as fully, as unquestionably, justified.

We are, then, in the presence of an ethos that vaunts, that gave itself and that Foucault accords the name of, an ethos of freedom. The freedom that this ethos celebrates, however, has as its inevitable and at once hated and loved twin, double, or companion, unfreedoms of a) parts of the free self, and b) yet more unqualified or unregretted unfreedoms of other selves. As to a), let us try to imagine a person who has so effectively deployed the technologies of the self that she no longer experiences desires or inclinations that, substantively or materially as it were, she judges to be unwelcome or unworthy. Although this might be regarded as the ultimate or highest objective of *enkrateia*, achieving it would in fact constitute a self-defeat, *une deception, peut-être même un trahison, de lui-même*, of the most serious and pervasive kind. The ethos of freedom in question has deeply embedded within it a version of the conceptual point discussed early in this work, namely that we think and talk about, value, the freedom to do X primarily or perhaps exclusively when we are aware of forces that operate to prevent us from doing X, forces that we have to defeat or overcome in order to do X. If A has banished from herself all dissonant or conflicting tendencies or dispositions, we others might say of her that she is therefore free to do those things that she continues to desire or to choose to do. But a condition of her saying this to or of herself, a condition of her experiencing herself as free, would have been eliminated. It would make sense for us to say of her that she was free, but it would not be meaningful for her to say this of herself. Stated somewhat differently, the ethos of freedom in question is an agonal ethos, an ethos that celebrates freedom not, or not exclusively, as unobstructed or unopposed thinking and doing but as a triumph over conflicting and antagonistic forces within the self (and between or among selves). This is presumably why, at bottom, Foucault rejects what he takes to be the Christian ideal of purgation or purification of the self, and this feature of his thinking dramatizes the fact that, insofar as he admired the Greek ethos, what he admired in it is better described as discipline or mastery or control than as freedom. As he says, this ethos requires a hermeneutics, a self-knowing of the self by itself, but it more importantly requires an "aesthetics," a "stylization" of the self by and for itself. It champions "dietetics" not "therapeutics," "regimen" not "purgation."[17]

Related points, but with a more potent political resonance, apply to b). In this regard, the analogous pertinent (Rousseauist) thought experiment is to imagine a polis or polity none of the members of which are in conflict with one another or with society, but who at the same time are regarded and regard themselves as properly or justifiably subject to the political and legal control of its norms, institutions, and practices. Just as the idea of a unified, a homogeneous self, eliminates the agonal quality necessary to meaningful thinking and talking about freedom, so the idea of a fully consensual polity, a polity among the members of which there may be occasional disagreement but warranted hierarchy and super- and subordination, deprives all participants of a condition essential to their thinking of themselves as free, as enacting their ethos of freedom. The biconditionality of freedom is formally the same as with the self, albeit substantively different. Freedom is meaningful to me as, say, citizen or ruler, only if 1) I exercise it against conflicting forces, and only if 2) I successfully or effectively discipline or control those forces. Thus on Foucault's account of the Greek ethos of freedom, *enkrateia* was not only rule over one's self, it was also preparation for ruling over others. If there were no others properly to be ruled by me, or if I failed in my attempts to subject them to my rule, I would be free in no more than a nominal, an existentially or aesthetically empty, sense of the word.

Foucault's evident if rarely explicitly stated preference for Roman as against Greek thinking and practicing seems to be due to the ways in which the Stoics and Epicureans developed the idea of self-mastery while largely eliminating or severely subordinating its relationship to political and other forms of mastery over others.

IV

Close to the end of Volume III of *The History of Sexuality*, Foucault summarizes his findings concerning Roman thinking and practicing in the following terms: "Now, in these modifications of preexisting [that is, Greek] themes one can see the development of an art of existence dominated by self-preoccupation. The art of the self no longer focuses so much on the excesses that one can indulge in and that need to be mastered in order to exercise one's domination over others. It gives increasing emphasis to the frailty of the individual faced with the manifold ills that sexual activity can give rise to. It also underscores the need to subject that activity to a universal form by which one is bound, a form grounded in both nature and reason, and valid for all human beings. It likewise emphasizes the importance of developing all the practices and all the exercises by which one can maintain self-control and eventually arrive at a pure enjoyment of oneself. It is not the accentuation of the forms of prohibition that is behind these modifications of sexual ethics. It is the development of an art of existence that revolves around the question of the self, of its dependence and independence, of its universal form and of the connection it can and should establish with others, of the procedures by which it exerts its control over itself, and of the way in which it can establish a complete supremacy over itself."[18]

Foucault's understanding of the most evident Roman departure from Greek thinking, which also signals what he seems most to admire in the Roman ethos, is expressed in the second of the foregoing sentences. Mastery of the self, as we might put it, is for the self's own sake, not for the sake of the quality of one's relations with others. Earlier in the volume he is yet more direct concerning what might be regarded as the anti- or at least apolitical character of the Roman views on which he concentrated his attentions. By comparison with Greek thinking, "The basic attitude [of the Stoics and to some extent the Epicureans] that one must have toward political activity was related to the general principle that whatever one is, it is not owing to the rank one holds, to the responsibility one exercises, to the position in which one finds oneself—above or beneath other people. What one is, and what one needs to devote one's attention to as to an ultimate purpose, is the expression of a principle that is singular in its manifestation within each person, but universal by the form it assumes in everyone, and collective by the community bond it establishes between individuals" (Ibid., 93). The last two clauses of the last sentence will require further attention just below, but it is clear that insofar as politics involves dominating or being dominated, ruling and/or being ruled, on Foucault's account of Roman thought and practice, political activities and involvements were relevant to the care of the self primarily in the negative sense that engagement in or with them deflects, diminishes, and in the worst cases perhaps destroys the individual's capacity to achieve and maintain self-mastery.

There are of course diverse uses of the concepts "politics" and "political." If we adopt the now influential view that "the personal is the political" (a view that Foucault seems to embrace in various places in his writings), the Roman ethos that he describes and appears to endorse cannot be characterized as apolitical or as indifferent to political arrangements and interactions. It is clear however, that on his account the Roman champions and practitioners of this ethos did not look to political relationships as the means by which or the settings in which to pursue their "ultimate purposes." Owing to the pronounced tendency of politics to produce dominance and subordination—both of which threaten or tend to diminish self-mastery—persons seeking to achieve and sustain the latter may indeed be advised to keep a wary eye on both their own political inclinations and the political dispositions of those others with whom they must share a time and a place. And they must be prepared to resist attempts by others to dominate them. But first, to the extent that the ideal of self-mastery comes to pervade the thinking of those around them, the threat of domination by others will recede and the corresponding need for other-regarding political vigilance and resistance will diminish. Second, if or to the extent that watchfulness concerning the tendency of others to seek political domination remains necessary, those who properly care for themselves will maintain such vigilance for defensive purposes rather than in the expectation that sustaining it will itself, directly as it were, constitute or contribute to self-mastery. Even if not threatened by subordination of self to political others, the self will still have to struggle to discipline desires and dispositions internal but alien to the self itself, the self as it has imagined itself and wishes itself to become. It follows, thirdly, that the self-discipline that represses or controls the self's impulses to political domination over others is but one dimension, perhaps a minor or marginal one, of the objective of self-mastery.

In short, in Roman thinking and practicing as Foucault analyzed and assessed them, there is not so much as a hint of the more soaring of the Republican, Participatory/Strong/Deliberative Democratic conceptions of politics as Humanizing or Ennobling. At most there are muffled echoes or anticipations of the weak Republican view according to which prudence requires that amount of political involvement circumstantially possible and necessary for the Self to defeat or deflect the attempts of others to use the authority and power of politics, government, and various governmentalities to subordinate It, that is to defeat or circumscribe the attempt by others to put their domination in place of the self's Self-mastery.

V

Assuming that the foregoing discussions present a more or less accurate account of the thinkings/practicings that Foucault foregrounds in his late writings, how should liberals and others devoted to freedom and individuality assess them?

The easiest part of this question concerns those formulations of the discipline/freedom relationship about which Foucault's own judgments are most easily discerned, that is, the Christian view (as he characterizes it), according to which the object of self-discipline goes beyond self-mastery to renunciation of the material or worldly self. There are of course no liberal grounds for arguing that individuals who are attracted to the monastic and confessional practices that Foucault briefly describes should be prevented, by law or by the force of general disapproval, from engaging in them, and no such grounds for arguing that the institutions and practices that sustain and help to enforce these forms of discipline should be legally prohibited or morally or otherwise condemned. Liberals can and should share and give expression to Foucault's view that these ideas and practices promote renunciation and subordination, not freedom of the self, but those who subscribe to the ideas and choose to engage in the practices should be at liberty to do so. If those of this disposition attempt to persuade others of doctrines such as "Perfect service is perfect freedom," liberals should not only follow but be more forthright than Foucault in contesting their formulations. Freedom is first and foremost a condition of individual persons, of subjects in the second sense in which Foucault uses the term. Persons should be free, should be at liberty, to renounce, subjugate, alienate their standing or character as subjects if they so choose. And they should be at liberty to regard doing so as enhancing their freedom (no one has authority, no one has proprietary rights, over or concerning the "proper" use of the "essentially contestable" concept "freedom"). But because the very objective of these practices and the conception of freedom that goes with them is the elimination of personality, agency, and the capacity for action (or the reduction of these to the end of self-renunciation), Foucault and Nietzsche (among numerous others, for instance Hume) are correct that widespread acceptance of such practices and conceptions (whether of Christian or other provenances) would signal the triumph of discipline over all freedoms save the freedom to alienate freedoms in favor of discipline. Returning to the questions raised earlier, we might say that truly successful practitioners of such forms of discipline would free themselves from the influence of desires and impulses concerning which they had previously experienced remorse as well as regret. But in doing so they at once take from themselves the possibility of a vast array of actions that they would otherwise have been free to attempt (and that are conventionally regarded as paradigms of free action) and eliminate from themselves that conflict among desires and objectives the recurrence of which was then and continues to be one of the usual conditions of meaningful thinking and talking about freedom. We can say of them that they are and should be free to think and act and refrain from thinking and acting in this or that way; but we should also say what they presumably want to be able to say, proudly, of themselves, namely that they have used their freedom to discipline themselves so as to eliminate all of the other freedoms they might otherwise have had.[19]

For reasons already partly explored, assessment of Greek and Roman thinking and practicing is less straightforward. Reflection concerning Foucault's presentations and commentaries concerning them presses us to confront complexities such as those noted at the outset of this essay.

Given the commitment, to *epimelia houtou, enkrateia, souci de soi,* and other forms of care and concern for the worldly and material self, attributed by Foucault to the Greek and Roman thinkers/actors that he studied, it comes as no surprise that Foucault's discussions—and hence my responses to them—are pervaded by terms such as the self, the self itself, the ego, the *je* and the *moi,* and related notions. As we have seen, care of the self, understood as pursuing or trying to enact an ethos of freedom, entailed "truth obligations," in particular the obligation to discover and be enlightened and guided by the truth or truths about oneself. *Souci de soi* has, importantly and perhaps predominantly, a self-referential, introspective, possibly even narcissistic quality or character. At the same time, however, the idea of culturally adopted and transmitted "technologies" through the use of which proper care is exercised strongly suggests that the truths about myself will also be truths about all or at least some considerable number of other selves with whom I share a position or status in a culture, society, or various vocational and avocational groups and practices. Thus I can learn about myself, at least in part, by learning about other selves. The practice of caring for the self, while in one degree or another (varying between the Greeks and Romans) self-referential in orientation or purpose, requires the development and employment of a generalizing psychology, perhaps a philosophical psychology or philosophical anthropology.

This somewhat uneasy combination of self- and other-directedness is particularly pronounced in Foucault's explorations of the Greek materials he consulted. It seems that primary among the "truth obligations" that I must discharge is to determine whether or to what extent I am capable of sustaining those forms of self-discipline that my culture makes a condition of living, of enacting, an ethos of freedom. In ways that anticipate the "substance" but less so the form or code of the Roman views, making this determination does have a dimension or component that is quite narrowly personal and introspective. I experience, notice in myself, various desires, inclinations, dispositions, for example, for various foods and forms of drink and sex, recreational or avocational activities, and the like. Over time I become aware that acting on some of these passions and desires regularly produces substantial and continuing satisfactions or gratifications, while acting on others among them frequently leads to frustrations, regrets, and perhaps feelings of remorse. I must then assess my capacity to discipline myself to continue with the former types of actions and to avoid or restrict the latter. (As noted above, if it becomes clear to me that I entirely or largely lack this capacity, the best way for me to care for myself is to submit to the discipline, indeed the domination, of some other or others who possess it.)

For the Greeks, however, much of this coming to know the truth about oneself, perhaps its largest part, is interpersonal and interactive in character, and involves coming to know the truth about others as well as oneself. Most generally, I must determine whether those others with whom I interact are or are not capable of self-discipline. If I determine that some among them—women, children, slaves, metics are said to be the easiest cases—do not have this capacity, I must discipline and control them. By contrast, as regards those who are themselves capable of *epimelia houtou*, I must assure both that they do not dominate me and that I do not dominate them. Because in both cases my judgments must be based on accurate, true assessments of the characteristics of others—characteristics that are largely given to rather than created or produced by me—it is importantly the case that in attempting to care for myself and hence to practice the ethos of freedom I must be guided by, to take my bearings from, the capacities and dispositions of others as well as by and from my own capacities and dispositions. On this understanding, care of the self is not only other-regarding but importantly other-dependent. If this vulnerability of the self to others is most emphatic in the domain of politics, on Foucault's readings it is a pervasive feature of Greek thinking and practicing. And if I am correct in my intuition that Foucault preferred Roman to Greek understandings (it is not easy to say with entire confidence), it is because in his judgment the former, in particular the understandings of the Roman Stoics, recognized but labored to minimize the respects in which the self and its freedom are hostage to the thinking and acting of selves other than itself.

The merits of this view—whether or not it was Foucault's—are addressed below. But as preparation for assessing the details of Foucault's construals of and responses to Roman materials it will be instructive to look a bit more closely at one of the most charged features of his engagement with Greek thinking, that is, his treatment of relationships between men capable of *epimelia houtou* and boys who have not yet fully developed this capacity but can be expected to do so as they mature.

Whereas Christians regarded desires and pleasures as bad or evil in themselves and hence to be extirpated or eschewed to the greatest possible extent, Foucault's Greeks affirmed their value to human life but thought of them as potentially dangerous and hence in need of control. The self was to engage in an active struggle to understand and achieve mastery over these of its characteristics and tendencies. The aim was not innocence or purity but "self-domination" or a "virile moderation" that allowed of enjoyments but subjected them to an "aesthetics," a "stylization," that distinguished the better from the worse, the transient from the abiding, and that thereby constituted and allowed the enactment of an ethos of freedom (Michel Foucault, 1990, 48, 50, 73). As indicated by terms such as "aesthetics" and "stylization," this self-government, indeed this "self-enslavement" (79), was only in part a matter of following general rules or formulae, of employing techniques that were the same for all capable of care of the self. "We are a long way from a form of austerity that would tend to govern all individuals in the same way. . . . On the contrary, . . . everything was a matter of adjustment, circumstances and personal position. . . . [T]he individual did not make himself into an ethical subject by universalizing the principles that informed his action; on the contrary, he did so by means of an attitude and a quest that individualized his action, modulated it, and perhaps even gave him a special brilliance by virtue of the rational and deliberate structure his action manifested" (62).

At the same time, because the "Moral askesis formed part of the paideia of the free man who had a role to play in the city and in dealing with others," the ascetics "that enabled one to make oneself into an ethical subject was an integral part, . . . of the practice of a virtuous life, which was also the life of a 'free' man in the full, positive and political sense of the word" (77). Accordingly, at the levels of both code and substance, there were certain general principles of conduct that applied to all capable of *epimelia houtou*.

This somewhat tense or at least awkward combination of characteristics obtained in respect to the desire for and the pleasures found in erotic relations (including the genitally specific pleasures—taking, what is apparently now controversial in various quarters, the anal and oral apertures as genitalia or at least as "erogenous zones") between adult men and adolescent (but presumably post-pubescent?) boys. Erotic relations, or more generally relations of "love," between men and boys were "free" in both legal and cultural respects. That is, engaging in such relationships was, as such, subject neither to criminal penalty nor to cultural condemnation (216).

This "freedom," however, was qualified by at least two general principles or requirements. The first was that the relationship had to be free in the further sense that it involved no coercion or domination; specifically, the adolescent boy had to consent to the relationship. (By contrast, wives— and perhaps slaves and metics?—were obliged to submit, had a duty to submit, to the erotic desires of their husbands and masters.) But, secondly, both the adult and the boy had a further and more demanding responsibility. The adult male had to recognize that using the boy for his pleasures could compromise or diminish the likelihood that the boy would, on maturity, achieve the manhood, virility, and hence self-mastery appropriate to him. Thus, even if the boy consented to the relationship, if the adult foresaw such a diminishing outcome he was obliged to discipline himself from pursuing his pleasures and also (thereby and in additional ways) to discipline the boy if the latter sought to continue the relationship. And the boy, insofar as he could anticipate his future as a "free man in the full, positive, and political sense of the word," was obliged to resist the man's advances if he judged them likely to compromise the manhood that was his proper destiny. Thus on both sides of this culturally salient type of relationship, but in ways reiterated in various forms throughout the domain of interactions among men capable of an ethos of freedom, mutual freedom and self- but also mutual discipline were inseparable. In a modulation of Sammy Cahn's memorable phrasing, you could not have the one without both of the others.

Abstracting a bit from the specifics of the man/boy, husband/wife, master/slave relationships, it was then and is now both common and tempting to regard these Greek understandings and practices as 1) well-grounded in the actualities of human experience, and 2) worthy or even demanding of our endorsement and allegiance. As to the first, I cannot care for myself unless I know and am attentive/responsive to the characteristics that set me apart from others. But knowing, understanding, and caring for myself requires that I recognize that I am what I am in important part owing to my interactions with others and particularly to the circumstances that I share with others. The obligation to know the truth about oneself is not reducible to seeking the truth about others but it cannot be fully or adequately discharged apart from attention to the latter. In the now influential phrasing (often explicitly indebted to Greek thinking), self-knowing and the care of the self of which it is an essential component are ineliminably and deeply situated.

VI

Does acceptance, recognition, acknowledgment of 1) commit us to or at least impel us toward acceptance of 2)? There is no doubt that in important respects the answer is yes, and hence to acceptance of the further view that the influences exercised upon us by others, including the disciplines that they attempt to impose upon us, are integral to our thinking and acting and therefore to our attempts to develop and practice an ethos of freedom (or, for that matter, any other ethos). To the extent, always important, that I am what I am because of my relations with others and my participation (or my resistance to participation in) shared practices, institutions, and activities, I cannot know who or what I am, hence cannot care for myself, without close attention and responsiveness to others and to arrangements that I share with them. In the practicing of freedom, mutual disciplining and self-disciplining go as closely together as do Sammy Cahn's horse and carriage.

But the, to me, most inspired and inspiring moments in Foucault's reflections concerning these matters occur when (as I permit myself to read him) he deploys Hellenic/Roman thinking/practicing to modulate and hence in part to challenge 2).

Epictetus and in general the Stoics of the first and second centuries agreed with their Greek predecessors that the self needs help from others in order effectively to carry out the "etho-poietic function" of transforming a true understanding of the self into an ethos of freedom. Individuals learn as they teach and vice versa. Care of the self "is a matter of bringing into congruence the gaze of the other and that gaze which one aims at oneself when one measures one's everyday actions according [primarily or at least initially] to the [culturally established] rules of a technique of living (Foucault, 1997, 208–9, 214–15, 221). In this or rather these respects Foucault discerns and seems to endorse substantial continuities between Greek and Roman thinking/practicing. But this is primarily to say that he discerns and endorses their common acceptance of my proposition 1) above.

As regards 2), however, he identifies substantial divergences or disparities between the two sets of thinking/practicing that he studied. "A Greek citizen of the fifth or fourth century would have felt that his *tekhne* for life was to take care of the city, of his companions. But for Seneca, for instance, the problem is to take care of himself" (260). Seneca and his fellow Stoics would have agreed with the Greek view that "the care of the self . . . implies complex relations with others," perhaps even that it is, in part, a "way of caring for others" (287).[20] On their understanding, however, ideally or rather properly, interactions among selves are the reciprocal relations among persons who, severally, "are . . . masters of themselves." For the Romans, "mastery of oneself is something that is not primarily related to power over others: you have to be master of yourself not only in order to rule others [or to prevent others not eligible to do so from ruling over you], as it was in the case of Alcibiades or Nicocles, but you have to be master of yourself because you are a rational being" (267). The following passage deserves to be quoted again. In "these modifications of preexisting themes one can see the development of an art of existence dominated by self-preoccupation. The art of the self no longer focuses so much on the excesses that one can indulge in and that need to be mastered in order to exercise one's domination over others. [Rather,] [i]t gives increasing emphasis to the frailty of the individual faced with the manifold ills that [for example] sexual activity can give rise to" (238). More specifically as regards political relations, "The basic attitude [of the Stoics and to some extent the Epicureans] that one must have toward political activity was related to the general principle that whatever one is, it is not owing to the rank one holds, to the responsibility one exercises, to the position in which one finds oneself—above or beneath other people. What one is, and what one needs to devote one's attention to as to an ultimate purpose, is the expression of a principle that is singular in its manifestation within each person, but universal by the form it assumes in everyone, and collective by the community bond it establishes between individuals" (93).

I conclude this chapter by elaborating upon and responding to several features of these heartening remarks.

First, as the last of the quoted sentences indicate, in foregrounding "self-preoccupation" Foucault is neither attributing to the Romans nor associating himself with a radically "unsituated" conception of individuality. When an interviewer raised with him the question whether passages such as that just quoted do not align him with Sartre's notions of authenticity, he responded by associating himself, rather, with Nietzsche: "I think that the only acceptable practical consequence of what Sartre has said is to link his theoretical insight to the practice of creativity—and not that of authenticity. From the idea that the self is not given to us [which, of course, Foucault accepts], I think there is only one practical consequence: we have to create ourselves as a work of art. In his analyses of Baudelaire, Flaubert, and so on, it is interesting to see that Sartre refers the work of creation to a certain relation to oneself—the author to himself—which has the form of authenticity or inauthenticity. I would like to say exactly the contrary: we should not have to refer the creative activity of somebody to the kind of relation he has to himself, but should relate the kind of relation one has to oneself to a creative activity. Q[uestion]: That sounds like Nietzsche's observation in *The Gay Science* that one should create one's life by giving style to it through long practice and daily work {no. 290}. F[oucault]: Yes. My view is much closer to Nietzsche's than to Sartre's" (1997, 262).[21]

Care, mastery, creation of the self by itself presumes conceptions or ideals of care, of mastery, of "style" by which the self can assess the merits of its "daily work" on itself. One of the clear implications of Foucault's rejection of Sartre is that these conceptions and ideals come to individuals first and foremost from the tradition, culture, society, and polity in which they have their being.[22]

The "individualism" before us, then, is not of the "atomistic" variety (mostly imagined) that contemporary Republicans, Communitarians, and Strong and Deliberative democrats so dearly love to hate. But this conclusion leads to two further elaborations/comments, and these have an importantly different tendency.

In rejecting Sartre and Descartes, Foucault is returning—in the context of his history of sexuality—to themes, the themes of power and governmentality, that had been central to his earlier studies. When he argues that the self works on itself in the setting of culturally, socially, and politically authoritative understandings, expectations, and requirements, he is reiterating and giving further detail to his view that subjects are subjected to relations of power, that they do their thinking and acting not in some epistemic, spiritual, or existential isolation but in response to the influences, pressures, and demands of the culture, society, and politics in which they have their being. Sartrean and Cartesian views are fantasies because "micro," "capillary," "pastoral" power is everywhere. And they are dangerous or rather disabling fantasies because they deflect the attentions of subjects from this fact, encourage them to think that they can achieve knowledge and self-mastery without engaging with the influences and forces that surround them and operate on them.

As we have already seen in part, however, Foucault never took this view as reason for despair, abject submission, or passive nihilism, and he certainly does not adopt such a stance in his discussions of the Romans. On the one hand, there were important respects in which the power relations—that is, the array of authoritative norms, established institutions, and disciplinary mechanisms—that pervaded Hellenic culture and society were enabling of care for the self and the pursuit of self-mastery. To be a

Stoic or an Epicurean, for example, was to have at one's disposal, and to think and act largely in terms of, ideas, orientations, dispositions, doctrines—in particular the idea of and disposition to self-preoccupation and self-mastery—that circulated in one's milieu and venues of activity. Some thinkers/practitioners contributed more notably to these persuasions than others, but when we identify them as Stoics, Epicureans, or more generally as Romans, we not only echo but underline their own, affirmative, sense of indebtedness to their culture and tradition.

But this is only one, and for present purposes the least engaging, dimension of Foucault's reports and reflections concerning power. In an interview conducted in the final year of his life, and with his Greco-Roman studies very much in his mind, he spoke as follows: "[P]ower relationships are . . . mobile, reversible and unstable. . . . [P]ower relationships are possible only insofar as the subjects are free. If one of . . . [the parties to such a relationship] were completely at the other's disposal and became his thing . . . there wouldn't be any relation of power. Thus, in order for power relations to come into play, there must be a certain degree of freedom on both sides. Even when the power relation is completely out of balance, when it can truly be claimed that one side has 'total power' over the other, a power can be exercised over the other only insofar as the other still has the option of killing himself, of leaping out of the window, or of killing the other person. This means that in power relations there is necessarily the possibility of resistance because if there were no [such] . . . possibility . . . there would be no power relations at all. . . . I refuse to reply to the question I am sometimes asked: 'But if power is everywhere, there is no freedom.' I answer [!] that if there are relations of power in every social field, this is because there is freedom everywhere" (1997, 292; see also note 15).

It is evident that this notion of freedom as resistance by the individual to demands made on her by cultural, societal, and political institutions is closely interwoven with the themes of situatedness or indebtedness to the disciplines imposed by established understandings and practices, and of self-discipline or care for the self as itself perhaps the primary cultural requirement or expectation. On the one hand, an individual unaware of or insensitive to cultural norms would not know what was expected/required of her and hence could "resist" those requirements only by happenstance or indirection. On the other hand, only those who have mastered the techniques of self-discipline, techniques that are themselves made available to them by their culture, are likely to have the further characteristics that enable resistance to demands that they find, generally or circumstantially, offensive to themselves.[23]

There emerges, then, a quite intricate and subtly nuanced combination or interwoven set of understandings concerning the relations among freedom, discipline, and resistance. Contrary to thinkers such as Sartre and Descartes, on the views Foucault is exploring and seems to be endorsing, self-discipline cannot be understood apart from modes of discipline that are encouraged if not demanded by culture and society (and hence by some number of other selves—even if the latter are not always readily assignable). We might say that the freedom, or better the capacity, to live a self-disciplined life depends upon or is at best barely conceivable apart from a disciplining society. We can certainly say that, on this view, the particular and distinctively important form of freedom that is resistance to cultural, social, and political discipline (domination?) is—if at all—only barely conceivable apart from a disciplining society. Discipline is one thing and freedom another.[24] But empirically, perhaps phenomenologically, perhaps ontologically, they are inseparable.

As regards what a few paragraphs above I designated proposition 1), I take this to be Foucault's general conclusion or assessment. I also regard it as a major contribution to identifying and exploring complexities in the discipline-freedom relationship such as those noted in preliminary terms earlier in this work. Certainly his reflections valuably supplement my own previous attempts to accommodate the "situated" character of thinking about and acting in the domain of freedom.

There remains, however, a certain puzzlement, an element of uncertainty or inconclusiveness that Foucault partially, but only partially, helps us to resolve. What is the motive, or whence cometh the impulse, to the "resistance" to power, authority, and authoritative norms and practices that Foucault thinks is always possible and that he clearly regards as essential to self-mastery and the ethos of freedom? If I am what I am, if my very conceptions of self-mastery and self-making are deeply indebted to my culture and its institutions and practices, how can we understand and on what grounds can we promote resistance to their requirements and expectations? We can say, and it is an admirable feature of Foucault's discussions of the Romans and in various other places in his earlier works, that resistance is itself one of the obligations that a culture deserving of my allegiance imposes upon me (or which I impose on myself by engaging affirmatively with a worthy culture).[25] On this view, resistance affirms the culture itself and at once manifests and reinforces my indebtedness and my commitment to it.

But Foucault's engagements with Roman ideas of care of the self offer an alternative, or at least a further (albeit relatively little developed) way of thinking about the puzzlement before us. One element of this further view is expressed in the already quoted phrases where Foucault says that Seneca and Epictetus held that you must be master of yourself because "you are a rational being" and that the principle that properly governs self-making is "universal by the form it assumes in everyone." Recall, however, that the latter reference to the frequently discussed rationalistic universalism of the Stoics is preceded by the remark that self-making is "the expression of a principle that is singular in its manifestation" in each and every person who properly cares for herself. And a few pages earlier in *The Care of the Self*, Foucault emphasized that the Stoics and Epicureans taught that each of us should seek to be able "to delight in oneself, as in a thing one both possesses and has before one's eyes," that we should please ourselves and "learn how to feel joy" (65–66).

These last remarks, which of course underline the differences between Roman and both Christian and Greek thinking, are consistent with the idea that there is a principle that is "universal in the *form* that it assumes in everyone" but they give the latter idea an importantly different emphasis or slant. I can know and act on the imperatives to "delight in myself" and to "learn how to feel joy" only if I have come to understand how I am or might become "singular" in the ways in which I "manifest" that which I share with the other members of my culture and perhaps at some level with all of humankind.

Read in the light of these remarks—but of course also in the perspective of his decided antipathy to Christian self-renunciation—Foucault's celebration of resistance as central to the care of the self and the ethos of freedom becomes more cogent and easier to understand. Even if I recognize and appreciate my indebtedness to the traditions and norms of my culture and society, even if in much of the work that I do on myself I employ techniques that are not only available to me from but urged upon me by my culture, my sense of and commitment to the reality or possibility of my distinctiveness, my desire to delight and experience joy in my singularity, may motivate me to resist not only unwarranted attempts to dominate me but also the subtler but more pervasive pressures and demands of micro or pastoral power and authority. Even if the preponderance of my experiences thus far tell me that I am what I have thus far become primarily because of the influences of my society on me, if I have a sense, a glimpse, of the actuality or possibility of a form of being that exceeds my experience up to now, I may have reason for, or rather may be inspired to, discipline myself to resist the universalizing, generalizing, homogeneity- and uniformity-producing prohibitions and requirements of power and authority relations in my culture and society.

If so, my self-discipline, my care of and for myself, might contribute importantly to my *freedom* from the control of disciplines imposed on me by society. It would also *enable* me, perhaps *empower* me, to pursue delights that, because they are a thing that *I* do or may possess and have before *my* eyes, I can enjoy in ways impossible for anyone other than *myself.*

These last thoughts are more sketched or hinted at than elaborated and defended in Foucault's texts.[26] It is undeniable, moreover, that they coexist with elements and tendencies that are in tension if not in antagonism with them. But if my emphasis on them owes much to my own proclivities, the discipline of engaging with Foucault has been of immense value in helping me to understand what my proclivities are and are not, should and should not be. Can one ask more of a thinker/writer?

No.

But I intend, in engagements to follow, to ask the same, on these topics, of Montaigne, of Nietzsche, and of Hampshire.

CHAPTER 3

The Self Against and for Itself: I
Montaigne on Freedom, Discipline, and Resistance

There are numerous indications that Montaigne understood freedom to mean the absence of effective obstacles to and constraints upon thinking and acting. In the last of his essays, "Of Experience," he says that he is "sick for freedom." From the surroundings of this remark it is clear that what he is sick *of* is the incessant actual or threatened interferences with his preferred attentions and activities, interferences produced by the religious and other conflicts of his time and place. He has been obliged to think and act other than he would prefer, to develop and continually practice a "small prudence" so as to keep the warring factions "from interrupting my freedom of coming and going."[1] Generalizing and perhaps deliberately exaggerating the thought, he says "if anyone should forbid me access to some corner of the Indies, I should live distinctly less comfortably. And as long as I find earth or air open elsewhere, I shall not lurk in any place where I have to hide. . . . If those that I serve threatened even the tip of my finger, I should instantly go and find others, wherever it might be" (Ibid.).

These sentiments, and the conceptualizations Montaigne employs in expressing them, make increasingly frequent appearances as the *Essays* progress. He flees "command, obligation, constraint" (F, II, 17, 493), despises censorship (F, II, 18, 506–510), and hates obligations to and dependency upon others (F, III, 9, 739). He endorses the traditional antithesis between freedom and all forms of slavery (F, III, 13, 831, 8434), and he regards his love of freedom and the discretion—even the idleness and laziness—that freedom allows to those fortunate enough to enjoy it, as among his most prominent and cherished characteristics and conditions (F, III, 9, 741, 759). In these respects, Montaigne emerges as a vigorous champion of freedom "negatively" understood. If the remarks considered thus far give us reason to expect him to favor resistance to constraints and restrictions imposed by others, they also suggest distrust of, apprehensions concerning, notions of discipline and control and perhaps to disciplinary practices and arrangements of all kinds.

These initial impressions, I will argue, are finally, that is, taking these extraordinarily diverse and complex essays as closely together as we can, both correct concerning Montaigne's views and a primary reason for admiring and taking counsel from them. But there are many things to be considered in order to support and, more important here, adequately to refine, these conclusions. Because Montaigne's much discussed (and debated) skepticism is among the most important of these considerations, we can make a beginning by considering aspects of the work of one of Montaigne's most important predecessors in the skeptical tradition, that is, Sextus Empiricus.[2]

I

Skepticism is commonly regarded as first and foremost an epistemological position, a stance concerning what we human beings can, and more important cannot, hope to know, correctly to judge or assess, and the like. Positions on these questions of cognitive and judgmental capacity and possibility are missing from neither Sextus nor Montaigne (they are particularly prominent in what is widely regarded that as the most skeptical of Montaigne's essays, the long "Apology for Raymond Sebond" [II, 12]), but another dimension or characteristic of "Pyrrhonian" skepticism à la Sextus is more pertinent to present concerns.

Sextus first characterizes skepticism as a "discipline,"[3] one "that is called 'zetetic' . . . from its activity of searching and examining . . . 'ephectic' (suspending) from the experience which the inquirer feels after the search," and sometimes "aporetic (doubting) . . . from the fact that their [those who are skeptics] doubting and searching extends to everything (the opinion of some), or from their inability to give final assent or denial" (Sextus, H, 32). In order effectively to practice this discipline, the skeptic must of course understand what it is to search, suspend, and doubt and to appreciate how these activities differ from those characteristic of non-skeptical philosophers and others given to dogmatism. As suggested by the terms "discipline" and "activities," however, it is not enough merely to grasp, understand, or otherwise to be cognitively competent concerning the differences between skepticism and other schools of thought. Rather, to *be* a skeptic, to practice skepticism, one must develop what Sextus calls an "ability."

Many pages of the *Outlines* and of Sextus's other works are devoted to identifying the elements and commending the advantages of this specifically skeptical "ability." Some of this detail, and comparable discussions in Montaigne, will be examined below, but I first consider Sextus's most general remarks concerning the key notion of ability. Although insisting that he is using the *word* in the ordinary sense of "being able" (as opposed, as Hallie explains, to any metaphysical notion such as potency, innate capacity, *energeia, dynamis,* and the like), it is clear that there is nothing ordinary, common, or to be taken for granted by being born with it or acquiring it in the ordinary course of growing up, being socialized, educated, and so forth, the ability necessary to skepticism must be deliberately and self-consciously cultivated and continuously sustained by disciplined practice. Large numbers of people never acquire it and some—in particular philosophers of the several dogmatic schools—positively disable themselves from or for it.[4]

Negatively described, the ability in question consists of disciplining oneself to avoid two logically distinct but frequently associated human tendencies: the first is to think that there must be a true answer to every question, a correct solution to every problem and hence that disagreement and uncertainty always betoken correctable errors in or remediable failures of inquiry and reasoning; the second is to insist, dogmatically, that the answer or solution at which I or we have thus far arrived is indisputably the true or correct one. More affirmatively, the skeptic trains herself not only to suspend judgment concerning rival doctrines and claims, but to expect and hence to look for considerations that at once oppose and balance one another, such that the only appropriate (defensible?) response is to suspend judgment concerning the merits of competing impressions, arguments, and conclusions. "Appearances [are] opposed to appearances, judgments to judgments, . . . appearances to judgments," leading—if the ability has been well cultivated and employed—to a "suspension of judgment," that is "a cessation of thought processes in consequence of which we neither deny nor affirm anything" and arrive at a state of "mental tranquility" or "an undisturbed and calm state of the soul" (H, 33–34).

The methods, techniques, skills (tropes) by which this suspension and stillness of mind and spirit (of body as well? Are the sensory and passionate as well as the cogitative mechanisms shut down? Certainly not for Montaigne) are best achieved, are elaborated in considerable detail in the *Outlines* but need not concern us here. For purposes of comparison and contrast with Montaigne, the salient point is the concurrent promotion to great prominence of an active, disciplining self and the withdrawal or re-treat of that self into a passivity that approaches hibernation if not self-nullification. The "ability" that the self is to cultivate is the power to monitor—to discipline and control—itself, to the point that its own native or congenital proclivities to seek, to inquire, to question, to assert, to insist, are curbed and bridled by itself. Skepticism as Sextus understands and pro-motes it involves, or rather requires, the simultaneous celebration and dis-dain, magnification and nullification, of the self by itself. The *ataraxia,* tranquility, stillness, of self that is brought about by skeptical discipline and perfected as that discipline produces an ever greater ability of the self to control itself results, one is tempted to say paradoxically, from quite in-tense, even violent activities of the self.

Much in the literature concerning freedom creates a powerful tempta-tion to invoke this concept here. The higher, purer, better part of the self frees its larger, cruder, more vulgar and dangerous self from disturbance, turmoil, distraction. And it frees itself as a whole for a life, a being(ness), of tranquility.[5] As I read them, however, Sextus's texts themselves do little to authorize the use of this language. Freedom and unfreedom, whether physical, political, moral, economic, or some other, are simply not issues for him, have no significant place among his concerns. But of course this is no impediment to our inquiring concerning the implications of Sextus's views for thinking about freedom and unfreedom. Doing so is facilitated by the fact that Montaigne adopts a strongly analogous notion of skeptical ability and is very much concerned with its implications for issues con-cerning freedom.

II

The form or manifestation of skeptical ability on which Montaigne most persistently prided himself, and the lack of which among his contempo-raries he most bitterly lamented, concerned the divine and virtually all religious matters. In the essay "Of Prayers" in Volume I, he takes an un-compromisingly fideist position, arguing that there is no role for reason or judgment in matters of faith and insists that the Bible "is not a story to tell, it is a story to revere, fear and adore" (F, I, 56, 232). He declares, proudly, his unqualified submission to the "Catholic, Apostolic, and Roman Church," the church "in which I die and in which I was born" (229) and in this essay, in the "Apology for Raymond Sebond," and in various other places, he objects strenuously not only to the Protestant doctrine of the priesthood of all believers but to the very fact that the Bible has been trans-lated into vulgar languages, and that church ceremonies are increasingly being conducted in vernaculars. As Villey says, from "Of Prayers" forward, "le divorce est complet entre les deux domaines de la raison et de la foi. La raison est Si faible, Si contraire par son essence aux verités surnaturelles, qu'il faut la tenir bien à l'ecart de tout ce qui est surnaturel" (V, 317 [the divorce is complete between the two domains of reason and of faith. The reason is so feeble, so contrary by its essence to the supernatural truths, that it is necessary to put it entirely to the side of all that is supernatural]. By disciplining himself to resist the temptation to meddle in matters beyond the ken of his reason and experience, Montaigne is able to live as tranquil a life as his time and place permit. By contrast, those who have not cultivated this ability are themselves disturbed and are the chief sources of disturbance, disruption, and often lethal conflict in their societies. If well cultivated, maintained, and employed, a kind of reason beyond or above reason can discipline us not to attempt to reason about religious matters.[6] In more traditional (for example, Socratic) epistemological terms, knowing what we cannot know, recognizing the limits of our knowledge, gives us a kind of knowledge of ourselves that enables us to avoid disruptive and destructive actions and to live a life of constancy and tranquility. What Sextus called the skeptical ability enables—empowers—a good deal more than skepticism itself.

Although articulated most insistently and continuously in respect to religion, this thematic recurs in Montaigne's work in respect to numerous other aspects of life, most particularly regarding what in a wide sense can be called the moral life. Here we must distinguish, as do most of Montaigne's recent commentators, between the earliest versions of the essays, comprising Books I and II, on the one hand, and, on the other, the later essays of Book III, and the later additions to the first published versions of the preponderance of the earlier essays. Numerous of the former do advocate a discipline, the cultivation of a form of ability, but rather than being skeptical, the ability is predominantly Stoical in character. That is, it does not rest on or proceed from doubt, uncertainty, and suspension of judgment concerning the right and the wrong, the best and the worst ways to live, but rather from a quite robust confidence in the teachings that he has absorbed from Seneca, Epictetus, and other Stoic masters and found to be confirmed by his own experience.

The clearest examples of Stoically inspired self-confidence are the several discussions of suicide and more generally of preparation for death (especially I, 14, 19, 20, 37; II, 3[7]), but there is a generalized emphasis on moderation and self-control with respect to the passions, steadfastness, and fortitude in the face of the endless, inevitable, and often agonizing and tormenting workings of fortune. His high praise of Socrates and of Cato the Younger (I, 37; II, 28) are good examples, and his confidence in the value of these virtues reaches a kind of crescendo in the essay "Of Virtue":

"I find by experience that there is quite a difference between the erratic impulses of the soul and a habit of resolute steadfastness. And I see very well that nothing is beyond our power: we can even, says someone [Seneca?— certainly not Paul or Augustine], surpass the deity itself—inasmuch as it is a greater thing to make oneself impassible by one's own efforts than to be so by one's natural condition—even combine with man's frailty a godlike resolution and assurance" (F, II, 29, 532–33). True, he immediately expresses pessimism about the likelihood that any but the greatest of humans can live steadily by these teachings (most of us can do so "only by fits and starts"), and goes on in the same essay to suggest that Pyrrho, who built his "amusing science [of living] out of ignorance" might offer more practicable advice.

In the essays to which I have been referring, however, these difficulties are not with the theory, not with the truth or wisdom of the Stoic teachings; rather, they are with us the practitioners, with the human weaknesses that deflect us from doing that which is undeniably wise and right. We know what disciplines we should impose on ourselves, what abilities we ought to cultivate. The shortfall or deficit is connative not cognitive; it is a failure of will and character not reason or mind.

Disciplines and abilities difficult to distinguish from the Stoical remained an object of Montaigne's admiration and personal craving to the end of his life. In the late and important "Of Husbanding Your Will" (III, 10), he praises Socrates for disdaining luxurious things and for saying, proudly, "How many things I do not desire." "Metrodorus," he continues, "lived on twelve ounces a day, Epicurus on less; Metrocles slept in winter with the sheep, in summer in the cloisters of the churches." In one of many late and often favorable appeals to Seneca (see the indexes in Frame and Villey), he quotes him as saying that "Nature supplies what it demands," and goes on to praise Cleanthes for living by his hands and for boasting that he could "feed still another Cleanthes" (772). A few pages later we find him admiring himself in strongly analogous terms: "We must not rush so frantically after our passions and our interests. Just as when I was young I opposed the progress of love, which I felt advancing too far upon me, and took care that it should not be so pleasing to me as in the end to overpower me . . . so I [now] do the same on all other occasions where my will is seized with too strong an appetite. I lean in the opposite direction from its inclination, as I see it plunging in and getting drunk with its own wine. I avoid feeding its pleasure to such an extent that I can no longer regain control of it without cruel loss" (776). At the same time, however, he rapidly lost confidence in the alleged rational or philosophical bases of these among his continuing convictions and commitments. At his most insistently skeptical moments, in the "Apology for Raymond Sebond" but also right up to and including "Experience," this leads him to expressions not only of disenchantment with the rational universalism of Stoicism but to despair and even to disgust with humanity and its self-proclaimed powers. In "Raymond Sebond," particularly in the early pages, many of these darkly pessimistic thoughts are presented through a contrast between "man alone, without outside assistance, armed only with his own weapons" and man supplied with God's grace (F, II, 12, 328, 326). The "weapons" with which unaided reason provides us are "puny" (327), and reason alone is "so lame and blind that there is nothing so clear and easy as to be clear enough to her" (328). Even the actions of the very paragons of rational virtue, that is Socrates and Cato the Younger, "remain vain and useless because they did not direct them toward the end of loving and obeying the true creator of all things, and because they did not know God; so it is with our ideas and reasoning: they have a certain body, but it is a shapeless mass, without form or light, if faith and divine grace are not added to it" (326–67).

Toward the end of "Raymond Sebond," and in later essays, the contrast between reason and grace becomes less salient, but the disparagement of reason not only continues unabated but is sharpened and extended. Echoing Sextus Empiricus, Montaigne argues that reason is and must remain inadequate as a basis for moral life. Reasoning necessarily begins with and cannot entirely go beyond the information provided by the senses, but the combination of the diversity and flux of the world and the weaknesses and variability of our sensory mechanisms prohibits us from placing full confidence in the testimony of the latter. Referring to what he takes to be Lucretius's view that distortion comes from the passions and reason, and that we should always cleave to the evidence the senses provide, he writes: "This desperate . . . advice means nothing else than that human knowledge can maintain itself only by unreasonable, mad, and senseless reason; . . . He [man] cannot escape the fact that the senses are the sovereign masters of his knowledge; but they are uncertain and deceivable in all circumstances" (447). Thus we must appeal from our senses to our reason. The latter, however, is no more reliable than the former. "To judge the appearances that we receive of objects, we would need a judicatory instrument; to verify this instrument, we need a demonstration; to verify the demonstration, an instrument; there we are in a circle" (454). Again, "Since the senses cannot decide our dispute, being themselves full of uncertainty, it must be reason that does so. [But because no] reason can be established without another reason; there we go retreating back to infinity" (454).[8]

Worse, reason and reasoning are dangerous, and reliance on them diminishes our humanity. "[W]e have strangely overpaid for this fine reason that we glory" because reasoning, or rather our overestimation of it, often excites the very passions it seeks to discipline (II, 12, 358), and the wisdom it yields easily becomes a kind of madness. "Of what is the subtlest madness made, but the subtlest wisdom? As great enmities are born of great friendships, . . . so are the greatest and wildest manias born of the rare and lively stirrings of our soul; it is only a half turn of the peg to pass from one to the other" (363). This subtle madness sometimes takes the form of an excess in the purity and perspicacity of our minds. "That penetrating clarity has too much subtlety and curiosity in it. . . . Therefore common and less high-strung minds are found to be more fit and more successful for conducting affairs. And the lofty and exquisite ideas of philosophy are found to be inept in practice" ("We Taste Nothing Pure" F, II, 20, 511).

The phrase "common and less high-strung minds" anticipates a theme that becomes prominent as Montaigne qualifies his pessimism and tries to identify resources that might allow us, despite the limitations and deficiencies of our senses and our reason, to live not only comfortable but "appropriate" lives. I return to this theme below. Of more immediate interest is the last of the sentences just quoted, and in particular the contrast between lofty philosophy and "practice." High philosophy as Montaigne characterizes and sometimes caricatures it, seeks to abstract from particulars, to subsume, categorize, and in other ways to generalize. When brought to bear on practice, it attempts to formulate and promulgate general precepts, rules, and laws that are intended to govern entire classes of circumstances, conditions, and modes of conduct. The disciplines it fosters consist importantly of submission to these general regimens and rules, and the ability it cultivates is a readiness to do so. As we have seen, in the earliest essays Montaigne showed himself well-disposed to this understanding and orientation; to the considerable extent that he remained to the end a "virtue theorist," he sustained that disposition. But nature and the ineliminable weaknesses of reason that we have been considering combine to make following this strategy both difficult and self-diminishing.

In an otherwise rather slight essay (II, 4, "Let Business Wait Till Tomorrow" as Frame translates the title; the French is "*À Demain les Affaires*"), Montaigne considers whether it is advisable to attend immediately to letters, messages, and other matters of business as quickly as they come to your attention or to be "nonchalant" and put off reading and responding to them until a convenient moment. As is his wont, he examines various examples of the two approaches, expresses some preferences of his own, but then concludes that "when all is said, it is hard in human actions to arrive by reasoning at any rule so exact as to exclude Fortune from her rights in the matter" (263). Later this somewhat casual remark emerges as a major claim directly pertinent to present concerns.

In the essay titled "Of Vanity" (III, 9), it emerges that one of the worst forms of the defect of character of that name is the desire to give the law to other people. Although he continues to find "many useful things" in Seneca, he has come to "dislike inculcation" and especially "the practice of his [Seneca's] Stoical school of repeating, in connection with every subject, in full length and breadth, the principles and premises for general use, and restating ever anew their common and universal arguments and reasons" (F, 734–35). In "Of Physiognomy" (F, III, 12) this critique is extended to a "scholastic probity," "that I see held in greater price than it is worth, . . . almost the only one practiced among us, a slave to precepts, held down beneath fear and hope" (811). And in "Of Experience" (III, 13), he extends it from ethics to government and law: "Since the ethical laws, which concern the individual duty of each man in himself, are so hard to frame, as we see they are, it is no wonder if those [laws] that govern so many individuals are more so" (F, 819). Although confessing that as he has grown older he has become increasingly a creature of fixed routines and rigid habits, he regrets this development and remains convinced that "there is no way of life so stupid and feeble as that which is conducted by rules and discipline" (F, 830).

It is in this mood, influenced by these convictions, that Montaigne issues his most dismissive and despairing assessments of the human condition and its possibilities. At the very end of "Sebond," he quotes Seneca's remark, "Oh what a vile and abject thing is man . . . if he does not raise himself above humanity," but immediately rejects this aspiration as absurd. "Nor can man raise himself above himself and humanity; for he can see only with his own eyes, and seize only with his own grasp. He will rise, if God by exception lends him a hand . . . by abandoning and renouncing his own means, and letting himself be raised and uplifted by purely celestial means. It is for our Christian faith, not for his Stoical virtue, to aspire to that divine and miraculous metamorphosis" (F, II, 12, 457). In another essay, I, 50, he describes Democritus as finding man "vain and ridiculous" and therefore going about with a "mocking and laughing face," while Heraclitus was filled with pity and compassion for the human condition. He himself prefers "the first humor; not because it is pleasanter to laugh than to weep, but because it is more disdainful, and condemns us more than the other; and it seems to me that we can never be despised as much as we deserve. . . . I do not think there is as much unhappiness in us as vanity, nor as much malice as stupidity. We are not so full of evil as of inanity; we are not as wretched as we are worthless. . . . Our own peculiar condition is that we are as fit to be laughed at as able to laugh" ("Of Democritus and Heraclitus," F, I, 50, 220–21).

In the passages I have been reviewing, Montaigne emerges not merely as skeptical and pessimistic but as something of a misanthrope. The diversity and flux of the world and of the senses by which we perceive it, together with the potent, often pulsating power of the passions, makes us wayward, errant, and rather foolish creatures. And when that "kill-joy reason" (F, III, 9, 762) attempts to take control and impose the discipline of rules and regimens, it more often than not makes matters worse. If or to the extent that freedom depends on the ability to discipline oneself and to resist the impulses and fashions of the moment, there is little hope of achieving it, virtually no prospect of sustaining it over any extended stretch of time or lengthy course of action. The self is primarily against itself, primarily one of the most potent of the many enemies of its own freedom.

III

Misanthropy is not necessarily a defect. Certainly it is to be preferred to the bovine optimism according to which this is the best of all possible worlds and to those various puffed-up versions of rationalism according to which reason can and should triumph over all non-, pre-, and extra-rational considerations. Although the bleakest, the most despairing moments in Montaigne's thinking were undoubtedly influenced by the senseless and murderous brutality of his own time and place, I at least do not see how we can read him without recognizing ourselves in his portrait of humankind.

As with his successor Hobbes, however, Montaigne held himself back from despair, refused to submit to passive nihilism. His search for human sources of comfort and encouragement led him, finally, back to himself and the freedoms and felicities he managed, often again heavy odds, to sustain for himself. But in speaking of and for himself he also and increasingly spoke of, to, and occasionally even for all of humankind. With a smile or two from Fortuna, human beings sometimes do and therefore sometimes can make their lives enjoyable and themselves worthy of their own self-esteem. How?

A modified Pyrrhonian skepticism plays an integral albeit not an exclusive role in what I will permit myself to call Montaigne's mature view of the abilities by the cultivation of which he himself had, intermittently but non-negligibly, accomplished this considerable feat and how others could best go about attempting to do so. To begin to understand and assess these developments in his thinking, let us return to his seemingly somewhat dismissive remark concerning Pyrrho's "amusing science" of virtue (F, II, 29, 533). What does Montaigne find "amusing" about a thinker and more generally a man for whom he evidently had considerable admiration? If we take "amusing" to mean laughable, and if we read the remark in the light of the views discussed in the previous section, the answer would seem to be provided by the words with which the sentence in question concludes:

"like all the others who were truly philosophers," Pyrrho tried to make theory rule practice, committed himself to the objective, generally fantastical and commonly leading to fanaticism, of making "his life correspond to his doctrine." As with all the other philosophers of this persuasion, he tried to write a book of rules for life and then to live by it. On this reading, Montaigne would appear to credit and indeed to offer an explanation for the numerous stories—with which this essay itself shows him to be fully familiar—concerning ways in which Pyrrho and other Pyrrhonian skeptics not only made themselves ridiculous but put life and limb in jeopardy by refusing to accept and follow well-established truths about humankind and the world.[9]

As Montaigne's discussion continues, however, it becomes clear that he is anything but disdainful concerning either Pyrrho or his "science." For starters, it should be noted that the French word that Frame translates as "amusing," namely "*plaisante*," is likened, for example in Larousse, to "*curieux*" and "*piquant*" as well as "*amusant*." If we render the former of these words by English terms such as *arouses, stimulates*, or *piques interest and attention*, we capture elements of Montaigne's presentation that *distinguish* Pyrrho from the other philosophers and display Montaigne's considerable esteem for both the doctrine and the man.

Unlike those philosophers who claimed that their sciences were grounded in allegedly rational foundations such as Stoical universalism, Pyrrho "maintained that the weakness of human judgment was so extreme as to be unable to take sides or lean either way, and would have it suspended in perpetual balance, considering and taking in all things as indifferent." This stance saved him from dogmatism and fanaticism. But rather than paralyze him or even diminish his capacity for action, it helped him to maintain great constancy in his day-to-day thinking and acting. True, he sometimes needed practical assistance from the less diffident of his friends; but he also had the ability, for example, to suffer "being incised and cauterized with such constancy that he was not seen even to blink" (F, II, 29, 533). Whereas Stoical and various religious forms of such resignation and impassibility stemmed from convictions as to what is right and wrong, good and bad, Pyrrho's indifference and steadfastness was grounded in the conviction that, most matters being undecidable, one might just as well go on as before.

More particular respects in which Montaigne followed Sextus's example will be discussed below. There are, however, important qualifications to his acceptance and use of the methods of Pyrrhonian skepticism. Although embracing the view that "There is no reason that does not have its opposite" (F, II, 15, 463) and hence that we should avoid assertiveness and especially vanity (III, 9) and presumptuousness (II, 17), he rejected the mechanical outlook according to which suspension of judgment can result from a literal equality in the weight of the arguments or evidence for opposing views. "[N]othing presents itself to us in which there is not some difference, however slight; and that either to the sight or to the touch, there is always something extra that attracts us, though it be imperceptibly. . . . [I]f we suppose a string equally strong throughout, it is impossible by all impossibility (*"il est impossible de toute impossibilité"* V, 611) that it should break; for where do you want the break to begin? And to break everywhere at once is not in nature" (F, II, 14, 463). Again, if we "imagine a mind exactly balanced between two equal desires . . . it is indubitable that it will never decide, since inclination and choice imply inequality in value; and if we were placed between the bottle and the ham with an equal appetite for drinking and eating, there would doubtless be no solution but to die of thirst and of hunger" (462). For all its limitations and weaknesses, "Judgment is a tool to use on all subjects, and comes in everywhere" (F, II, 50, 219); if exercised with due care it can yield and inform the use of precepts and predilections that will help us to create "Our great and glorious masterpiece," which "is to live appropriately" (F, III, 13, 850).

Judgment requires criteria by which to choose among those differences that experience and reason call to our attention. For reasons already considered, the criteria available to us are never fully satisfactory, always disappoint us from time to time. (Compare Cavell: We cannot do without criteria, but they will always disappoint us. Cavell, Stanley, 1979, especially chapter 2.) Thus we must not sublime them, must not invest them with superstrong standing or apply and follow them like mindless automata. But much of the time we will do as well as can be hoped (as well as Fortuna allows), by taking our bearings from them, following their cues and leads.

What are the sources of suitable, humanly serviceable, criteria of judgment and what warrants our qualified but nevertheless substantial confidence in them? We already know that Montaigne rejects the view that they do, could, or should come from abstract, philosophical, or universal reason. Following Sextus and the Pyrrhonians generally, he insists that our criteria must be practical, not theoretical. Sextus distinguishes between the dogmatist's understanding of "criterion" as "the standard one takes for belief in reality or non-reality" and the skeptic's view that "it is the standard of action the observance of which regulates our actions in life." He then goes on to identify four particular "heads" under which, for the skeptic, the "observance of the requirements of daily life" should properly fall. They are "the guidance of nature, the compulsion of the feelings, the tradition of laws and customs, and the instruction of the arts (H, 39–40).[10] Montaigne's construals of these four sources of orientation often differ from Sextus's, but each of the latter figures importantly in his reflections. And as the essays continue, the first and second assume increasing prominence and distinctiveness.

Let us begin with the third, laws and customs handed down by tradition, the salience of which in Montaigne's thinking is largely responsible for his partly deserved reputation as a highly conservative thinker. The least qualified of his counsels to follow established custom and law, indeed to make doing so a deeply ingrained habit, concern those dimensions of human affairs that he thinks (as have and do numerous others) often are and always ought to be firmly institutionalized. Given his radical fideism and categorical rejection of all forms of Protestantism, it is not surprising to find some of his bluntest expressions of this view in his discussions of organized religion, but his comparatively sparse remarks concerning law, government, and to some extent politics not infrequently approach the former.

Some of the most potent but also most general expressions of this species of conservatism occur in I, 27, titled "It Is Folly to Measure the True and False by Our Own Capacity."[11] To begin with what Montaigne might well have intended as the chief practical upshot of the essay, he intones that "We must either submit completely to the authority of our ecclesiastical government, or do without it completely. It is not for us to decide what portion of obedience we owe to it" (134). Since "doing without it" would of certainty cast us into "execrable atheism" and the dark and bloody chaos unleashed by Luther (F, II, 12, 320), there can be no mistaking which of these options we should "choose." Although making it clear that he is thinking first and foremost about religion, he generalizes this view as follows: "It is a dangerous and fateful presumption, besides the absurd temerity that it implies, to disdain what we do not comprehend. For after you have established, according to your fine understanding, the limits of truth and falsehood, and it turns out that you must necessarily believe things even stranger than those you deny, you are obliged from then on to abandon these limits." Thus, as already seen, it's all or, literally, nothing. "[W]hat seems to me to bring as much disorder into our consciences as anything, in these religious troubles that we are in, is this partial surrender of their beliefs by Catholics" (F, I, 27, 134).

In "Of Presumption" (II, 17) he argues that what is true of religion and religious governance is substantially correct throughout the domain of "public affairs." "To my mind, in public affairs there is no course so bad, provided it is old and stable, that is not better than change and commotion." It is not that, in content or substance as it were, that which is old and established is therefore wise or good. "Our morals are extremely corrupt, and lean with a remarkable inclination toward the worse; of our laws and customs, many are barbarous and monstrous; however, because of the difficulty of improving our condition and the danger of everything crumbling into bits, if I could put a spoke in our wheel . . . at this point, I would do so with all my heart" (F, II, 17, 497). He is convinced that "the worst thing in our state is instability, and the fact that our laws cannot . . . take any settled form. It is very easy to accuse a government of imperfections, for all mortal things are full of it. It is very easy to engender in a people contempt for their ancient observances; never did a man undertake that without succeeding. But as for establishing a better state in place of the one they have ruined, many of those who have attempted it have achieved nothing for their pains" (498; I take "state" here to mean the human estate generally, not only, certainly not merely, the state in the sense of a territorially bounded and politically and juridically organized entity that was only just emerging in Montaigne's time).

In the next paragraph, and more fully in "Of Experience," he continues and formalizes this thought into a general and now familiar doctrine about authority and obedience. "Obedience is not pure . . . in a man who reasons and argues" (498). "[L]aws remain in credit not because they are just, but because they are laws. This is the mystic foundation of their authority; they have no other. And that is a good thing for them. They are often made by fools, more often by people who, in their hatred of equality, are wanting in equity; but always by men, vain and irresolute authors. . . . Whoever obeys them because they are just, does not obey them for the reason he should" (F, III, 13, 821). This understanding of the relation between authority and obedience is commonly but mistakenly attributed to Hobbes. It is developed with considerable subtlety by Michael Oakeshott in respect to that mode of politically organized society that the latter calls *societas* or civil society, and it is articulated with exemplary clarity—following Kant—by Jacques Derrida. (For discussion and references, see my *Reflections of a Would-Be Anarchist*, Chs. 4–5. Flathman, 1998.)

Montaigne claimed to have followed precepts such as the foregoing in his own public conduct, and he had little hesitation in recommending his example to others. Going back to our starting point, the counsels just discussed constitute perhaps the most important part of that "little prudence" which he employed to prevent the civil wars of his time "from interrupting my freedom of coming and going."[12] To understand the relationship between the norms of this "prudence" and what we might call Montaigne's larger philosophy of life, we need to consider his thinking about those other sources of practical guidance that Sextus calls nature and feeling. We can prepare the way for doing so (and begin to put Montaigne's "conservatism" in perspective) by looking briefly at the qualifications he explicitly makes to the prudence thus far outlined. Doing so will also lead us into his comments concerning the guidance that should be provided by "the arts."

As to custom and convention generally, while we should accept them as general guides to action, we should not do so "blindly" or "slavishly." In "Of Ancient Customs" (I, 49), he opens with a compilation, drawn primarily from Plutarch, of differences among the more or less settled tastes and preferences of various times and places, but then expresses himself as follows: "I should be prone to excuse our people for having no other pattern and rule of perfection than their own manners and customs; for it is a common vice, not of the vulgar only but of almost all men, to fix their aim and limit by the ways to which they were born. . . . But I do complain of their particular lack of judgment in letting themselves be so thoroughly fooled and blinded by the authority of present usage" that, like chameleons, they change their colors with every passing social fancy and are entirely incapable of appreciating the ways and mores of other peoples (215–16). Again, in the much later "Of Experience," we find him asserting that "We should conform to the best rules, but not enslave ourselves to them. . . ."[13]

The dissonances, the sharply drawn and never resolved tensions between these last remarks and those quoted earlier, are perhaps at their most extreme in I, 23, "Of Custom, and Not Easily Changing an Accepted Law." As in I, 49, we again have an extended assemblage of beliefs and practices drawn from ancient and contemporary sources. And running through much of this essay there is a strong suggestion that the question whether to accept and follow, even blindly, the customs of one's time and place is one that does not and for the most part cannot arise in a meaningful, that is to say a practical, way. Habit, he contends, "stupefies our senses" (78). "[T]here is nothing that custom will not or cannot do; and with reason Pindar calls her . . . the queen and empress of the world" (83). We are told that customs and conventions should be brought before the bar of reason or conscience. But Montaigne prefers to align himself with those doctors "who so often abdicate the reasonings of their art to the authority of habit,"[14] and he is convinced that the "laws of conscience" are themselves "born of custom. Each man, holding in inward veneration the opinions and the behavior approved and accepted around him, cannot break loose from them without remorse, or apply himself to them without self-satisfaction" (83). "[T]he principal effect of the power of custom is to seize and ensnare us in such a way that it is hardly within our power to get ourselves back out of its grip" (83).

Here as elsewhere in the *Essays*, however, Montaigne draws back from what threatens to become not only dogmatic and determinist rather than Pyrrhonic skepticism but disdainful and despairing pessimism. Exempting himself from the generalizations just quoted, this essay is pervaded by his own judgments both of this and that, these and those particular customs and conventions, and of the role of custom and convention in human affairs. Of the innumerable things that custom and its executive agent habit can and will do, many are barbaric, repugnant, despicable, shameful, and the like. And when Montaigne was asked, or asked himself, to justify "one of our observances," that is a custom "received with steadfast authority far and wide around us" (and apparently by Montaigne himself), he found its "foundation so weak that I nearly became disgusted with it, I who was supposed to confirm it in others" (84). (He does not identify the custom in question.)

On the other hand, the last pages of the essay give eloquent expression to his judgment that the empire of Queen Habit is for the most part beneficial to humankind and in particular to views concerning authority, law, and obedience such as those discussed above. Nor are these convictions presented as mere prejudices, mere manifestations of the sway of custom and convention over his own thinking. The "considerations" that show the injustice, barbarism, monstrosity, and indecency (85–86) of practices ranging from the highest matters of law and justice, religion and family, to "indifferent things such as" styles of dress "do not deter a man from following the common style. On the contrary, it seems to me that all peculiar and out-of-the-way fashions come rather from folly and ambitious affectation than from true reason . . ." (86). He is "disgusted with innovation, in whatever guise, and with reason, for I have seen very harmful effects of it." Praising Socrates's refusal to "save his life by disobedience even to a very unjust and iniquitous magistrate," he argues that "it is [no less than!] the rule of rules, and universal law of laws that each man should observe those of the place he is in: 'It is a fine thing,'" he approvingly quotes Crispin as saying, "'to obey your country's laws.'"

Throughout Montaigne's work, counsels, admonitions, even imperatives such as just quoted coexist with robust condemnations of blind or slavish conformity, obedience, and submission. Custom and habit do and should rule over much of human conduct, but they can and sometimes should be subjected to scrutiny by the arts of practical judgment. Remembering what reason is not and cannot be, we should also bear in mind that "it has pleased God to give us some capacity for reason, so that we should not be, like the animals, slavishly subjected to the common laws, but should apply ourselves to them by judgment and voluntary liberty" (F, II, 8, 279). As mention of the animals leads us to expect, this advice also applies to those "common laws" that we—often mistakenly—take to be laid down by Nature itself. While "we must indeed yield a little to the simple authority of Nature," we ought not "let ourselves be carried away tyrannically by her: reason alone must guide our inclinations." As regards, for example "the affection that," it is widely held, fathers should bear for their children (the title of this essay is "Of the Affection of Fathers for their Children"), Montaigne declares he has "a taste strangely blunted to these propensities that are produced in us without the command and mediation of our judgment. For example, . . . I cannot entertain that passion which makes people hug infants that are hardly born yet, having neither movement in the soul nor recognizable shape to the body by which they can make themselves lovable. And I have not willingly suffered them to be brought up near me" (279–80). (So much for Montaigne the strictly orthodox Roman Catholic.)

IV

Montaigne offers no encompassing, no comprehensive view or perspective from which to harmonize these often conflicting convictions and dispositions. His emphasis on the diverse and fluctuating character of human experience, and on the limitations and weaknesses of human judgment, would seem to forbid any very general doctrine concerning when and why to go with the flow of custom and convention and when to critique and resist it. Returning, however, to the fact that under the headings of custom and convention, law, and authority, we are primarily concerned with public, with institutionalized, aspects of life, Montaigne makes further distinctions that ease somewhat the tensions, muffle somewhat the dissonances that we have encountered in following his discussions of them. Underlining these distinctions will help us to foreground what is most estimable in Montaigne's thinking concerning the topics before us.

Recall the passage from I, 23, in which he argues that the absurd and even monstrous character of many laws and customs ought not deter the "man of understanding" from conforming to them. This is in part because such a man, for example Socrates, will understand the higher-order reasoning according to which obedience is "the rule of rules," the "law of laws." This reasoning, however, concerns what Montaigne calls "externals"; it concerns "our actions, our work, our fortunes, and our very life," all of which we must "lend and abandon" to society. (For reasons that will appear immediately and again later, I take "our very life" to mean no or little more than staying alive.)

Encompassing and consuming as these notions appear to be, there is much in human experience that is not only outside of but properly independent of their domain. In particular, "society in general can do without our thoughts, and in respect to them the wise man will withdraw his soul within, out of the crowd and keep it in freedom and power to judge things freely" (86). Just as Socrates ennobled rather than compromised his soul by knowingly and intentionally submitting his body and his life to an unjust magistrate, so those of understanding can conform to law and custom and yet sustain and perhaps enhance that which is distinctive and distinctively important to them as individual persons. There is tension and conflict between the internal and the external, between the personal and the public dimensions of life, but those who understand both can achieve and sustain a modus vivendi between them. (Readers of Hobbes will recognize the similarities between Montaigne's distinction and Hobbes's distinction between *in foro externo* and *in foro interno*.)

Appearing as it does in an early essay, we might take this distinction between "externals" and the inner life of the soul to be an expression of the Stoical notion of the "retreat to the Inner Citadel" (as Isaiah Berlin has scornfully called it) that, I have argued above, Montaigne later abandoned. But strongly analogous distinctions not only recur in later essays but acquire a far greater prominence and articulation than they are accorded in the all but parenthetical remark just noted in "Of Custom and Not Easily Changing an Accepted Law." And while they do not entirely escape the difficulties with the Stoic notion of retreat, they present a conception of the inner self and its relationships to various "externals" that is far more fruitful and engaging than the latter.

Recall that in "Of Democritus and Heraclitus" (I, 50), Montaigne gives expression to some of his most disdainful and dismissive assessments of human beings and their modes of conduct. But one of the most pathetic of the human tendencies he noted there is precisely to pretend indifference toward distinctions such as between body and soul, internal and external, personal and public. Although hardly one either to diminish the role of Fortuna in human affairs or to exaggerate the possibility of human control over the flow of events and outcomes, Montaigne nevertheless insists that there are dimensions or domains of life that depend more on us than on the circumstances into which Fortuna flings us. Notwithstanding his numerous diminishing assessments of our powers of judgment, indeed underlining their limitations in describing the always partial and tentative character of the judgments he himself advances in his *Essays*,[15] he insists that "it is a tool to use on all subjects, and comes in everywhere" (219). For various practical purposes we may agree that, viewed externally, things "in themselves may have their own weights and measures and qualities" (220), qualities, moreover, that must be taken into account in making pragmatic judgments concerning events and the actions appropriate in response to them. But even in the lowliest of its practical/empirical functions, the soul (which Montaigne often treats as the seat of judgment) "treats a matter not according to itself, but according to herself," allotting to each its "qualities as she sees fit" (220). And because souls differ enormously from person to person, "Death is frightful to Cicero, desirable to Cato, a matter of indifference to Socrates. Health, conscience, authority, knowledge, riches, beauty, and their opposites—all are stripped on entry and receive from the soul new clothing, and the coloring that she chooses— . . . and which each individual soul chooses; for they have not agreed together on their styles, rules, and forms; each one is queen in her realm" (220).

To deny the role of personal or subjective judgment in these matters is at least self-deceiving and in most cases hypocritical. "Wherefore let us no longer make the external qualities of things our excuse; it is up to us to reckon them as we will. Our good and our ill depend on ourselves alone" (220).

This subjectivism or, better, radical perspectivalism, coexists with rather than contradicts or annuls Montaigne's repeated insistence on the ways in which our judgments and our dispositions are shaped and directed by custom, convention, and the often transient opinions of those around us. Without denying the reality or diminishing the value of the latter, he insists not only on the possibility but the reality of an ineliminable plurality of judgments and hence of dispositions, tendencies, and orientations toward thinking and acting. Empirically or perhaps phenomenologically, this aspect of his argumentation can be construed as an expression, even an outcome, of his skeptical rejection of the dogmatic view that "the external qualities of things" are given, dispositively and indisputably, by impersonal or intersubjective Nature or Reason. But it is clear that Montaigne also has a heavy normative or axiological investment in the distinctions I am considering and in particular in the conception of a self (or the possibility of selves) that not only cannot be reduced to a resultant of the forces that play upon it but that celebrates, revels in, and seeks to make the most of its particular, distinguishing, perhaps even unique characteristics.

We have seen Montaigne's view that those who deny or attempt to explain away this self are guilty of a kind of *mauvaise foi*. We now must explore the respects in which those who recognize this self, but seek to suppress, shrivel, or even apologize for it fall short of and perhaps betray their humanity. Yet more important, we must appreciate Montaigne's intense appreciation for those, high and low according to conventional assessments, who, each in their own way, embrace, celebrate, and seek to enhance a self that is for as well as against itself, a self that recognizes and combats its weaknesses and deficiencies but that does so in the name of and for the sake of enhancing itself.

We may begin by gathering a number of the passages in which Montaigne presents variants on the theme of external submission accompanied by internal independence. As with the remarks already noted, most of the pertinent passages concern relationships between self and other, and particularly more or less institutionalized relations between self and others. These passages do not take us all the way into the self that is for itself (*le soi pour lui-même*), but they manifest Montaigne's concern to protect the latter from the many forces and pressures that threaten to diminish, denature, or destroy it.

Montaigne never seriously entertained the notion of a way of life or of being untouched by or unindebted to tradition, culture, society, neighbors, fellow citizens, and so on. In an extended series of figures, however, he attempted to convey his understanding of the ways in which one should maintain what Nietzsche was to call a "pathos of distance" from others. The essay "Of Husbanding the Will" (III,10) is pivotal in this regard, and its opening paragraphs present carefully articulated expressions of his thinking. "[F]ew things touch me, or to put it better, hold me; for it is right that things should touch us, provided they do not possess us" (766). He cultivates this "privilege of insensibility" and "in consequence grow[s] passionate about few things" and does not "engage" himself "easily." He particularly opposes those passions "that distract me from myself and attach me elsewhere." His conviction is "that we must lend ourselves to others" but "give ourselves only to ourselves." When "pushed . . . into the management of other men's affairs," he has been willing "to take them in hand, [but] not in lungs and liver, to take them on my shoulders, not incorporate them into me; to be concerned over them, yes; to be impassioned over them, never." "We must husband [*mesnager*] the freedom of our soul and mortgage it only on the right occasions; which are very small in number, if we judge sanely" (767).

Although clearly expressed in respect to relationships and attachments such as marriage, the family, and involvements with neighbors,[16] this sensibility was especially marked as regards affairs that are public in the sense of involving formally delineated institutions and obligations, in particular government and politics. No doubt influenced by his two unsought and happily relinquished terms as Mayor of Bordeaux, he believed that life that is "public" in this sense is inherently depraved, requiring "offices which are not only abject but also vicious." The morally iniquitous actions that they often demand may sometimes "be excusable . . . inasmuch as we need them and the common necessity effaces their true quality," but this is an insidious and corrupting way of thinking and even when it is justified he prefers to leave it and the actions it condones to others (III, 1, 600). When he was young he sometimes plunged avidly into public affairs, but, "Since then I have often avoided becoming involved in them, rarely accepted them, never asked for them, keeping my back turned on [this sort of] ambition" (603). With more than a little irony, he remarks that he would leave this part in the human drama to "be played by the more vigorous and less fearful citizens, who sacrifice their honor and their conscience, as those ancients sacrificed their life, for the good of their country. We who are weaker, let us take parts that are both easier and less hazardous. The public welfare requires that a man betray and lie and massacre; let us resign this commission to more obedient and suppler people" (600).[17] Consistent with his recognition that public life sometimes requires and justifies actions that would otherwise be properly condemned, Montaigne also allows that a passion that often animates rulers and other actors on the public stage, namely the craving for glory, can be "salutary" and sometimes must be cultivated even by the dissemination of fables and myths that, if believed, inspire heroism and sacrifice ("Of Glory," II, 16, 477–8). With the possible exception of its close cousins vanity and arrogance, however, Montaigne regards the quest for glory as the worst of the human attributes or dispositions. He favorably cites Chrysippus and Diogenes as "the first and firmest exponents of the disdain for glory" ("Of Glory," II, 16, 468). "[A]ll the glory in the world," they argued, "did not deserve that a man of understanding should so much as stretch out his finger to acquire it:

What's in the greatest glory, if it be but glory? Juvenal (469).

Worse, the quest for glory and honor demeans and diminishes the self because "of all of the pleasures there was none more dangerous or more to be avoided than what comes to us from the approbation of others" (468).[18]

V

These last thoughts, particularly the thought that even apparently high-minded forms of other-regardingness or other-directedness are deflecting, diminishing, and finally corrupting, lead Montaigne to give favorable consideration to an extreme version of the view that the self should be solely for itself—should direct its attentions and concerns exclusively to living tranquilly—"tranquilly not according to Metrodorus or Arcesilaus or Aristippus, but according to me. Since philosophy has not been able to find a way to tranquility that is suitable to all, let everyone seek it individually" (471). He goes so far as to entertain "one of the principal doctrines of Epicurus," namely "CONCEAL YOUR LIFE," a precept that "forbids men to encumber themselves with public charges and negotiations" and thereby "necessarily presupposes . . . contempt for glory, which is an approbation that the world offers of the actions that we place in evidence." Accordingly, Epicurus counsels himself and his followers "not to regulate [their] . . . actions at all by common opinion or reputation" except out of the consideration of small prudence "to avoid the . . . accidental disadvantages that men's contempt might bring him" (469). Montaigne pronounces these precepts of Epicurus to be not only clearly superior to those of Aristotle and Cicero but "infinitely true . . . and reasonable" (469). What is more, the apparent consequence, namely that each of us, certainly every "person of understanding" among us, should accept them and endeavor to live by them, is powerfully reinforced as the essay continues. "I do not care so much what I am to others as I care what I am to myself. I want to be rich by myself, not by borrowing." "[A]ll these judgments . . . founded on external appearances are marvelously uncertain and doubtful; and there is no witness so sure as each man to himself." "I hold that I exist only in myself; and as for that other life of mine that lies in the knowledge of my friends . . . , I know very well that I feel no fruit or enjoyment from it except by the vanity of a fanciful opinion" (474–5).[19]

As with other doctrines that are, abstractly, "infinitely true . . . and reasonable," however, as a practical matter the Epicurean principles are easier to formulate and articulate than steadfastly to apply. Epicurus himself betrayed them by writing a testament that made no sense apart from his concern for his reputation after his death (469–70), and the rest of us (Socrates may be the only genuine exception thus far, albeit truly strict Augustinian Christians who disdain the earthly life and leave the question of the afterlife entirely to God's grace would seem to be possible candidates) are "I know not how, double within ourselves, with the result that [in these and numerous other regards] we do not believe what we believe, and we cannot rid ourselves of what we condemn" (469). Thus the notion of a concealed, entirely private solitary life, while worthy and indeed inspiring as an ideal, will of itself provide few if any of us with a sufficient guide to thought and action or criteria by which to assess the day to day conduct of ourselves and others.

How then can/should the self supplement its concern for itself? With what considerations can the latter be combined consistent with and complementary to its proper self-preoccupation? Elements of the answers to these questions are already before us and are quite straightforward. So long as we do not do so vainly and presumptuously, as do the Protestants, we should hearken to God's will for us as it is made available to us in and through the teachings of the church that is established in our society. Again, as long as we do not do so blindly or slavishly, we can and should let secular custom, convention, and law direct much of our conduct. If or to the extent that we can accomplish the difficult feat of sustaining the freedom of our internal judgment concerning the merits of the rules to which we conform, the guidance with which they provide us could well answer many of the quotidian questions of conduct with which we are confronted.[20]

In respect to these sources of guidance in "external" matters, Montaigne, the mature champion of the self for itself, supplements and qualifies positions discussed above primarily by invoking a view of "nature" and of following the "natural" as distinct from and often as opposed to the artful and the artificial, the abstract and the theoretical, the contrived and the needlessly convoluted. Somewhat surprisingly, a significant element of the theme of following nature is salient in the first formulation of the early and primarily Stoical essay "Of Moderation" (I, 30). Much of the essay is in praise of moderation and temperance, especially with regard to sensual pleasures, and it reaches what could easily be its conclusion with the generalization that "there is no sensual pleasure so just that excess and intemperance in it are not a matter of reproach" (148). In fact, however, this is not Montaigne's final or apparently even his strongest conviction on the matter. Speaking "in good earnest," he continues as follows: "[I]sn't man a miserable animal? Hardly is it in his power, by his natural condition, to taste a single pleasure pure and entire, and still he is at pains to curtail that pleasure by his reason: he is not wretched enough unless by art and study he augments his misery." Later he supported this thought by quoting Propertius's line, "We have increased by art the troubles of our lot," and in the final revisions of the essay this quotation is followed by these remarks: "Human wisdom very stupidly exercises its ingenuity to reduce the number and sweetness of the sensual pleasures that belong to us . . ." (148). Moderation, yes, monkish abstinence and abnegation, no. The sensual pleasures are ours by nature and we should let ourselves enjoy them.

Montaigne returns to this theme many times, perhaps at greatest length in the long, wandering, and frequently bawdy "Of Some Verses of Virgil" (III, 5). After a characteristically extended exploration of attitudes and practices concerning sexual relations, he complains that those who are learned or philosophically disposed treat "of things too subtly, in a mode too artificial and different from the common and natural one." His page "makes love and understands it. Read him Leon Hebrero and Ficino; they talk about him, his thoughts, and his actions, and yet he does not understand a thing in it . . ." If Montaigne himself were "of the trade" of men such as Ficino and Aristotle he "would naturalize art as much as they artify nature" (666). More specifically as regards sexual intercourse, "Nature pushes us on to it, having attached to this desire the most noble, useful, and pleasant of all her operations." But she leaves us free to assess it as we see fit and, stupidly, we "shun it as shameless and indecent, blush at it, and recommend abstinence. Are we not brutes to call brutish the operation that makes us? . . . What a monstrous animal to be a horror to himself, to be burdened by his pleasures, to regard himself as a misfortune" (669–70).

True, the body is often a source of pain and misery, and there is no reason to think that Montaigne opposed all of those forms of bodily self-discipline studied and apparently endorsed by Foucault (for example,

"Dietetics"). Manifesting his oft-repeated scorn for the medical practition-ers of his time, however, Montaigne sought to lighten this burden on him-self and his friends, neighbors, and acquaintances. "Alas poor Man! You have enough necessary ills without increasing them by your inventions, and you are miserable enough by nature without being made so by art. You have real and essential deformities enough without forging imaginary ones" (670).[21] He rejected any very sharp distinction between the corpo-real and the mental or spiritual (see III, 13, 849, as well as the discussion about to be cited), but insofar as he followed the convention of treating the "soul" as the seat of judgment he argued that, rather than being cool to-ward bodily pleasures, it should "hatch them and foment them, to offer and invite herself to them." "For it is indeed reasonable, as they say, that the body should not follow its appetites to the disadvantage of the mind; but why is it not also reasonable that the mind should not pursue its appetites to the disadvantage of the body?" (681).[22]

Although clearly no unvarnished sensualist or hedonist, in these pas-sages Montaigne strongly associates nature and the natural with the body and its pleasures.[23] This association shows up again but in broadened form in other places where he expresses his preference for the natural over the artificial. In "On Experience" he says: "I, who operate close to the ground, hate that inhuman wisdom that would make us disdainful enemies of the cultivation of the body. I consider it equal injustice to set our heart against natural pleasures and to set our heart too much on them" (F, III, 13, 849). How, then, in addition to being respectful and responsive to our bodies, does one go about "operating close to the ground"? What, in addition to our bodies, constitutes the "ground" to which we should remain "close"?

An important part of the answer to these questions can be gleaned by looking at Montaigne's several discussions of cannibals, peasants, and other "primitive" or "simple" peoples. In "Of Cannibals" he admits to ac-cording great trust to the reports of his Brazilian informant precisely be-cause he "was a simple, crude fellow" and therefore a "character fit to bear true witness; for clever people observe more things and more curiously, but they interpret them; and to lend weight and conviction to their inter-pretation, they cannot help altering history a little. They never show you things as they are but bend and disguise them according to the way they have seen them; and to give credence to their judgment and attract you to it, they are prone to add something to their matter, to stretch it out and amplify it. We need a man either very honest, or so simple that he has not the stuff to build up false inventions and give them plausibility; and wed-ded to no theory. Such was my man" (F, I, 31, 152). Although not easy to harmonize with what I earlier called Montaigne's radical perspectivalism, this stance accords well with his suspicion of art, artifice, and purported sophistication and it is in even closer harmony with his assessments of what was reported to him concerning life among denizens of the New World.

He describes the material conditions of these peoples as exceptionally pleasant by European standards (152–55), but what is far more striking to him is what he calls their purity. They have been, he opines, "fashioned very little by the human mind, and are still very close to their original naturalness. The laws of nature still rule them . . . and they are in . . . a state of purity" far superior to the forms of innocence imagined by European state of nature thinkers such as Plato and Lycurgus, thinkers who "could not imagine a naturalness so pure as we see by experience; nor could they believe that our society could be maintained with so little artifice" (153). In remarks that directly anticipate some of the most famous sentences of both Hobbes and Rousseau (did either or both of them know this essay?) except that it reverses Hobbes's and apparently endorses Rousseau's valorizations of the circumstances it describes, Montaigne asserts that among the "barbarians," "there is no sort of traffic, no knowledge of letters, no science of numbers, no name for a magistrate or for political superiority, no custom of servitude, no riches or poverty, no contracts, no successions, no partitions, no occupations but leisure ones, no care for any but common kinship, no clothes, no agriculture, no metal, no use of wine or wheat. The very words that signify lying, treachery, dissimulation, avarice, envy, belittling, pardon—unheard of" (153). The "naturalness" that Montaigne discerns and admires among the primitives, the respects in which they live (as he says he aspires to do) "close to the ground," then, is contrastive and partly negative or privative, partly positive and attributive: they have avoided or been spared characteristics that afflict those who regard them as barbarians, and they retain and sustain valuable traits and tendencies that the latter have lost.[24]

With qualifications that anticipate Rousseau's regrets concerning the inegalitarian and unjustifiably inequitable features of self-styled civilized societies, Montaigne descries, if only vestigially and precariously, comparably admirable positive and negative characteristics among the "simpler" folk (including Socrates and himself!) of his own more direct and extensive acquaintance. Rather than pursuing the "vain and superfluous," the subtle but deceptive niceties of the learned, "Let us look on the earth at the poor people we see scattered there, heads bowed over their toil, who know neither Aristotle nor Cato, neither example nor precept. From them Nature every day draws deeds of constancy and endurance purer and harder than those that we study with such care in school. How many of them I see all the time who ignore poverty! How many desire death, or meet it without alarm and without affliction!" (F, III, 12, 795). Following Socrates, who like himself is of the common sort in every respect except that he knows it (II, 17, 481), he asserts that "We need hardly any learning to live at ease. And Socrates teaches us that it is in us, and the way to find it and help ourselves with it. All this ability of ours that is beyond the natural is as good as vain and superfluous" (III, 12, 794). Although he likes nothing so much as to retire to the solitude of his book-filled tower, he is convinced that "Most of the instructions that learning uses to encourage us are more showy than powerful and more ornamental than effective. We have abandoned Nature and we want to teach her her lesson, she who used to guide us so happily and so surely. And yet the traces of her teaching and the little that remains of her image—imprinted, by the benefit of ignorance, on the life of that rustic, unpolished mob—learning is constrained every day to go and borrow, to give its disciples models of constancy, innocence and tranquility." Regrettably, "men have done with Nature as perfumers do with oil: they have sophisticated her with so many arguments and farfetched reasonings that she has become variable and particular for each man, and has lost her own constant and universal countenance." Accordingly, we must seek among the untutored and indeed the animals for the "evidence of her that is not subject to favor, corruption, or diversity of opinion" (803; and compare III, 13, 844). Resisting and disciplining himself against this degrading and indeed depraving tendency, he has "very simply and crudely adopted for my own sake this ancient precept: that we cannot go wrong by following Nature, that the sovereign precept is to conform to her." And this means, he claims, that "I let myself go as I have come. I combat nothing. My two ruling parts [presumably body and soul], of their own volition, live in peace and good accord" (F, III, 12, 811).

VI

These discussions of Nature and the Natural provide me with a convenient route to return to my questions concerning freedom, discipline, and resistance. As various scholars have noted, the passages just considered seem to be distinctive in that in them Montaigne appears to be generalizing quite freely concerning the human condition and to be quite prepared, on the basis of those generalizations, to advance principles and precepts that should be followed by all of humankind. Whereas he frequently claims that his essays are written solely for himself and a few friends, proudly announces that "I do not make it my business to tell the world what it should do—enough others do that—but what I do in it" (F, I, 28, 142), says he desires the well-being of his country but "without getting ulcers and growing thin over it" (F, III, 10, 778–9), and so forth, we have now been seeing him claim to be "guided by the general law of the world" (F, III, 13, 821) and to present himself as quite prepared to guide the world by giving general laws to it. He knows the truth about how the world is and how it should be, and that knowledge makes him free. And since others do not have that knowledge, resist accepting it and acting on it, it is for Montaigne to do what he can to bring them under the sway of its discipline. He acts for himself importantly if not primarily by acting against the proclivities of others to act in ways that are harmful to him.

It is undeniable that there are changes of tonality and emphasis in the later essays and additions, but it is important to be clear about the content and especially about the addressees of the more generalizing of Montaigne's remarks. As to the former, the characterizations of the human condition are highly general and entirely consistent with great variations from society to society and person to person. If it is true that "Each man bears the entire form of man's estate" (F, III, 2, 611), it is no less the case that "Men are diverse in inclination and strength; they must be led to their own good according to their nature and by diverse routes" (F, III, 12, 805). To whom, then, are the general counsels addressed? Because they are based on what comes naturally to the primitive and simple among us, the rest of us, including or rather especially Montaigne himself, learn from rather than teach them. And presumably those who remain vain, presumptuous, or otherwise dogmatic will pay little or no heed to Montaigne's advisings.

I conclude, then, that they are addressed primarily by Montaigne to Montaigne himself and perhaps to those akin to him. Having experienced the temptations of learning, philosophizing, and dogmatizing, hence no longer able to rest his head on that "sweet and soft and healthy pillow" that is "ignorance and incuriosity" (III, 13, 822), Montaigne must teach himself, discipline himself, to attend to himself, to make the study of himself both his "metaphysics" and his "physics" (821). "There is nothing so beautiful and legitimate as to play the man well and properly; no knowledge so hard to acquire as the knowledge of how to live this life well and naturally; and the most barbarous of our maladies is to despise our being" (852). "It is an absolute perfection and virtually divine to know how to enjoy our being rightfully. We seek other conditions because we do not understand the use of our own, and go outside of ourselves because we do not know what it is like inside. Yet there is no use our mounting on stilts, for on stilts we must still walk on our legs. And on the loftiest throne in the world we are still sitting on our rump."

There is, then, much need for discipline, there are numerous temptations, inclinations, and dispositions that must be resisted. To live "appropriately," to sustain a life with as much freedom as Fortuna allows, requires that we discipline ourselves against many of the "disabilities" that our socialization, acculturation, and education urge on us and attempt to instill in us. But if it is not an easy thing to let one's self go as it comes, to let the self be first and foremost for itself, this is because the idea of doing so is not merely an idea but a soaring ideal, a vision of what fully human, fully humane, lives—in all of their diversities—would be like. This is the ideal that Montaigne urged upon himself and whoever else had or was prepared to cultivate the ability to celebrate and pursue it. A life relieved of, freed from, self-diminishing forms of "combat" requires struggle with and against elements and forces that, given the unavoidably situated character of our selves, are almost certain to have installed themselves deeply within us. The possibility of sustaining that second form of combat depends above all on sustaining—no easy thing to do—the conviction that

> "You are as much a god as you will own
> That you are nothing but a man alone."
> Amyot's Plutarch (III, 13, 857)

CHAPTER 4

The Self Against and for Itself: II
Nietzsche as Theorist of Disciplined Freedom
of Action and Free-Spiritedness

Foucault is more than generous in his acknowledgments, on the issues here in question and numerous others, of his indebtedness to the thinking of Nietzsche. And Nietzsche, as part of his repeated expressions of admiration for the thinkers of the Renaissance, gives high praise to the "bold and light-hearted skepticism of a Montaigne," contrasting the latter's outlook and temperament with the "insipid backwoodsman's problems" that preoccupied Martin Luther (*Will to Power*, I, 93: 57; hereafter *WP* followed by book, section, and page numbers. And cf. *Human All Too Human*, I, 1: 12; hereafter *HATH* followed by volume, section, and page numbers). There is therefore reason to expect substantial continuities to emerge from explorations of and engagements with these three thinkers. But just as we found significant differences between Foucault and Montaigne, so we will find that the nuances and inflections of Nietzsche's thinking about freedom, discipline, and resistance depart importantly from those of Foucault and Montaigne. These differences should help us to enlarge and refine our own reflections concerning these topics. Moving through a number of issues and topics of concern to all three thinkers, I explore some of the salient continuities and commonalities but intersperse comments concerning respects in which Nietzsche's positions—as one would expect in relations among thinkers all of whom are committed perspectivalists—diverge from the reflections thus far discussed.

For present purposes, the most salient commonality among Montaigne, Foucault, and Nietzsche is the high ranking they each give to human freedom. We have seen the views of Montaigne and Foucault on this topic and strikingly similar thoughts are prominent in Nietzsche. In *Human All Too Human,* for instance, he says: "What . . . we may call ourselves in all seriousness (and without being in any way defiant) is 'free-ranging spirits,' because we feel the tug towards freedom as the strongest drive of our spirit and, in antithesis to the fettered and firm-rooted intellects, see our ideal almost in a spiritual nomadism—to employ a modest and almost contemptuous expression" (Vol. II, Section One: 263). A little earlier in the same section, and anticipating a theme that we will explore below, he proclaims that "When thought and inquiry have become decisive—when, that is to say, free-spiritedness has become a quality of the character action tends to moderation" (Ibid.: 169). Again, in *The Gay Science,* as a part of singing the praises of polytheism and the freedom the Greeks attributed to the several gods vis-à-vis one another, he asserts that this outlook "was the inestimable preliminary exercise for the justification of the egoism and sovereignty of the individual: the freedom that one conceded to a god in his relation to other gods—one eventually also granted to oneself in relation to laws, customs and neighbors" (Book III, paragraph 143: 191–2; hereafter *GS* followed by book, paragraph, and page numbers).

These notions of freedom and free-spiritedness are present throughout Nietzsche's works and become increasingly prominent and emphatic in his later writings. His numerous formulations of them are anything but uniform or self-explanatory and we will have to return to them at greater length below. I mention a few of the passages concerning them at this juncture to quell any initial suspicions that, as distinct from Montaigne and Foucault, for Nietzsche, freedom was at best a subsidiary concern. But, as with the other thinkers engaged, we cannot understand and assess Nietzsche's thinking about freedom without first critically considering the wider theoretical and rhetorical settings in which remarks such as those just quoted take their place. Our first step in conducting this wider inquiry and reflection will be to take up the topics identified by the title of the following subsection.

I

Cognition /Conation: Reason, Passion, and Other Sources of Thought and Action

Let us begin with a passage that sketches several of the main elements of what can fairly be called Nietzsche's epistemology. Early in Book Three of *The Will to Power* (Section I of this book is titled the "Will to Power as

Knowledge"), Nietzsche declares his hostility to what he takes to be the view of knowledge acquisition that is dominant in his century and indeed has prevailed in one form or another throughout much of the history of Western philosophy. "Against positivism," the positivist "halts at phenomena" and insists that "There are only *facts.*" Nietzsche responds as follows: "No, facts is precisely what there are not, only interpretations. We cannot establish any fact 'in itself': perhaps it is folly to want to do such a thing" (III, 3: 267).

He then imagines the positivist objecting that on this view "Everything is subjective," thereby introducing the notion of the subject—and the subject-object divide—into the philosophy of cognition. Nietzsche's response is to say that "even this is interpretation. The 'subject' is not something given, it is something added and invented and projected behind what there is. Finally, is it necessary to posit an interpreter behind the interpretation?" The positivist, he thinks, will answer this question with an emphatic "yes." But "even this is invention, hypothesis" (Ibid.). "In so far as the word 'knowledge' has any meaning, the world is knowable; but it is *interpretable* otherwise, it has no meaning behind it, but countless meanings." And the view that this is the case is called "Perspectivism" (Ibid.).

It is important to underline the subversive character of the idea that the world can be said to be knowable only insofar as the word "knowledge" has any meaning. "Knowledge" being a word in one or more languages, its meaning(s) are given by the customs and conventions that govern its use(s) in this or that language. Thus claims that this or that is the case, that these or those are the facts, in addition to being variously interpretable in every case,[1] invariably put a screen of artifice or invention between knowledge claims and the world that those claims purport to be about.

What are the sources of our interpretations and the conventions that are necessary to forming and articulating them? Nietzsche addresses this question at numerous places in his writings and the answers he gives to it vary somewhat among the several discussions. But the answer he gives in the brief but pregnant subsection that I have been discussing warrants rejection of any very clean distinction between cognition and conation, between knowledge and belief, thinking and feeling. In a passage that echoes Montaigne, he says that "It is our needs that interpret the world; our drives and their For and Against." He then continues in terms that Montaigne would use, if at all, only of a limited subset of drives: "Every drive is a kind of lust to rule; each one has its perspective that it would like to compel all the other drives to accept as norm" (*WP* III, 481: 267).

This last sentence is of course an expression of his view that seeking knowledge is an expression of the will to power and that the claim to have acquired it includes the claim that some of one's drives have triumphed over the others or that one's drives have triumphed over the drives of other persons. Thus, to look ahead a bit, the activities called by such names as inquiry, reflection, and contemplation require the freedom to act on some among one's drives but also require discipline and resistance. I must discipline myself to act, at least here and now, on one and only one subset of my drives and I must resist the attempts by other persons, institutions, and so on to impose their drives on me. Even the domains of inquiry and reflection, often characterized as peacefully contemplative, are arenas of conflict and discord. And to the extent that my quests for knowledge involve me in interactions with other persons, those relationships will always have a competitive or conflictful as well as a sometimes cooperative character. Nor should these characteristics be regretted. If they infuse a certain pathos into the quest for knowledge, for the free spirit they also give that quest force, vivacity, and a certain zest. If we use the word "science" to stand for all attempts to augment knowledge, then all science should be "gay."

It hardly needs to be said that the foregoing elements of Nietzsche's epistemology will be deeply disturbing to the gray, somber types (for example, Darwin and Spencer) that Nietzsche thought dominated the "scientific" scene in Britain and elsewhere. The latter will resist the free spirit's attempts to promote a gay science, and proponents of such a science must be prepared to resist their resistances. But Nietzsche deepens and it should be said darkens the skepticism of his epistemology in several respects that need to be considered.

One respect in which he does so is with his thoughts about reason. In the tradition he is contesting, reason is sharply distinguished from and opposed to passion. Reason is to control the passions and it is reason and reasoning that allow us to arrive at the truth and the good and to avoid the false and the evil. But, as with Montaigne, Nietzsche rejects any sharp distinction and argues that, insofar as we can differentiate the two, reason plays a distinctly limited rule in our thinking and acting. "The whole conception of an order of rank among the passions: as if the right and normal thing were for once to be guided by reason—with the passions as abnormal, dangerous, semi-animal. . . . The misunderstanding of passion and reason, as if the latter were an independent entity and not rather a system of relationships between various passions and desires; and as if every passion did not possess its quantum of reason—" (*WP*, II, 387: 208). After claiming that he has restored "His Lordship At-Random [the aleatory] to all things," with characteristic hyperbole Zarathustra pronounces that, therefore, "With all things only one thing is impossible—rationality!" He goes on to qualify this extreme view, but only minimally. "A little reason, to be sure, a seed of wisdom scattered among the stars: such leavening has been intermingled with all things: for folly's sake, wisdom has been intermingled with all things. A little wisdom is quite possible—but in all things I found the blissful certainty that they would rather—dance on the feet of chance." Again, this is a condition or circumstance to be welcomed, indeed celebrated. "Oh sky above me, you pure high sky! Your purity means to me that there are no eternal spiders and spider webs of reason—" (*Thus Spake Zarathustra*, Third Part: 194; hereafter *TSZ*, followed by part and page numbers). Thus insofar as reason and reasoning can be distinguished from passion, they will play no more than a minimal role in maintaining the discipline and resistance necessary to freedom.

The doctrines discussed thus far resonate with might be called Nietzsche's metaphysics or cosmology. We should beware, he says, "of positing generally and everywhere anything as elegant as the cyclical movements of our neighboring stars; . . . The total character of the world . . . is in all eternity chaos—in the sense not of a lack of necessity but a lack of order. . . . Judged from the point of view of our reason, unsuccessful attempts [at finding an order] are by all odds the rule. . . ." (*GS*, Three, 109: 167–68). The flux and disorder of the world is itself an obstacle to, or at least places severe limitations upon, the possibility of attaining, through investigations and reflections governed by reason, knowledge concerning it. As Montaigne and Foucault put it, the world is not made for us, and our reason is not made such that it can steadily and widely provide us with reliable access to and knowledge concerning our world.

We have not yet reached, however, Nietzsche's most radical and disturbing critique of and alternative to positivist and rationalist epistemologies. In Section 333 of *The Gay Science* he introduces what he evidently thinks is his most profound thought on the matters we have been discussing. "For the longest time, conscious thought was considered thought itself. Only now does the truth dawn on us that by far the greatest part of our spirit's activity remains unconscious and unfelt" (*GS*, 333: 262). He then reiterates his view that thinking, apparently even the pre-, post-, or extra-conscious thinking that he is going to discuss, is full of conflicts among "instincts" and can lead to exhaustion. But he then returns to the theme presented in the passage just quoted: "*Conscious* thinking, especially that of the philosopher, is the least vigorous and therefore also the relatively mildest and calmest form of thinking; and thus precisely philosophers are most apt to be led astray about the nature of thinking" (Ibid.).

In Section 354 he returns to this theme at greater length. We not only could but for the most part do without, "as one says metaphorically," consciousness. "The whole of life would be possible without, as it were, seeing itself in a mirror. Even now, for that matter, by far the greatest portion of our life actually takes place without this mirror effect; and this is true even of our thinking, feeling, and willing life . . . " (Ibid.: 297).

What, then, is this in principle (but not, as we see below, in practice) superfluous something that is called consciousness? Nietzsche's answer is that it is the "*capacity for communication*" and that its presence or absence is always proportionate to the "*need for communication.*" "Consciousness is really only a net of communication between human beings; it is only as such that it had to develop; a solitary human being who lived like a beast of prey would not have needed it." That some of our actions, thoughts, and feelings "must" enter our consciousness is the result of a must "that for a terribly long time lorded it over man. As the most endangered animal, he *needed* help and protection . . . and for all of this he needed 'consciousness' . . . needed to 'know' himself, what distressed him . . . how he felt, . . . what he thought" (Ibid.: 298).

In order to develop the capacity to communicate with oneself and to others, it was necessary to develop means or media of communication, that is, to develop those "signs of communication" some of which are called words but that include numerous other communicative devices that can also be called languages. "[T]he development of language and the development of consciousness (*not* of reason but merely of the way reason enters consciousness) go hand in hand" (Ibid.: 299). Thus, "from the start," consciousness and language "was needed and useful only between human beings (particularly between those who commanded and those who obeyed); and . . . it developed only in proportion to the degree of this utility" (Ibid.: 298).

We might say that for Nietzsche language and consciousness are teleological and its uses perlocutionary in character. Realizing their vulnerability, and by instinct grasping that making themselves more secure required mutual assistance, human beings thought—perhaps felt—their way to the devices that came to be called language. Thus at bottom language and consciousness take their character from the end to which they contribute. Thus, again at bottom, Nietzsche's account has a reductive tendency. Language and hence consciousness primarily serve this utilitarian purpose. Analyzing any instance of language-cum-consciousness requires identifying the ways in which it contributes, was/is expected by its users to contribute, to providing them with a degree of protection or security. Because language-cum-consciousness as we now experience and use them have a long and complex history, analyzing them requires the often arduous and complex form of investigation called genealogy.

Nietzsche presents a partial summary of his genealogical investigations in the paragraph under consideration. Without ever denying the utility of language-cum-consciousness, as we have begun to see, he claims that humanity has paid and continues to pay a high price for them. Language serves not only "as a bridge between human beings [the famous rainbow bridge of concepts?] but also a mien, a pressure, a gesture." "[C]onsciousness does not really belong to man's individual existence but rather to his social or herd nature." Thus consciousness, rather than facilitating the achievement of knowledge, becomes a barrier to arriving at it and particularly to arriving at that most important kind of knowledge, knowledge of the self. Given "the best will in the world to understand ourselves as individually as possible, 'to know ourselves,' each of us will always succeed in becoming conscious only of what is not individual but 'average'. . . . Fundamentally, all our actions are altogether incomparably personal, unique, and infinitely individual; there is no doubt of that. But as soon as we translate them into consciousness *they no longer seem to be*" (299). The "world of which we can become conscious is only a surface and sign-world, a world that is made common and meaner; whatever becomes conscious *becomes* by the same token shallow, thin, relatively stupid, general, sign, herd signal; all becoming conscious involves a great and thorough corruption, falsification, reduction to superficialities, and generalization. Ultimately, the growth of consciousness becomes a danger; and anyone who lives among the most conscious Europeans even knows that it is a disease" (299–300). To look into the mirror that is consciousness is to see into a darkened glass.

To repeat, Nietzsche never denies the value, indeed the indispensibility, of language and the consciousness constituted by using language. He is not, in this or any other respect, a passive nihilist whose only objective is to destroy that which he finds objectionable or distasteful. He recognizes, in so many words as it were, its utility and of course by his own doctrine he himself can communicate his thoughts to others only by putting them into words and thereby making himself conscious of them. As with so many of the "extravagant" surmises (297) that he advances, his objective seems to be to shake up (at least some of) the complacent and to exhume and breathe life into possibilities that have been buried under the detritus of centuries of overly conscious culture.

It of course might be objected that he is not as clear as one might wish concerning the origin, character, or standing of that non- or extra-conscious "knowledge" (a kind of awareness?) that he ranks so highly. He would reply that he is as clear as the superficial and falsifying character of the language he must use allows him to be. And he might further rejoin that any attempt to say more and more clearly would not only fail but might diminish the likelihood that he and others would be attentive and receptive to those forms of being that exceed the experiences that we can have in the several houses of language. It should be added that when Nietzsche offers negative characterizations of language-cum-consciousness he captures an experience common among us. We often find that language is an imprecise, an unsubtle, and even a falsifying medium in which to encounter and express ourselves and our world. This feeling of being diminished by our language, of "running against the boundaries of language . . . against the walls of our cage" (as Wittgenstein put it), seems to presuppose some sense, however dim or ineffable, of a domain of experience that is prior to or apart from language. This may be mysticism, but if there are benign and possibly creative forms thereof, Nietzsche's is a good candidate.[2]

II

Discipline and Control: By Others and by the Self Itself

The thoughts discussed in the previous section articulate radical respects in which the self is against but might make itself, at least in part, for itself, for its own freedom. Insofar as the self submits to, becomes dependent upon and, hence, complicit with the herd mentality that is inscribed in language, it is against the possibility of its knowing itself as a "unique and infinitely individual person." But "there is no doubt" that human beings "are"—at least in the sense of having the potential to become—such persons, and it may even be that the experience of feeling constrained and diminished by language can assist this or that person in loosening somewhat the hold of language upon them. To the extent that Zarathustra speaks for Nietzsche, it seems clear that the latter's quest for free-spiritedness, for a spiritual nomadism, was aided in this way. In ascending to peaks and dancing on the edge of abysses, Zarathustra rises above language and consciousness and peers into depths in which they cannot exist. The self is disciplined, controlled, and also importantly enabled by language, but retains the possibility of resisting *that* discipline and disciplining itself to accept the uncertainties and rigors and also releasing itself to the exhilarating joys and delights of free-spiritedness.

In the respects just iterated, there are substantial continuities between the ideas canvassed and those now to be considered. Even for the free spirit—we might say especially for the free spirit—life in a society and culture (and for Nietzsche there is no such thing as human life altogether apart from a society and culture) involves a plethora of positive and negative demands and requirements, pushes and pulls. Understanding language to mean not just words but that vast array of devices in and through which these imperatives are expressed and these forces deployed, we can say that all of them reach and impact the members of society through or under the sway of language. Famously, however, Nietzsche does not content himself with this general view. He details numerous particular respects in which societies and cultures have, do, and of certainty will continue to control and direct the thinking and acting of their members. And just as he recognizes the "utility," even the indispensibility, of consciousness, so he acknowledges and even celebrates many of the further sources of discipline and direction that have evolved through human history. As we will see, just as Nietzsche is no passive nihilist, neither is he a champion of "*laisser-aller*," of that "letting go" that he thought was promoted by Romanticism. There is much that we not only do but should accept and to which we ought to conform ourselves. As with language, however, Nietzsche is never far from the thought that human life is at its best when or to the extent that it maintains an always precarious but precious balance or accommodation between accepting the controls and restraints of social and cultural life and the self-discipline necessary to resist them so as to achieve and sustain free-spiritedness. I begin with the former and work toward his thoughts as to how and why the latter—in all its diversity—can be accomplished.

In perhaps the most widely discussed passage in *The Genealogy of Morals*, Nietzsche argues that "man's true problem" is to find ways of breeding "an animal with the right to make promises" (Second Essay, Section I: 189; hereafter *GM* followed by essay, section, and page numbers). At least three aspects of this remark deserve comment. First, it is implicit that "unbred" animals, including the animals that are human beings, do not have this right. Second, Nietzsche's use of the language of breeding makes it clear that acquiring this "right" is not something that individuals can do entirely for themselves, that there must be "breeders" who know what it takes to deserve this right and who can engender or otherwise install the necessary characteristics in the animals they breed. Third, this latter point is perhaps part of the reason that Nietzsche asks whether this problem of generating animals with this right "is [not] the paradoxical problem nature has set itself with regard to man?" (Ibid.) Answering yes to this question, he says that it is paradoxical because by nature human beings do not have the characteristics necessary to deserve the right and hence there is a puzzle as to when, where, and how the "breeders" could or did emerge. It is also paradoxical in that—unless Nietzsche is thinking about genetic engineering, which is unlikely—there is a puzzle as to why an animal who lacked the necessary characteristics would submit to the demands of the breeders. (As usual with such paradoxes, to the extent that Nietzsche attempts to dissolve or at least diminish them—often he simply lets them stand and not infrequently relishes them—he does so by presenting a genealogy of the emergence of animals with this right, hence with the capacity to engender them in others, and the emergence of other animals willing to submit to the training of the breeders. On this point see the discussion just below.)

As one would expect from what we have seen thus far, Nietzsche expresses surprise that "the problem has in fact been solved to a remarkable degree" (Ibid.). It is surprising for reasons already considered but more particularly because promise-making, or rather promise-keeping, is opposed by "a strong force, the faculty of oblivion" or forgetting. "The role of this active [force of] oblivion is that of a concierge: to shut temporarily the doors and windows of consciousness; . . . to make room for the nobler functions and functionaries of our organism which do the governing and planning." It "represents a power, a form of strong health" without which "there can be no happiness, no serenity, no hope, no pride, no *present*" (Ibid.).

Clearly, if breeding an animal with the right to make and the capacity to keep promises destroyed or overwhelmed the faculty of oblivion, doing so would be a disaster for humankind.

But "this naturally forgetful animal . . . has created for itself an opposite power, that of remembering, by whose aid, in certain cases, oblivion may be suspended—specifically in cases where it is a question of promises" (Ibid.: 189–90). This remembering must also be an active force, "an active not wishing to be done with" a pledge once made. It must be a "'veritable memory of the will'; so that between the original determination and the actual performance of the thing willed, a whole world of new things . . . can be interposed without snapping the long chain of the will" (Ibid.: 190).

The faculty of oblivion provides the self with a place of quiet, of solitude as Nietzsche is fond of saying, in which the freedom of free-spiritedness can be cultivated and exercised. But this solitude must coexist with remembrance and commitments, to others, into the future and in an important sense to the past. And this requires, "presupposes," the breeding and sustaining of qualities that are in strong and ineliminable tension with the power of oblivion. "A man who wishes to dispose of his future in this manner must first have learned to separate necessary from accidental acts; to think causally; to see distant things as though they were near at hand; to distinguish means from ends. In short, he must have become not only calculating but himself calculable, regular even to his perception, if he is to stand pledge for his own future as a guarantor does." (Ibid. Note that most if not all of these capacities are developed and exercised in the domain of the conscious.)

In a highly complex and readily misunderstood passage, Nietzsche first underlines the importance of the development of calculating and calculability and then, as usual, issues a caution or warning concerning taking such a development to excess. What, he asks, is the greatest danger threatening humankind? His initial answer is as follows: "If the majority of men had not always considered the *discipline* of their minds—their 'rationality'—a matter of pride, an obligation, and a virtue, feeling insulted or embarrassed by all fantasies and debaucheries of thought because they saw themselves as friends of 'healthy common sense,' humanity would have perished long ago" (*GS*, Two, 76: 130, italics added). He calls the absence of such discipline madness and says that it "means the eruption of arbitrariness in feeling, seeing, and hearing, the enjoyment of the mind's lack of discipline, the joy in human unreason" (Ibid.) He then explains why he had put "rationality" in scare quotes (and might well have employed the same graphic device with "unreason"). "Not truth and certainty are the opposite of the world of the madman, but the universality and the universal binding force of a faith; in sum, the non-arbitrary character of judgments" (Ibid.).

Where does this "faith" come from and what sometimes sustains it? In answering this question Nietzsche again underscores the point that, as with the closely related power of remembrance, it is not a faith that an individual can create and sustain entirely by or for herself. "[M]an's greatest labor so far has been to reach agreement about very many things and to submit to a *law of agreement*—regardless of whether these things are true or false. This is the discipline of mind that mankind has received; but the contrary impulses are still so powerful that at bottom we cannot speak of the future of mankind with much confidence" (Ibid.: 130–31). The agreement is interpersonal in standing and the disciplines that it imposes on this or that individual come at least in part from the others who are parties to it.

This last point is underlined but also further called into question as the passage continues. "Continually this faith, like *everybody's* faith, arouses nausea and new lust in subtler minds; and the slow tempo that is here demanded for all spiritual processes, this imitation of the tortoise, which is here recognized as the norm, would be quite enough to turn artists and thinkers into apostates. It is in these impatient spirits that a veritable delight in madness erupts because madness has such a cheerful tempo" (Ibid.: 131). We will not be surprised to find Nietzsche extolling impatient spirits (such as himself). But they depend upon, we might even say are parasitic upon, a large number of "virtuous intellects." "What is needed is *virtuous stupidity*, stolid metronomes for the slow spirit, to make sure that the faithful of the great shared faith stay together and continue their [slow, closely regulated, not a Zarathustrian] dance. It is a first-rate need that commands and demands this" (Ibid.).

What, then, about the impatient, the free, spirits? "We others are the exception and the danger. . . ." In part because the stupidly virtuous will misunderstand and resent the free spirits, it follows for Nietzsche that "we need eternally to be defended" and this is possible because "there actually are things to be said in favor of the exception. . . ." But they can be defended only on a condition that brings the free spirit, at least in part, back into the grid fashioned by the law of agreement. They can be defended "*provided that* [they] *never want* . . . to become the rule*" (Ibid.). There is a place for madmen, for the *idiot savant*, but only on condition that her thinking and acting do not disrupt the disciplinary forces on which the future of humankind depends. This requires that the free spirit at once resist the requirements of the law of agreement and discipline herself not to disrupt the workings of the latter. (No easy feat! Try it!)

It is not to be thought that in talking about a law of agreement Nietzsche is putting himself in company with social contract or modern constitutional thinkers who imagine, or claim the historical reality of, a moment in time at which an agreement was arrived at which was thereafter held to be binding into the indefinite future. In the Second Essay of *The Genealogy of Morals* he addresses the issues just discussed, this time using the wider language of "responsibility" as well that of promising. His reflections have brought him "to the long story of the origin or genesis of responsibility" (II: 190). The tremendous achievement "of rendering man up to a certain point regular, uniform, equal among equals, calculable." Referring to his discussion in the book entitled *Daybreak*, he attributes this achievement to "'the custom character of morals,' that labor man accomplished upon himself over a vast period of time. . . . With the help of custom and the social strait-jacket, man was, in fact, made calculable" (*GM*: 190–91). Given that this process occurred "over a vast period of time," we have to assume—as Nietzsche obviously does—that the custom character of morals has undergone numerous changes in substance. It remains the same in that in important respects it defines the virtues and the obligation to enact and otherwise to honor them, but what counts as virtuous changes from time to time and place to place. Thus a certain adaptability is necessary even on the part of the stupidly virtuous.

The sequel to the remarks just quoted speaks to rule versus exception, virtuous intellects versus impatient free-spiritedness, and hence discipline, resistance, and freedom. It will therefore repay us to follow a bit further his discussion in *The Genealogy of Morals*. Immediately following the remarks just considered, he presents a thought that at first glance appears to have an oddly Hegelian ring and that might be taken to offer support for readings of Nietzsche as a thinker of the end of history, the last man, and the like. "If we place ourselves," he says, "at the terminal point of this great process, where society and custom finally reveal their true aim, we shall find that the ripest fruit of that tree is. . . ." (Ibid.: 191). Readers of the preceding remarks might expect this sentence to end with something like "societies and cultures populated by fully calculable and unfailingly responsible persons."

In fact, however, the "terminal point" to which Nietzsche somewhat misleadingly refers is not the end of history but is more appropriately regarded as the true beginning of a history that is genuinely human or humane. The ripest fruit of the development of the custom character of morality is, rather, "the sovereign individual, equal only to himself, all moral custom left far behind. [The last phrase is of course an exaggeration.] This autonomous, more than moral individual (the terms *autonomous* and *moral* are mutually exclusive) [another exaggeration!] has developed his own, independent, long-range will, which *dares* to make promises; he has a proud and vigorous consciousness [a kind of awareness, perhaps subliminal?] of what he has achieved, a sense of power and freedom, of absolute accomplishment" (Ibid., italics added).

There follow a number of unpleasing remarks concerning the deserved dominance of these sovereign individuals, these "overpersons" who are characterized by *virtu* rather than virtue, over their inferiors, the stupidly virtuous. As with the elitist-sounding remarks in the related observations in *The Gay Science*, remarks such as these, which are of course liberally sprinkled throughout Nietzsche's writings, raise the question of the place of the notion and the value of equality in Nietzsche's thinking. I touch on this question at intervals below, but I have discussed it in some detail elsewhere (see Flathman 1992, Part Two) and will not address it at length here. But we should note that those parts of the *Genealogy* passage already discussed, as with the remarks in *The Gay Science*, put Nietzsche's much criticized elitism in a perspective often not noticed by his critics. It was Nietzsche's insistence that the exceptional persons owe a great deal to the law of agreement and must not disrupt it that I had in mind in interjecting the word "exaggeration" in the passage just quoted. But the same thought is forwarded in a different idiom in that very passage. When Nietzsche says that the autonomous individual is the ripest fruit of the tree of customary morality he is not only emphasizing but importantly celebrating customary morality. To change figures slightly, if the overperson tried to destroy such morality, she would be sawing at the branch on which she sits. In however many respects some persons are superior to others, they are all alike in that (among numerous other respects) without customary morality there would be little or nothing between them and a madness for which no defense could be given.

We can end this section by considering some examples of the advice that Nietzsche gives to free spirits, some of his characterizations of the *virtus* that they should cultivate and enact.

In a passage that connects directly with the argument that we are all indebted to and should not disrupt customary morality (and one that aligns him closely with a central theme in Montaigne), Nietzsche addresses the role of habit in the life of free spirits such as himself. He first observes that he loves "brief habits and considers them an inestimable means for getting to know *many* things and states, down to the bottom of their sweetness and bitternesses" (*GS*, Four, 295: 237). Even if "brief," and Nietzsche does not specify a proper duration, habit requires remembrance and at least a temporary readiness to do again what one has done before. "But one day its time is up; the good thing parts from me, not as something that has come to nauseate me but peacefully and as sated with me as I am with it—as if we had reason to be grateful to each other as we shook hands to say farewell" (Ibid.: 238).

What he hates is *enduring* habits, and he is grateful even to "all my misery and bouts of sickness and everything about me that is imperfect, because this sort of thing leaves me with a hundred backdoors through which I can escape from enduring habits" (Ibid.). But what he hates even more, what is "most intolerable . . . and the terrible par excellence would be for me a life entirely devoid of habits, a life that would demand perpetual improvisation. That would be my exile and my Siberia" (Ibid.). Habits are indispensable, and sustaining them for the appropriate period of time requires the free spirit to resist her tendencies to forgetfulness and to discipline herself against an arbitrary waywardness of conduct. But this discipline and resistance in turn engenders the need for another, the discipline to be done with a habit when its time has passed. (See also the two next paragraphs—296–97—in Ibid. in which Nietzsche discusses the value and dangers of a "firm reputation" (238) and "the ability to contradict" oneself as well as others. The latter ability "is still more excellent and constitutes what is really great, new and amazing about our culture; this is the step of steps of the liberated spirit." And he asks, somewhat sardonically and in apparent contradiction with the view that "our culture" encourages and celebrates this ability, "Who knows that?" (Ibid.).

This back and forth between admiring and denigrating the culture of his time and place, a veritable leitmotif in Nietzsche's work, finds dramatic expression in his discussion of "European Nihilism" in Book One of *The Will to Power*. "I have as yet found *no* reason for discouragement. Whoever has preserved . . . in himself . . . a strong will, together with an ample spirit, has more favorable opportunities than ever. For the trainability of men has become very great in this democratic Europe; men who learn easily and adapt themselves easily are the rule: the herd animal, even highly intelligent, has been prepared" (*WP*, One, 128: 79). The words "adapt themselves easily" and "highly intelligent" suggest that even the herd animals have the ability to give up outworn habits and perhaps even cheerfully to contradict themselves. Somewhat more generously, in a slightly earlier passage he allows that "there are signs that the European [at least the "good European," which is how Nietzsche sometimes liked to style himself] of the nineteenth century is less ashamed of his instincts; he has taken a goodly step toward admitting to himself his unconditional naturalness, that is, his immorality, *without becoming embittered*—on the contrary, strong enough to endure only this sight" (120: 74).

Once again, however, he hastens to issue a warning. The "instincts of decadence should not be confused with *humaneness*; the means of civilization, which [can?] lead to disintegration and necessarily to decadence, should not be confused with culture; the libertinage, the principle of *laisser aller*, should not be confused with the will to power (which is the counter-principle)" (Ibid.: 75).

Thus far his advice is cast in general terms, in terms sufficiently broad that his counsels might apply to persons who are comfortable with customary morality and do not desire the more refined but challenging delights of free-spiritedness. A number of his more specific admonitions and recommendations are gathered in Book Four of *The Will to Power*. Here are a few examples: "Blind indulgence of an affect [for example, a passion, a lust], totally regardless of whether it be a generous and compassionate or a hostile affect, is the cause of the greatest evils. Greatness of character does not consist in not possessing these affects—on the contrary, one possesses them to the highest degree—but in having them under control" (928: 490). Again, "*In Summa: domination* of the passions, *not* their weakening or extirpation!—The greater the dominating power of a will, the more freedom may the passions be allowed. The 'great man' is great owing to the free play and scope of his desires and to the yet greater power that knows how to press these magnificent monsters into service" (Ibid., 933: 492).

How does the free spirit maintain this delicate, constantly threatened equilibrium between the free play of desires and control over them? Perhaps surprisingly, one means of doing so is to cultivate what Nietzsche calls prodigality. "True graciousness, nobility, greatness of soul proceed from abundance; do not give in order to receive—do not try to exalt themselves by being gracious;—prodigality as the type of true graciousness, abundance of personality as its presupposition" (935: 493). Along with prodigality he recommends a careful choosing of one's enemies and magnanimity as well as fierceness toward them. Zarathustra says, "I love the courageous, but it is not enough to be a fighter. One must also know *whom* to fight. Often there is more courage in containing oneself and passing by—in order to save oneself for a worthier enemy! . . . You must be proud of your enemies" (*TSZ*, Part Three: 248). In the often intemperate *The Anti-Christ*, Nietzsche says that he struggles to maintain "a large tolerance, that is to say a *magnanimous* self-control" (38: 149; hereafter *AC* followed by section and page numbers).

Returning to *Will to Power*, Number 943 of Book Four offers a number of further counsels, including the following: Apparent frivolity but underneath it a "stoic severity and self-constraint"; endurance of poverty, want, and sickness; maintaining an "incognito" ("if God existed, he would, merely on grounds of decency, be obliged to show himself to the world only as a man"); "Pleasure in forms; taking under protection everything formal, the conviction that politeness is one of the greatest virtues; mistrust for letting oneself go in any way . . . ;" "Ability to keep silent: but not a word about that in the presence of listeners" (496–97). And a little later: the free spirit "*always maintains poise*" (948: 499).

Many of these thoughts bring to mind Foucault's discussions of the means appropriate to caring for the self, and of course also much of Montaigne's advice to himself and to anyone else who cares to listen. Some of the most important of them are condensed, and the similarities with Montaigne and especially with Foucault underlined, in Nietzsche's highly favorable invocation of the Stoic philosopher Epictetus. "The human being after the model of Epictetus would certainly not be to the taste of those [Christians, for example] who strive after the ideal nowadays. The constant tension of his being, the unwearied glance turned inward, the reserve, caution, uncommunicativeness of his eye . . . ; not to speak of his silence or near silence: all signs of the most resolute bravery. . . . In addition to all this, he is not fanatical, he hates . . . display and vainglory . . . ; his arrogance, great though it is, has nonetheless no desire to disturb others, it admits a certain mild intimacy and wants to spoil no one's good humour—it can, indeed, even smile! [T]here is very much of the humanity of antiquity in this ideal. [T]he fairest thing about it is, however, that it lacks all fear of God, . . . that it is no penitential preacher" (*Daybreak*, Book V, Paragraph 546: 219; hereafter *DB* followed by book, paragraph, and page numbers).

The passage continues in a manner pertinent to the question of Nietzsche's thinking about equality. "Epictetus was a slave: his ideal human being is without class and possible in every class, but is to be sought above all in the depths of the masses as the silent, self-sufficient man within a universal enslavement who defends himself against the outside world and lives in a constant state of supreme bravery" (Ibid.). Among numerous other differences between him and the Christian, "he does not hope and does not accept the best he knows as a gift—he possesses it, he holds it bravely in his own hand, he defends it against the whole world if the world wants to rob him of it" (Ibid.). Of course Nietzsche was not a slave in the same jural or technical sense as Epictetus, and he rarely identified with the masses. But he thought that most of humankind, including himself to the extent that he did not effectively resist it, were enslaved by Christianity; and if I read him correctly there is nothing in his ideal of free-spiritedness that prevents members of the mass from aspiring to and perhaps achieving some one of its many and diverse variants.

In those dimensions of his thinking that manifest his indebtedness to Stoicism, Montaigne was apparently more influenced by Seneca than by Epictetus (there are vastly more favorable references to the former than to the latter), but his one citation of Epictetus by name anticipates more than a little of what Nietzsche admired in the Roman Stoic. "It seems in truth that nature, for consolation of our miserable and puny condition, has given us as our share only presumption. This is what Epictetus says, that man has nothing properly his own but the use of his opinions" (Montaigne, *Essays*, Vol. II: 360). Of course Nietzsche would add "and those of our actions that follow our own opinions," but since for Montaigne actions proceed from opinions, in this regard there is no great difference between the two thinkers. It should be added that the similarities between the two become yet more pronounced as Montaigne begins to incorporate Epicurean elements into his thinking.

In *The Care of the Self*, Foucault makes numerous references to Epictetus. And because he ties his borrowings from him directly to the ideas of freedom and resistance, looking at a few of the relevant passages will serve as a transition to our concluding section. "Seneca," he says, "commands a whole vocabulary for designating the different forms that ought to be taken by the care of the self and the haste with which one seeks to reunite with oneself" (46). Marcus Aurelius, he says, is repeatedly concerned with the same issue, but "It is in Epictetus no doubt that one finds the highest philosophical development of this theme. Man is defined in the *Discourses* as the being who was destined to care for himself. This is where the basic difference between him and other creatures resides. . . . Man . . . must attend to himself: not, however, as a consequence of some defect . . . but because the god [Zeus] deemed it right that he be able to make free use of himself" (46). Recall that Nietzsche praised Epictetus for having no fear of God, a view that Foucault shares. But Epictetus is referring to one among many gods and the fact that one of them "deemed it right" that human beings should care for themselves creates not fear but "a privilege-duty, a gift-obligation that ensures our freedom while forcing us to take ourselves as the object of all our diligence" (Ibid.).

A little later in the same text, Foucault speaks of Epictetus's notion of self-examination, preferring it to the Socratic "know thyself" on the ground that the aims of the latter are to recognize ignorance and, if possible, replace it with knowledge. In this respect, Foucault seems to suggest, Socratic self-examination directs the self's attention outside of itself to some reality the truth about which does not depend on its being affirmed or embraced by the self itself. "The examination Epictetus talks about is completely different. . . ." (63). Its objective is to differentiate "between that which does not depend on us and that which does. . . . This inspection is a test of power and a guarantee of freedom: a way of always making sure that one will not become attached to that which does not come under our control" (64). The several disciplines of self-control and -care, including resistance to the impositions attempted by others, are sources of power and hence, possibly, of "freedom to" as well as "freedom from."

III

Control, Resistance, and Freedom

As suggested, Nietzsche's remarks about Epictetus present in compressed form many of his thoughts concerning control and discipline. And the appropriations from Epictetus by Montaigne and Foucault underline some of the ways in which, for the two latter as well as for Nietzsche, control and discipline are essential to power and hence to freedom.[3] Their thoughts in these regards, to indulge an anachronism, have a strong Nietzschian accent.

One of the numerous ways in which Nietzsche follows Epictetus and Montaigne (and anticipates Foucault) in connecting control and discipline with freedom is articulated in the following remarks from early in Book Four of *The Will to Power*: "The faith in the pleasure of moderation—that pleasure of the rider on a fiery steed—has been lacking hitherto.—The mediocrity of weaker natures has been confused with moderation of the strong!" (870: 466). In this regard, he goes on to say in the next section, there is "a confusion [that] is quite natural, although its influence has been fatal: that which men of power and will are able to demand of themselves also proves a measure of that which they may permit themselves" (Ibid.). Instancing some "great" men, he says that Handel, Leibniz, Goethe, and Bismarck existed "blithely among antitheses, full of that supple strength that guards against convictions and doctrines by employing one against the other and reserving freedom for itself" (471–72).

Employing a phrase that became popular among twentieth-century thinkers influenced by him, Nietzsche asserts that every doing is a forgoing. But he turns this sometimes disheartening and even enervating idea to the advantage of his conception of free-spiritedness. "What we do should determine what we forego; *by* doing we forego—that is how I like it, that is my *placitum* [principle]" (*GS*, Four, 304, p. 244, first italics mine). Self-control is of great importance, but "those moralists" who make of it our first and foremost duty afflict those who submit to their demands with "a peculiar disease." Whenever a person who has embraced such teaching experiences a desire, a push or a pull, "it will always seem to him as if his self-control were endangered. No longer may he entrust himself to any instinct or free wingbeat" (Ibid.). To the extent that I adopt the doctrine or dogma of self-control, I must also resist it and "lose . . . [myself] occasionally" (Ibid., 305: 244–5). That magnanimity toward enemies discussed above must extend to that part of the self that is the enemy of the self's choosing what to do and what to forgo; that is the enemy of one's free-spiritedness and hence one's most valuable freedoms of action. But the magnanimity must be proud and strong, not submissive—even to the teaching that commends it. To return briefly to the thoughts considered in my Section I above, this recommendation applies to doctrines and dogmas concerning what is true as well as what is good and virtuous. Referring to a slogan that is often used against him, Nietzsche asserts of "Nothing is true; everything is permitted," that "Here we have real freedom, for the notion of truth itself has been disposed of" (*GM*, Third Essay, XXIV: 287).

What, then, are free-spiritedness and the freedom of action that is among its chief expressions or manifestations? As we would expect from the opinions and arguments we have been considering, Nietzsche presents numerous examples and characterizations of both, but nowhere to my knowledge does he offer a definition of these terms or concepts. To define them would be futile because we experience them and their absence in a great and constantly changing variety of situations and circumstances. It would also be dangerous because definitions are always restrictive and narrowing; they blind those who accept them to the fluid multiplicity of free-spiritedness and freedom of action in our lived and imagined experience. In part for this, or these, reasons, it is difficult to locate Nietzsche's thinking on the grids or in the schemas that for many centuries have organized thinking about and disputations concerning these concepts.

To take instances of typologies that have been with us for several centuries, it would be not only difficult but misleadingly reductive to classify him, exclusively as it were, as a theorist of "negative" as opposed to "positive" freedom or as solely concerned with the "conditions" as distinct from the "ends" of freedom or the reasons for valuing it. Elements in the formulations of the several proponents of these sorting devices are all prominent in his thinking.

It is clear from the considerations rehearsed here, for example, that numerous among Nietzsche's discussions are directed against restrictions on and obstacles placed in the path of individual thinking and acting, placed by hegemonic social, cultural, and occasionally political norms and values, and by institutional and other controlling mechanisms and forces. Free-spiritedness and freedom of action are importantly "negative" in character; they consist importantly in escaping from or breaking the hold of such impositions and constraints. The clearest case is of course the imperium imposed and sustained by Christianity and its agents and operatives.

Nietzsche thought that the preponderance of Christians were no less than enslaved by Christianity; reduced to a herd that was not merely informed and guided but indoctrinated, controlled, and directed, and their potential for freedom deeply diminished by Christianity and its shepherds. The thought that the Christian God was dead did not mean that, literally, everything is permitted, but it did mean that the hold of a myriad of unjustifiable constraints had been broken by those who had convinced themselves of this "death" and might someday be removed from all or most of those now under the Christian yoke. In this respect, to use a word that most proponents of "positive" freedom abhor, the death of the Christian God was a liberation.

Although less vituperative concerning them than are many of his remarks about Christianity, Nietzsche had similar reactions to rationalism, customary morality, and to political doctrines such as nationalism, socialism, and what might be called democratism. We have seen that he placed substantial value on the first two and especially the second, but taken to excess they too could stifle thinking and reduce action to the dogmatic, the rote, and the formulaic. The thinking and often the acting of free spirits are importantly (but not exclusively) characterized by spontaneity, inventiveness, and unpredictability. When doctrines such as those just mentioned harden into dogmas, free spirits must resist their demands and assert their own individuality and independence. Their thinking and acting, as with Zarathustra's, thereby become distinctive, unorthodox, even idiosyncratic. Doing so of course arouses the ire of many. Accordingly, free spirits must summon their strength and stand against the attempts of the scientistic and stupidly virtuous to control and direct their thinking and acting.

Although only rarely addressing topics conventionally regarded as political, in *Human All Too Human* and a few other places, Nietzsche had some choice words for the doctrines mentioned above. "Socialism is the fanciful younger brother of the almost expired despotism whose heir it wants to be." Because it "expressly aspires to the annihilation of the individual," "it requires a more complete subservience of the citizen to the absolute state than ever existed before" and seeks to improve the individual into "a useful *organ of the community*." It is therefore "in the profoundest sense reactionary" (One, 473: 173). Nationalism and its pet entity the nation itself are sources of the same and some additional evils. The nation "is in its essence a forcibly imposed state of siege and self-defence inflicted on the many by the few and requires cunning, force, and falsehood to maintain a front of respectability" (174). When heated up by nationalisms it has many of the same repugnant characteristics and effects as socialism. Thus one "should not be afraid to proclaim oneself simply a *good European* and actively to work for the amalgamation of nations" (475: 175). And those many who want to make Nietzsche into an anti-Semite and a proto-Hitlerian would do well to consider the following: "the entire problem of the *Jews* exists only within national states, inasmuch as it is here that their energy and higher intelligence, their capital in will and spirit accumulated from generation to generation in a long school of suffering, must come to preponderate to a degree calculated [albeit not by the Jews] to arouse envy and hatred, so that in almost every nation—and the more so the more nationalist a posture the nation is again developing—there is gaining more ground the literary indecency of leading the Jews to the sacrificial slaughter as scapegoats for every possible public or private misfortune" (174–75). Thus in the name of individuality and individual freedom of action, the free spirit will resist the nation, nationalism, and anti-Semitism. (Incidentally, Nietzsche's self-identification as a good European and a proponent of "the strongest possible European mixed race" is one of the few instances in which he embraces an ideal that he is willing to share with as many others as possible. More on this below.)

Nietzsche's thoughts about democracy are more complex and nuanced than those concerning the doctrines just discussed, and there are remarks that are, if somewhat grudgingly, supportive of it. (See, for example, 438: 161.) But he shared the fear of many mid- to late-nineteenth- (and not a few twentieth-) century thinkers that democracy, often in alliance with religious forces, promotes a state every bit as absolute and destructive of individuality as nationalism and socialism. What I have called democratism, now widely know as popular, direct, deliberative, or participatory democracy, forwards a conception of government "as nothing but the instrument of the popular will, not as an Above in relation to a Below" with those Below prepared to resist its overweening tendencies, "but merely as a function of the sole sovereign power, the people" and looked to by the people to solve their every problem and to satisfy their every desire. Where this attitude and these expectations have become widely adopted, "the unknowledgeable will think they see [in the state] the hand of God and [will] patiently submit to instructions from above. . . . " Democratic government may then ensure, at least temporarily, "internal civil peace and continuity of development," but at the cost of a "unity of popular sentiment" assured by "the fact that everyone holds the same opinions and has the same objectives" (472: 170–71). Although for the most part urging that free spirits maintain a "pathos of distance" vis-à-vis the state and the politics engendered by its authority and power, Nietzsche seems to recommend that they engage themselves to resist and promote resistance to the democratic as well as to the nationalistic and socialistic state. Here again, resistance is necessary to sustaining and enhancing freedom of thought and action.

Thus resistance, and the discipline required to achieve the power neces-sary to make it effective, are conditions of free-spiritedness and freedom of action. They are not the same as and should not be confused with the latter two because other conditions are often also necessary to make attempts at resistance successful and because there are forms of discipline that are in-imical to freedom in both senses. It is, I think, fair to say that for Nietzsche discipline and resistance are necessary conditions of free-spiritedness in any culture or society that Nietzsche can imagine. And for those who suc-ceed in maintaining a goodly amount of "solitude," of sustaining a "pathos of distance" vis-à-vis not only politics and government but society and culture more generally, they may be both necessary and sufficient condi-tions of becoming and remaining an "overperson." They are also strongly contributive to the freedom of action. But they are neither sufficient for nor necessary to the latter. They are not sufficient for reasons already stated, and they are not necessary to all freedoms of action because govern-ments, societies, and cultures may be indifferent or even favorably dis-posed to many of the latter. There is, however, plausibility to the thought that freedoms of action of the latter type will not be held in high esteem by those who have them.

Thus far, and with the qualifications concerning the conditions of free-dom just entered, there are good reasons for thinking of Nietzsche as im-portantly a theorist of "negative" freedom, a theorist who thinks that unfreedom consists in a person being under restrictions and controls im-posed by others, finds herself confronted with substantial obstacles to the thinking she desires to do and the acting in which she has an inclination or a will to engage. Unfreedom is undesirable because it is due to the presence of effective constraints—"brake-shoes" as Zarathustra calls them (*TSZ*, Second Part: 108)—freedom is valuable because the individual is able to resist and overcome those constraints and hence is able to think and act as she is disposed to do. To recur to a formulation that I proposed in an ear-lier writing, on the considerations thus far examined, Nietzsche can be said to advance a notion of freedom and unfreedom the elements of which, schematically, are: "Action attempted by an agent plus the possibility of im-pediments to that action placed or left by another or other agents acting with the intention of placing or leaving those impediments" (Flathman, 1987: 322). Freedom in this, I think familiar, sense consists in the agent successfully overcoming the impediments, unfreedom consists in the agent's being prevented from the desired action by the impediments. Of course Nietzsche places more emphasis than I did on the discipline and re-sulting strength that allows the agent to resist the impediments placed by others, but otherwise this formula captures much of what he says in pursuing the thought that "the tug towards freedom . . . [is] the strongest drive of our spirit."

As anticipated, however, further qualifications need to be made to this reading—and hence this appropriation—of Nietzsche's thinking. The kind of qualification necessary is presaged when Nietzsche speaks of "Virtue [*virtù?*] as pleasure in resistance, will to power. Honor as recognition of the similar and equal-in-power" (*WP*, Book Two, 255: 148). Resistance to custom, convention, and authority is necessary to open up spaces for freedom and hence to give outlets for the will to power, outlets that are socially and culturally significant. But even if it does not have this other-regarding effect, resistance and the will to power that it discloses are sources both of visceral pleasure and the pleasure of being honored by those who deserve to be honored.

Enlarging on this point, the forms of discipline that enable resistance to others also contribute importantly to the possibility of saying, *con brio* as Nietzsche encourages us to put it, "yes to life." Looking back on his lifetime of thinking, in *Ecce Homo*, he says that he had "become the first to comprehend the wonderful phenomenon of the dionysian," which he here characterizes as the readiness to make a "*supreme affirmation* born out of fullness, of superfluity, an affirmation without reservation even of suffering, even of guilt, even of all that is strange and questionable in existence. . . . This ultimate, joyfullest, boundlessly exuberant Yes to Life is not only the highest insight, it is also the *profoundest*, the insight most strictly confirmed and maintained by truth and knowledge" (*Ecce Homo*, 79–80).

Of course this affirmation, which is enunciated in a great variety of locutions and rhetorics throughout the writings primarily consulted here, would not be possible without disciplined resistance to the array of "degenerated" instincts "which turn . . . against life with subterranean revengefulness . . . " (Ibid.). If we take the readiness to make the dionysian affirmation as the distinctive, the differentiating characteristic of the free spirit and the overperson, we can reaffirm the above reading that discipline and resistance, and hence freedom from degenerate outlooks, are necessary conditions of free-spiritedness. And if the free spirit must enact, must act upon, this affirmation, we can also say that a significant measure of freedom of action is also among the necessary conditions of free-spiritedness. But now freedom from and freedom to, rather than being for their own sake, are of inestimable value because they enable the affirmation, the Yes to Life. Removed from this Weltanschauung or Weltgeist, freedom to engage in action and perhaps freedom from constraints and controls might be trivial and perhaps diminishing.

At first and perhaps at second sight this construal is supported by some of the more pungent remarks of Zarathustra. "You call yourself free? I want to hear your sovereign thought, not that you have escaped from a yoke. Are you one of those who are *entitled* to escape from a yoke? There are some who cast off their ultimate value when they cast off their servitude. Free *from* something? What does Zarathustra care? But let your clear eyes show me you are free *for* something" (*TSZ*, First Part: 69).

To return to my earlier formulations, in the passages now under consideration Nietzsche can be read as advancing a notion of freedom as autonomy and unfreedom as heteronomy, when these notions are explicated as follows: "Action attempted by an agent in the pursuit of a self-critically chosen plan or project that the agent . . . believe[s] is consonant with defensible norms or principles [or ideals], plus the possibility of impediments to that action placed or left by another agent or other agents acting with the intention of placing or leaving those impediments" (Flathman, op. cit.). It would appear that an agent is entitled to be free of the yoke or yokes placed or left by others, to be free in a sense that a free spirit such as Zarathustra *would* care about, only if she has a "sovereign thought" that is and deserves to be genuinely her own. If she lacks such a thought, or perhaps thoughts, her unfreedom, her being heteronomized, may be beneficial to her.[4]

There is a temptation to go yet further and read Nietzsche as promoting a conception of freedom close to what I have called Fully Virtuous freedom (except that of Nietzsche we have to say "fully virtu-ous"). In this formulation, the above words "believes is consonant with defensible norms or principles" are followed by "chosen to satisfy, and in fact satisfying, certifiably worthy norms or principles [or ideals]." This reading is responsive to what is sometimes called Nietzsche's perfectionism. It is not enough that the individual's sovereign thought(s) be unquestionably her own; rather, that thought or those thoughts must be affirmed "without reservation" and this must be *because* it or they are "confirmed and maintained by truth and knowledge." Echoing widely circulated slogans such as "Ye shall know the truth and the truth shall make your free" (the motto of my university is *Veritas Vos Liberabit*), thus construed Nietzsche is a proponent of one of the most soaring versions of the "positive" theory of freedom, a version that not only distinguishes between higher and lower, better and worse selves—distinctions that Nietzsche unquestionably makes and that move him toward a conception of freedom as autonomy—but that specify that a self can be regarded as high or good only if its sovereign thoughts accord with truth.

This further interpretation, however, is clearly mistaken. There is no denying or wishing away the fact that in the passage quoted from *Ecce Homo*, Nietzsche makes a direct connection between the merits of a supreme affirmation and the fact that it is confirmed and maintained by truth and knowledge. But whose truth and whose knowledge? For reasons that have been rehearsed in detail above, it cannot be truth and knowledge as conventionally accepted in this or that society and culture. But we have also seen that Nietzsche identifies himself as a perspectivalist, as holding that truth and knowledge are always and necessarily determined from the perspective of some person or persons and that the idea of a higher theory, a metatheory, that can and should arbitrate among perspectives and determine what is TRUE and what counts as KNOWLEDGE is not only a fantasy but a dangerous delusion. (On this topic, in addition to works already discussed, see especially his "On Truth and Lies in a Non-Moral Sense" and the other early papers collected in Daniel Breazeale, editor and translator, *Philosophy and Truth.*)

Nietzsche is a "perfectionist" in the sense that he has formed and aspires to the realization of an idea, or rather an ideal, of a self or of selves that soars above the traditional, the conventional, and the orthodox. Moreover, he heaps derision and scorn not only on idealisms in the philosophical sense but on numerous of what we might call the ideals of life with which he was familiar. But while he gives various names to the ideal(s) that he admires—the free spirit, the overperson, and several others—he repeatedly insists that there is no single version of this generic ideal that should be preferred to all others. Just as he shared William James's admiration for polytheism and its diverse, fluctuating, and often conflicting conceptions of the divine or superhuman, so he thought that there are, and believed passionately that there ought to be, an irreducible multiplicity of ideals of life. As he put the latter conviction—with unequaled verve and exuberance—"Whatever kind of bizarre ideal one may follow . . . one should not demand that it be *the* ideal; for one therewith takes from it its privileged character. One should have it in order to distinguish oneself, not in order to level oneself. . . . 'This is what *I* am; this is what *I* want:—*you* can go to hell' " (*WP*, Book Two, 349: 190–91*).

IV

Concluding Thoughts

As with Montaigne, Nietzsche gives us no single, unified answer to our questions concerning how we should think about, and act concerning, the relationships between freedom on the one hand and discipline and resistance on the other. For both of them, and especially for Nietzsche, freedom is a multivalent concept and idea and it and various nearly cognate terms and related ideas such as liberty, liberation, and *laissez-aller* are used in a great variety of contexts and in respect to diverse circumstances. Moreover, ideas of freedom often appear without the word or words being used, their presence in Nietzsche's thinking being indicated by his use of the various notions that he regards as opposed to or in contrast with freedom. In these respects, his linguistic and rhetorical practices—leaving aside terms distinctive to him such as "free-spiritedness" and "overperson"—are for the most part familiar to us from our own discourses. If we find his thinking convincing we can readily appropriate it to our own and if we find it engaging but unacceptable, we can readily dispute it.

The opening sentences of the previous paragraph notwithstanding, there are several respects in which major tendencies in Nietzsche's thinking about the ideas and issues of concern here, if not systematic or even notably orderly, is not only accessible but quite clear. For present purposes, perhaps the three most important of his themes are those that I proceed to discuss.

First, there is no categorical or across-the-board opposition between freedom and discipline. Discipline is often necessary to both freedom of action and free-spiritedness and it often contributes to those desiderata even when it is not necessary to them. Nietzsche obviously prefers self-discipline to disciplines imposed by others, and for the free spirit this preference for it is categorical, in that the free spirit, even if she finds the particulars of disciplinary regimens in and takes them from social or cultural norms, must subject them to critical examination. If she accepts them she must in this way internalize them and in this sense make them her own. For the free spirit, disciplines not internalized in this way are antithetical to her freedom.

The free spirit will almost certainly recognize that numerous of the members of her society or culture are not given to or are incapable of critical assessment of social and cultural norms, and she will acknowledge that her own freedom may be enhanced by their uncritical submission to them. She may also feel some gratitude toward the "virtuous intellects" both for the reason just stated and because their compliance with the law of agreement and customary morality, and their attempts to impose them on her, will multiply the occasions on which she experiences the need to exercise a further discipline on herself, the discipline necessary to resisting their demands and realizing the pleasures that such resistance, perhaps only such resistance, can afford.

The second and third themes are partly stated by or implied in the first, but go beyond them. Resistance, at least in the sense of standing against the demand that conventional disciplinary regimens be accepted uncritically, and often in the further sense that they often must be actively resisted, is essential to free-spiritedness and in many instances to freedom of action. Moreover, it is clear from Nietzsche's brief discussions of the state and politics that the possibility of a politically organized society that we might call livable or tolerable depends on the readiness of some considerable number of citizens—including citizens who may not qualify as free spirits in the strongest sense—to resist the government and its commands. In this respect, Nietzsche deserves to be numbered among those who give at least—but not more than—two cheers for democracy, and he sometimes appears to be friendly toward anarchism if it is the only alternative to despotism.

Third, Nietzsche recognizes that discipline and the strength necessary to resistance are almost certainly necessary to any considerable measure of freedom of action and contribute importantly to the vigorous and fruitful pursuit of his ideal of free-spiritedness. He does not, however, equate the third with either of the first two. It is possible to have numerous freedoms of action and not formulate an ideal for oneself, and if one has imagined and wished for an ideal, freedom of action does not guarantee that it will be effectively pursued. A further and quite vital point is that there are ideals—for example the Christian ideals as Nietzsche understands them—that manifest not disciplined free-spiritedness but despotic impulses on the part of their champions and uncritical submissiveness on the part of those who follow their promoters. (The passage that begins "Whatever bizarre ideal you may follow" notwithstanding, the pluralism of Nietzsche's idealism is not without its limits.) Free-spiritedness is almost certainly a condition of formulating and pursuing any ideal about which Nietzsche would say "This is what *You* are, this is what *You* want. *I* can't have it and you can tell me to go to hell," but it is not a sufficient condition of doing so. Formulating and pursuing an ideal that passes this test requires imagination and creativity, that is qualities of mind and more especially of spirit that cannot be analyzed—as free-spiritedness importantly is—in terms of what the free spirit is not and what she is against. We are on safe ground in saying that any ideal that Nietzsche would judge worthy would feature a strong commitment to overcoming those parts of the self that are against its idealized self, to self-making, and hence to some version of individuality. Exactly how individuality does or should manifest itself, however, cannot be predicted and certainly cannot be prescribed.

If this brief summary captures the main themes in, and theses advanced by, Nietzsche's thinking about freedom, discipline, and resistance, how should we assess them? It should be evident from the foregoing pages, from their tonalities and from the delight (which no doubt some will think excessive) that I evidently take in quoting from Nietzsche's work on these and related topics, that my own assessment is largely favorable. That this is the case, at least in regard to the relationship between freedom and discipline, came initially as something of a surprise to me. When I began these reflections, I was suspicious of the view that the various familiar forms of discipline are necessary for freedom, contributive to it, or even compatible with it. (This suspicion did not extend to the idea that resistance is often not only contributive but frequently necessary to freedom. Given that discipline is almost always necessary to effective resistance, I was closer to accepting something like Nietzsche's view than I then realized.) Somewhat suspicious of my own suspicion, and knowing from previous readings that Foucault, Montaigne, Nietzsche, and Hampshire are enthusiasts for freedom but also for various types of discipline, the thought occurred to me that engagements with their formulations would be a fruitful way to test both of these suspicions.

Even as I complete this project, my present judgments must remain provisional, open to challenge and reconsideration. With one major exception with which I conclude, however, I now agree with much of what Nietzsche thought about these matters. Beginning with the third of the themes or theses summarized just above, I strongly agree—indeed in this respect have long since agreed—with Nietzsche's thoughts, both negative and positive, concerning ideals and the place that they should and should not have in our affairs.

An ideal is an idea or more or less integrated array of ideas to the realization of which an individual or some number of individuals aspire. It is regarded by those who embrace it as providing a standard of excellence or accomplishment, an excellence exceeding that which has as yet been achieved in their lives and in most cases in the lives of those with whom their lives are regularly involved or engaged. The ideal gives inspiration and a degree of direction to those who are committed to its realization and it provides a basis on which to critique arrangements and patterns of conduct that fall short of its demands.

As sources of inspiration, direction, and critique, ideals are valuable, and sometimes—as in the case of Nietzsche's ideal of free-spiritedness—of supreme value to those who espouse them. In providing grounds on which to critique conventional understandings and orientations, they provide those who hold them with reasons for distancing themselves from them, with the courage and strength necessary to resist the demands with which they are presented and to overcome the obstacles with which others confront them. For Nietzsche and for numerous other promoters of ideals, a person without an ideal, without a "sovereign thought," may be (perhaps by chance) free from many restrictions and hence may be free to do many things. But lacking a sovereign thought to inspire and captain their thinking and acting, their thoughts are likely to be commonplace and their actions lacking in self-control and self-chosen orientation.

As Nietzsche would emphatically say ("we exceptions to the rule" are the glory of but also one of the chief dangers to humane life), ideals can be and often are not only dangerous to but destructive of a "decent regard for the opinions of [hu]mankind" and hence the possibility of a minimal decency in human relations. The Christian ideals have enslaved much of Europe and more recently prominent ideals such as socialism and nationalism threaten a despotism unknown for several centuries. Even worthy ideals can engender dogmatism and fanaticism. Lacking any commitment to moderation, politeness, and poise, any appreciation for the pleasures that come from respecting "forms," their proponents run a brutal roughshod over those who do not accept—and not infrequently a few of those who do—their ideal.

Since he was intensely aware of these dangers, one of the most appealing aspects of Nietzsche's conception of his ideal is his insistence on guarding it against its being put, by himself or others, to these nefarious purposes. The most striking example of this insistence is represented by the passage I quoted at the end of section III. If you can't have my ideal, the last thing I would want to do would be to level myself by imposing it on you. But this resounding and perhaps unprecedented declaration is surrounded by admonitions, to himself as well as to others, to discipline oneself to maintain *virtu's* of form such as those mentioned again in the previous paragraph. The ideal is of supreme value, but it can be realized only if those who cherish and promote it discipline themselves to enact these formal or adverbial virtues.

One final point regarding ideals as Nietzsche understands them. He is right, both conceptually and (if this is a distinction) normatively, to refuse to *identify* forming and pursuing his ideal with freedom. Freedom in the two main senses discussed here is a high-order value for Nietzsche, but— as with the *virtu's* just mentioned—it is to be kept distinct from his ideal. It is a condition of being in a position to enact one's ideal and it can contribute valuably to the ability to formulate an ideal that one wishes to embrace. By refusing, however, to identify acceptance and pursuit of an ideal—his or anyone else's—with freedom, he protects others from the enormities perpetrated in the name of forcing others to accept and live by an ideal they do not accept, the enormity of "forcing them to be free."

These appreciations of what I called the third of Nietzsche's themes also capture much of what I think merits endorsement in the two that precede it in my summary discussion. Nietzsche is correct that there is no categorical opposition between freedom and discipline. As Montaigne and Foucault also understood, in the entire absence of the various forms of discipline that they both strongly favor, thinking and acting deteriorate into "letting go," very likely into a form of self- and mutually destructive madness. (In this respect their thinking has many affinities with the thinking of Hobbes.) For Montaigne these forms of discipline are especially important for those who seek to make themselves—for example, to make oneself, as Montaigne essayed to do, in large part by writing oneself. For Nietzsche they are especially important for those who aspire to the closely related ideal of self-overcoming and free-spiritedness. But for reasons already discussed, it is also important, including to the free spirit, that they be exercised by those who aspire to other ideals or to none. In the absence of discipline there may be various freedoms of movement, but there is little if any freedom of action. (I return to this distinction below.)

Nietzsche is also correct to argue that self-discipline is to be preferred to disciplines imposed by others. This is, again, particularly the case with the free spirit but it is also true of anyone who aspires to achieve and maintain some degree of individuality. To repeat, it is unavoidable that some forms of discipline will be found in and adopted from norms already widely shared. But the free spirit, and anyone else who recognizes the sometime need for resistance to such norms, must be capable of critiquing and standing against them. Disciplines never subjected to such critique are antithetical to the freedoms of the free spirit and endanger the freedoms of anyone and everyone.

As regards anyone and everyone, I write "endanger" rather than "antithetical to" for two reasons, the second and more important of which leads to the disagreement with Nietzsche that I anticipated above. The first is that the demand for a continuous and universally critical stance toward established conventions and norms is almost certainly unrealistic. Although claims that all freedoms are deeply situated and all selves deeply embedded are (dispiriting) exaggerations, they are exaggerations, not generally mistaken propositions. As Nietzsche himself repeatedly and in my judgement rightly insists, a recognizably civil society depends on a "law of agreement" and a customary morality that are not continuously or widely questioned. In railing against those exceptional, those "impatient" ones, who seek to "disrupt" these arrangements and conventions, and in saying that his hell would be a life of constant improvisation, he brings this understanding to bear on himself. And in acknowledging, gratefully we may say, the numerous respects in which he is benefited by the presence of a large number of readily trainable persons, he not only recognizes but endorses a conception of society and culture that includes these characteristics.

What, then, is there to disagree with? We might begin by saying that to the extent that Nietzsche generalizes his demand for a continuous critical stance toward the received and the conventional, he blurs a part of his own distinction between the free spirit and those who do not accept this ideal of life. For present purposes, a better way to put the objection may be that he risks violating his own strictures against imposing (a part of) his ideal on others. And if or insofar as he does so in the name of freedom, he moves his conception and valorization thereof in the direction of a notion of autonomy versus heteronomy rather than a conception of freedom of action.

In order to conclude discussion of this point it will be helpful to develop somewhat further the tripartite distinction among differing senses or uses of "freedom" and "unfreedom" already mentioned.[5] In the first, that is freedom of *movement*, freedom consists in the movement of a body or its parts not effectively impeded or obstructed by other persons or physical things. Unfreedom, accordingly, consists in attempts at or impulses to movement that are prevented by other persons or other bodies. Distinctive to this conception of freedom is that it requires, indeed allows, no reference to *why* the person or other body wants, desires, is disposed to, has the objective or purpose, to move in a particular direction. The clearest examples of freedom and unfreedom in this sense are reactions to stimuli or other causes such as the blink of an eye in response to a bright light and the jerk of a leg struck on the patellar tendon. If unimpeded, the movements are free, if effectively prevented by some other body or force, they are unfree. The theory called behaviorism (and not a few kindred theories) treats all or a very large number of the movements—the behaviors—of human beings as instances of movements and aims to explain as many of them as possible on this model or understanding (the (in)famous Stimulus-Response theory). It treats "mentalist" explanations as delusions, impossibilities, or both.

By contrast, the theory of freedom and unfreedom of *action requires* reference to the "mentalist" components of actions. On the now widely accepted (generic) analysis of actions as distinct from movements, an action involves four main elements, namely a belief, a desire to act on that belief, the formation of an intention to do so, and the adoption of a purpose, goal, or end that the agent expects or hopes to be achieved by doing so. As with freedom of movement, unfreedom consists in the agent's attempt at action being effectively prevented. In most of its versions, however, unfreedom of action is brought about by the actions of other agents and hence requires attention to the beliefs, desires, intentions, and purposes of the agents who prevented the first party from successfully taking the action she attempted.

As already indicated in part, freedom in the sense of autonomy, and unfreedom in the sense of being heteronomized by other agents or agencies, adds further requirements to saying that an agent acted in freedom. These further requirements vary among the numerous theorizations of autonomy and heteronomy, but all of those known to me specify that the acting agent must be aware of (conscious of, as Nietzsche might say) her beliefs, desires, and so forth, and must subject them to some degree of critical assessment. If she has no self-critical awareness of the "why" of her attempted conduct she cannot be said to be autonomous and hence, on this conception of freedom, cannot be said to be free. And as her self-critical awareness diminishes, her autonomy and hence her freedom diminish with it.

By contrast with freedom as unimpeded movement, both freedom as unprevented action and freedom as autonomous conduct deserve to be regarded as ideals. But the latter is by far the more demanding of the two and for this reason allows of a fewer number of instances in which an agent can properly be said to have acted in freedom. Perhaps for this reason, champions of freedom as autonomy, including Nietzsche and perhaps Montaigne and Foucault, regard it as the higher of the two ideals. It is not difficult to understand the attractions of this view. Notions such as "the unexamined life is not worth living" and imperatives such as "know thyself," "overcome thyself," and "make thyself" all weigh in its favor. Anyone who places a high value on her own individuality will be attracted to it. Certainly such a person will be attracted to it as an ideal *of her own and for herself.*

There are nevertheless reasons to hesitate before the ideal of autonomy. One such reason is the following: Even if I regard the ideal as exclusively mine, make no attempt to convince others of its merits or hold them to it, in some of its versions it involves such a radical distancing from others as to amount to a disregard for them and possibly a readiness to appropriate them to my objectives. My quest for autonomy becomes so unqualifiedly self-regarding that I either isolate myself from others or treat them as means to my ends.

It might be thought that this objection applies to Nietzsche. His repeatedly expressed craving for solitude could be taken to indicate an indifference regarding others, and his enthusiasm for the opportunities and other advantages made available to him owing to the "trainability" of most Europeans might suggest a crassly instrumental attitude toward them. I think, however, that this reading, while admittedly finding some support in his texts, is mistaken. He does seek to distance himself from others, but what he seeks is not isolation but a "pathos of distance." A person indifferent to others would experience no pathos in her relations and especially her non-relations with or to them. And the passages that suggest that he is prepared to "use" others for his own purposes must be read along with, and against, his many injunctions to politeness, fastidiousness, magnanimity, and like *virtu's* of form. These and many other of his injunctions apply not only to the stance he should take toward other exceptional persons but to all human beings. (This is one of several indications that there is a strong egalitarian component in his thinking.)

A second reason for hesitation before this ideal is the one already sketched above. If or to the extent that I hold others to the ideal of autonomy, that ideal becomes a weapon, at least a rhetorical and perhaps a more material weapon against them. If another person claims to have taken an action freely or in freedom, and if I am convinced that her action did not satisfy criteria of autonomy such as having subjected her beliefs, desires, and so on to appropriately critical scrutiny, I can deny that she acted in freedom. And if I further think that it is a mark against her that she fell short of autonomy, I may convince myself that I am justified in interfering in her thinking and acting so as to remedy this defect. I may show disrespect for her and I may convince myself that it is my duty to interfere in more material and potentially more efficacious ways.

Here again there are elements in Nietzsche's thinking that warrant bringing this objection against him. There is no shortage of remarks in which he evinces what has to be called disdain for the stupidly virtuous and those herd-like many whose lives consist in sheep-like submission to some shepherd. Here also, however, this criticism must be qualified. The *virtù's* on which he repeatedly and avidly insists may permit of expressing disdain in a philosophical treatise, but commitment to them, to standing pledge for one's word, to scrupulously avoiding actions that disrupt the workings of the law of agreement, are incompatible with the kinds of direct interference under discussion.

Consider in this regard a remark of his concerning politics, one that is relevant to the above discussion of democracy or democratism and that will lead us to a third objection to the conception of freedom as requiring autonomy: "[I]f the purpose of all politics really is to make life endurable for as many as possible, then these as-many-as-possible are entitled to determine what they understand by an endurable life; if they trust to their intellect also to discover the right means of attaining this goal, what good is there in doubting it? They *want* for once to forge for themselves their own fortunes and misfortunes; and if this feeling of self-determination, pride in the five or six ideas their head contains and brings forth . . . there is little to be objected to, always presupposing that this narrow-mindedness does not go so far as to demand that *everything* should become politics in this sense, that *everyone* should live and work according to such a standard" (*HATH*, Volume I, 8: 161). Disdain, yes. But with regard to a chief source of interference with the beliefs and actions of the many, Nietzsche explicitly counsels against it, requiring only that their beliefs and chosen forms of action not be made mandatory for him.

Briefly stated, a third objection to the ideal of autonomy and the conception of freedom that its proponents frequently advance is that it underestimates or otherwise mischaracterizes action and acting, tending to assimilate them to movements or behaviors. Otherwise stated, ideas of autonomy and of freedom as (conceptually) requiring autonomy exaggerate the differences between autonomy and action. No one among the four generic components of action are merely unconsidered responses to stimuli. Beliefs, desires, intentions, and purposes are always chosen from among alternatives and, typically, are chosen among and often against alternatives that compete with or are either conceptually or materially (or both) incompatible with those chosen. Moreover, framing an intention and adopting a purpose rarely if ever will tell the agent which among alternative courses of action will best enact the intention and achieve the purpose. Of course awareness of alternatives, critical reflectiveness as to why one among them is here and now chosen over the others, and the self-discipline to act as one thinks best, vary from action to action and agent to agent. Deeply ingrained beliefs, strongly felt desires, conventional and habitual intentions and purposes may reduce awareness and reflectiveness to minimal proportions. But if there is no awareness and no reflectiveness we are in the presence of a movement not an action.

Some may think that this is no more than, is "merely," a conceptual point. But if there is such a thing as a "merely" conceptual point, the one before us is not an example. Insofar as we recognize persons as agents attempting to engage in action we attribute—accord—to them qualities that are different, if at all, only in degree from those exalted and privileged by theories of autonomy and of freedom as requiring autonomy. Such differences as there are between the actions of agents and the actions of those who are autonomous are far from sufficient to justify the view that only the successful attempts at action of the latter deserve to be thought of as done in freedom. They are obviously insufficient to justify preventing the actions of agents on the ground that doing so is necessary to make them free.

Is Nietzsche guilty of underestimating action and exaggerating the differences between it and autonomy? The answer is at once a No and a Yes. When, in passages such as the one just quoted, he speaks of "intellect," self-determined wants, ideas of the endurable and the unendurable, and the like, he attributes characteristics of agency and action to the many. In respect to these dimensions of his thinking and others rehearsed in considering the previous two objections, the answer is No. When he indulges himself in expressions of contempt for the abjectly submissive herd, of those who "let themselves go" and descend into madness, the answer is Yes. There no doubt are human beings about whom these characterizations are apt. But if thinkers from Aristotle to Hampshire (see the following chapter) are correct that action is the staple ingredient in, an elemental feature of, human life, generalizations of the latter sort are as misleading as they are dangerous to human freedom.

For now I can say that my brief attempt at an assessment of Nietzsche's thinking has led to a balance strongly in favor of his views concerning freedom, discipline, and resistance. Where his formulations prompt objections, I very often find that in other passages he responds effectively to them or gives me reasons to qualify my concerns. As with Foucault and Montaigne, my engagement with his thinking has strengthened my commitment to views I earlier held and has also convinced me that reservations I previously had to positions akin to his are either unwarranted or less damaging than I earlier thought. It is of course my hope that others who follow my explorations of his extraordinarily rich and supple reflections will arrive at a similar conclusion. Further consideration will be given to related matters in the pages that follow.

CHAPTER 5

Stuart Hampshire on Freedoms and Unfreedoms of Mind and of Action

The British philosopher Stuart Hampshire makes no references to Foucault, but one to Montaigne, and not more than a few (but, as with the reference to Montaigne, not unimportant) references or allusions to Nietzsche. Nor to my knowledge has his thinking been discussed along with or as pertinent to understanding and assessing the work of the other thinkers considered here. It is nevertheless a secondary aim of this and the following chapter to show that, along with important differences, Hampshire's numerous writings address many of the same issues, and evidence important formal and substantive continuities, with the ideas and ideals of the three philosophers primarily engaged in the previous chapters. The most obvious of these commonalities is Hampshire's persistent concern with the concept of freedom and with the various conceptions thereof that have been formulated and advanced in the long history of thinking about it. But his construals of and arguments concerning concepts such as thought and action, reason, custom and desire, language, community and individuality, all of which are central to his thinking about freedom, also resonate with ideas salient in Montaigne, Nietzsche, and Foucault. Thus in engaging with his thinking we can continue and enlarge upon the reflections essayed thus far. Because the discussions are lengthy and complex, in both chapters I provide, at the outset, footnotes that outline the topics and subtopics that organize them.[1]

Freedoms and Unfreedoms of Mind

With respect to freedom, it is fair to say that Hampshire's abiding concern has been with what, in the title and lead essay of one of his books, he calls the freedom of mind. (Stuart Hampshire, *Freedom of Mind and Other Essays*, 1971; hereafter *FOM*, plus page number.) We must, however, resist several temptations to which this shorthand phrase might attract us. The first is to think that "mind" in this phrase refers to one unified or fully integrated entity. As will emerge in some detail below, the concept of mind and its operations encompasses a diverse and sometimes complementary, sometimes conflicting, variety of powers, processes, and limitations. These include various forms of thinking (including, but by no means exhausted by, reasoning or deliberating); forming desires, beliefs, and judgments about ourselves, the world around us, and what we can, should, and must do in it; framing intentions and purposes and deciding to act on them; imagining worlds in some ways different from those with which have thus far become familiar. Ideally or at their best, the foregoing powers of the mind are most often exercised or enacted self-consciously and in a more or less coherent or at least recognizably connected fashion. But Hampshire repeatedly insists that in many instances (perhaps most notably in respect to imaginings) beliefs, intentions, desires, and the like are formed subconsciously and even unconsciously.

A second temptation that must be resisted is to think that his concern with the *freedom* of the mind led him to focus his attentions exclusively or primarily on questions commonly understood as freedom versus determinism, the freedom of the will, autonomy versus heteronomy, and the like. It is not that he neglected these familiar issues. Negatively, he does reject views such as that a fully adequate scientific "charting" of the brain will or could in principle render the concept of the mind superfluous, that a rigorously scientific behaviorism will do the same for thought and action, and that thinking, intending, believing, desiring, and like capacities and operations of the mind can be adequately explained by neuroscientific, physiological, psychological, linguistic, or social scientific or historical investigations.[2] Although an ethical "naturalist" and universalist of sorts, he also rejects those forms of universalistic naturalism which contend that, again in principle, a thoroughgoing understanding of our "nature" could provide us with a unified and indisputably correct or appropriate morality or politics. While conceding something to each of these familiar views, he contends that all of them are indefensibly reductive or overly deterministic in ways that deny what we know to be the actualities and possibilities for freedom of the mind and the freedoms of thinking and acting of which some degree of freedom of mind is in most cases an integral part.

Thought and Thinking

Beginning with the ideas of thought and thinking, it will be well to start by noticing other aspects of human life that may be necessary or contributive to them but that should not be confused with thinking. Doing so will also briefly continue the foregoing discussion of views that Hampshire rejects. Although regarding thinking and its usual close ally speaking (and other uses of language) as the capacity and form of activity most distinctive of (but only usually, not always most valuable to) human beings and their actions, he recognizes respects in which thinking is possible only if or to the extent that other human attributes and circumstances are available to the would-be thinker.

1. Conditions of and limitations on the mind and on thinking
The most generic of these further attributes is an at least minimally functioning body, including but not limited to the brain and the sensory organs. In a statement of direct relevance to questions of freedom and unfreedom—and that connects recognizably to views of Nietzsche and Foucault—early in *Thought & Action*, Hampshire argues that "I find myself from the beginning able to act upon objects around me. In this context to act is to move at will my own body, that persisting physical thing, and thereby to bring about perceived movements of other physical things. . . . To doubt the existence of my own body would necessarily be to doubt my ability to move . . . I find myself living in a medium of physical action and reaction, and I do not need to infer from my observations alone that I have made a movement of some particular kind. I find my power of movement limited by the resistances of objects around me. . . . This felt resistance . . . defines for me, in conjunction with my perceptions, my own situation as an object among other objects" (47–48). This combination of perceptions and sensations (also passions and wishes, 106, 149), neither of which necessarily involve thinking, do not fully account for the "elementary discover[ies] just described. To them, and to thinking and acting in response to them, must be added elements of thinking such as identifying objects as, in Wittgenstein's phrase, "somethings not anythings or nothings" and also operations of the mind such as believing, intending, and trying, operations conditioned by but not reducible to perceptions and sensations. "I know directly, that I tried, or set myself, to move, or that I did not try, but was moved by something else. No knowledge is more direct and underived than this knowledge of the fact of my own intention to move or to bring about a change" (48).

The last two sentences move us on to concepts and ideas that require detailed attention. But Hampshire's repeated emphasis on the corporeal or somatic should be underlined by quoting two further passages. "I do not know how I would identify myself as a disembodied being"(50). More generally, and developing what he calls the "double aspect theory of personality," he argues that "The circuits of the brain function in accordance with the laws of physics, as do the sense organs and limbs and the human body as a whole" (*Morality and Conflict*, 55; hereafter *M&C*). On the other hand, "Thoughts are only adequately explained by thoughts"; thus, "There are two utterly distinct, but indispensable, schemes of explanation with a common subject matter, which is the total activities and reactions of human beings" (56). Hampshire credits Spinoza with formulating, against Descartes, a double aspect theory and says that its strength lies in the fact that according to this theory "there is no incompatibility, and no competition, between the two systems of explanation, the immaterialist and the materialist. . . . They are both valid and indispensable, and each is independent of the other and complete in itself" (63).

The last clause—"independent of the other"—is, on Hampshire's own showing, an overstatement. The double aspect theory is itself a product of thinking, and for reasons already discussed the scientist must employ thinking in identifying the elements that compose the material world and in discerning and generalizing concerning the laws that order that world. A central element in his repeatedly articulated criticisms of empiricism is the view that "reality by itself sets no limit" to identifications and descriptions of it, that "any element in reality . . . may always be classified in an indefinite number of alternative ways," and that "we," a we that presumably includes scientists, "are . . . constantly changing our standpoint" or the perspective from which we make our identifications, descriptions, and generalizations.[3] (The same should be said of the passages concerning corporeality discussed just above. The passages just considered, however, underline Hampshire's view that an at least minimally functioning body is a necessary condition of, and places limitations on, thought and thinking. No particular thought or pattern of thinking can be sufficiently explained by reference to the material world, but the possibility of thought cannot be fully explained without such reference. It is in part in this sense that he advances "a kind of materialism" (*FOM*, last essay).)

Hampshire also argues that there are events and activities that occur in the mind but that either do not involve thinking or that heavily influence and often limit it. As to the first, he argues that "Any human mind is the locus of unquestioned and silently formed intentions and of unquestioned and silently formed beliefs" (*T&A*, 101). This argument is relevant to the claim that there are mental events that do not involve thinking, especially if it is viewed in company with his numerous discussions of sub-conscious and pre-conscious thoughts. Again, although one cannot act on a desire, a want, or a wish without the agent evaluating it by some criterion that she endorses, they sometimes simply "occur" (*Freedom of the Individual*, 38, hereafter *FOI*). "One may simply want to do something at a particular time, without the desire to do it being attributable to any line of thought or calculation" (48, 93).

There are at least two further respects in which operations of the mind should be distinguished from thinking. The first concerns the exercise of "imagination," the second the role of language and convention in human affairs. As to the first, it is true that acting on an imagining, as with acting on a preconscious or subconscious wish or want, requires "a making up of one's mind; and even in respect of the works of imagination . . . an artist [and all other agents] must still self-critically make up his mind on the merits of his realised conceptions, however these were arrived at" (*FOI,* 107). "In stressing the role of decision, I am not . . . depreciating the imagination, and I am not depreciating the undirected and pre-conscious workings of the mind. The most profound and fruitful discoveries of truth may present themselves to a man in an apparently unconnected manner, and without any apparent source in his own directed thinking. If one distinguishes between that which occurs in the mind, without the subject's conscious agency, and one's own directed thinking, aimed at appropriateness and with precautions against misguidedness, one is not thereby bound to underrate the imagination. . . . There may indeed be truths, and insights of many kinds, which typically are arrived at in some state of passivity of mind, and not as the conclusions of the kind of thought that conforms to a norm of logical order and directedness. [Indeed] as only a minority of our actions are the conclusions of deliberation, and only a minority are the outcome of considered decisions, so not all our significant beliefs are the discoveries of an ordered inquiry." Extending this theme in ways further considered below, he adds that it is not "a requirement of rationality that a process of deliberation should usually be the precursor either of action or of belief" (Ibid. For further discussions of imagining, see: *Public & Private Morality*, 53, hereafter *P&PM*; *M&C*, 130–131; *Innocence and Experience*, 30–31, hereafter *I&E*).

Turning to the second limitation on or precondition of thinking, language, and the wider notion of conventions, customs, and ways of life, are among the most pervasive topics in Hampshire's writings. He sees them as among the salient features of human affairs, features that often require thinking and that in innumerable instances not only enable thinking but are integral components of both thinking and acting. The many ways in which they are not only necessary but strongly contributive to both is a main theme in later discussions. First, however, attention must be given to the respects in which, as Hampshire sees it, language and other conventions precede and limit or otherwise importantly influence thinking. After considering this important aspect of Hampshire's theorizing, it will be possible to move to closely related questions that have been before us throughout these essays, namely, "What is the mind free from and what is it free to do?" It will then be possible to address the somewhat wider question, namely, "What are *persons* who enjoy some degree of freedom of mind free from and free to do?"

Language, Hampshire argues, is necessary to thought (*T&A*, 11–12). He does not mean this or that known or imagined language, but some language or other. Nor, in saying this, does he contradict claims considered above, claims that there are mental powers and events that are pre- or extra-linguistic and hence he does not deny that we sometimes have experiences of ourselves and the world without using language. (On this theme, compare Nietzsche's discussions of the unconscious as compared with the conscious or consciousness.) As was seen above, however, we can have experience of a this or a that, a so-and-so or a such-and-such, if and only if we have available to us words or other signs—words or signs that have a more or less definite and more or less continuing meaning in our community of language users—that we can use to differentiate this's from that's and hence identify commonalities among the various perceptions and sensations that, often despite noticeable differences among them, we denominate in a particular way. Of course languages vary importantly and for the most part unpredictably from place to place and time to time in any one place. (They vary, as he frequently puts it, both within and between "ways of life." See *P&PM*, 12–13, 31; *M&C*, 7, 149.) Regarding language as conventional or customary, Hampshire categorically rejects all versions of the notion that there is, could, or should be a single language that is what it is because it accurately tracks or mirrors nature or reality.

There are, however, two inseparable types of feature that all languages must possess in some form or other, certain uses to which all languages are and must be put. In abstract terms, the first is rules of language "that single out elements in reality as being of the same kind, and that identify recurring kinds of thing: secondly, rules that single out one specimen of a certain kind of thing from another, and identify the same one as recurring or appearing again. Rules of the first type may be called principles of classification: rules of the second type . . . principles of individuation. Rules of the two types are systematically connected" (*T&A*, 12). It is exclusively in language that we can identify a this or a that such that we can differentiate it from others which, in our perceptions, may appear to be importantly similar to it. In making such identifications—whether of a genus or a species—however, we always and necessarily classify the this or that as a *kind* of thing. We identify it as a something that has recurred in our experience and that does or could recur in our future experience, and that we classify in the same way despite what may be notable changes in it. (Thus memory is necessary to all but the most evanescent identifications. See below for discussion of the place of memory in thinking and acting.)

Contrary to many philosophers, including Kant, who advanced a conception of necessary kinds, but also earlier philosophers who advanced theories featuring notions of natural kinds, these identifications-cum-classifications are made by, not given to, human beings. (On Kant and the earlier philosophers just alluded to, see *T&A*, especially 13–14.) Hampshire does briefly entertain the idea that certain generalizations can be made as to the substance as opposed to the form of languages and their rules (21). But there are no necessary or given starting points to the succession of identifications and classifications that we make. In one of his strongest statements insisting on the conventional or customary character of all language, and hence of all thinking, Hampshire argues that this succession "must depend on our permanent and common interests, and the forms of our social life. . . . It depends on the form of civilization, of which the language is a part, as one social institution among others." Continuing this argument in ways that underline continuities with his discussions of features of mental life that owe little or nothing to conscious, directed, thinking, he says that "The institution of language presupposes a background of non-linguistic convention, the social world of conventionalized gesture, expression and habits of agreement" (20).

Comparing uses of language to following rules and norms of polite and morally defensible conduct, he says that the agent doing either of the latter "has learnt his variations of behaviour in the same way that he learnt to speak his native language: by imitating others and by being corrected, with greater or less generality, when he goes wrong. He does not need to have learnt a code of manners, explicitly formulated, any more than he need have learnt the rules of grammar applicable to his native tongue. In both cases one could speak of the rules and conventions being internalised" (*P&PM*, 27, 37). As with all conventions, customs, and traditions, these presuppositions, these features of the background, can and do change. "There is no theoretically determinable limit to the variety of new types of classification that may be introduced. There will be as many new types of classification as there will be new forms of social life and of co-operation among men" (21). Some of these changes will be proposed as a result of critical assessment of the established conventions. But the idea that each and every one of them could be made objects of critical analysis, either all at once or successively, is a fantasy, often one of many manifestations of "innocence" as distinct from "experience."

As the last quoted passage indicates in part, Hampshire is not arguing that language creates a "cage" against the bars of which we can do no other than, in futility, butt our heads. In company with numerous philosophers of language from Vico to Wittgenstein and up to the present, he argues that languages and their rules are characterized not only by porosity to directed and undirected change but by open texture, aporias, and other indeterminacies. Unlike the rules programmed into a computer or other machine, "When [a man] . . . intends to follow some prior instructions in his actions, that which he intends to do is not completely stated in the instructions themselves. The instructions may be complete, in the sense of sufficient, [but only] given certain assumptions about the normal capacities of men. . . . The 'instructions' fed into a machine . . . could be complete, in the sense that the 'adoption' of the instructions by the machine in itself brings about the intended achievement. Only [if at all] in ritual and magical uses of language—e.g. 'Repeat these words after me . . .'—can a man become rather like a machine. Otherwise the man . . . must have some practical knowledge that is not contained in the instructions" (*T&A*, 217–18). In sum, language is necessary to all thinking, but language rarely fully determines any particular thought or succession of thoughts.

Hampshire distinguishes between important conventions, those that are properly regarded with deep seriousness, and others that, again often properly, are accorded less significance by the participants in a form or way of life. Among the clearest cases of such serious conventions, the violation of which usually arouses feelings of shock and repugnance in those who witness them, are certain rules of morality that distinguish this way of life from others. Many such conventions are "imbedded" in the languages of the participants in ways of life, and hence linguistic violations of them double in brass as moral transgressions. But the "seriousness" with which conventions of language are viewed is not restricted to rules that are widely viewed as having moral standing.

Rather, "[j]ust as any natural language has to satisfy the common requirements of language as such, being a means of communication, so on the other side a language has to develop in history and over a period of time, its own distinguishing forms and vocabulary, if it is to have any hold on men's imagination and memory. The project of Esperanto, the generally shared and syncretistic language, does not succeed. A language distinguishes a particular people with a particular shared history and with a particular set of shared associations and with largely unconscious memories, preserved in the metaphors that are imbedded in the vocabulary" (*M&C*, 135). As with all others, these serious conventions do change and can be changed by deliberate thought and action. But they form "the bedrock of my moral [and other] dispositions, upon which I must build differently" (Ibid.).

2. Operations and capacities of thinking; its relations to action

If we accept Hampshire's assessments of the conditions of and limitations on thinking (as, with minor disagreements, I do), what of a more positive or affirmative character can we say about it?

"Thought" and "thinking" are very general concepts and are put to a variety of uses. For this reason we cannot expect to arrive at a general theory that identifies and orders all of their established and interpersonally cogent or intelligible employments. But they are not empty, are not "free-floating signifiers." The most familiar and unchallenged of their uses display commonalities that for the most part distinguish them from other concepts with which they are sometimes confused. Usually, for example, we are able to distinguish thoughtful action or conduct from thoughtless movements or behaviors. Elaborating on the idea that pre- or sub-conscious events in the mind, as well as imaginings, can themselves provide an impetus to but not the sufficient conditions of action, Hampshire writes: "The concept of thought, fully secularised and separated from God, does not become so general as to be without content. An activity [movement?] has become unthinking or thoughtless when we have neglected to apply any standard of rightness and mistake to the performance, when we have just gone ahead without reflection and control" (*I&E*, p. 39). As a practical matter, "In general it is reasonably assumed that thoughtlessness in the performance of any valued activity is a recipe for failure." More generally, "Reflection and control are the necessary features that constitute thought across all domains of thoughtful activity; and 'reflection' is a word that can be used to represent a distinct phenomenon in conscious experience. We unavoidably know the difference in conscious experience. We unavoidably know the difference in experience between the thoughts [impressions?, inclinations?, imaginings?] that from time to time occur to us and the line of thought that we pursue while we are concentrating on some thought-controlled activity. This is the familiar distinction between activity and passivity of mind, to which many philosophers have referred but which no one, I think, has succeeded in analysing. The distinction, with a scale from active to passive thinking, is an incontestable phenomenon, and is not an invention of philosophical theory; there is the felt difference between doing something with care and attention and doing it while thinking of something else, or the difference between concentrating on a problem and its possible solutions and just drifting and allowing one's thoughts to stray" (Ibid.: 39–40).

Two features of this important passage must be underlined. The first is that the distinction is scalar in character. That is, in practice the distinction between thoughtfulness and thoughtlessness is a matter of degree, varying from activity to activity and person to person. Moreover, there are some persons who are thoughtless over large and important stretches or domains of their activity.[4] The second is that the distinction, while undoubtedly carrying normative implications, is first and foremost conceptual/analytic in character. Most particularly, and for reasons already seen in part, it is decidedly not Hampshire's view that activities that do not manifest thinking are therefore without value. (The subordinate clause, "fully secularised and separated from God," also deserves comment. Surely the characteristics that distinguish thinking for Hampshire are sometimes evident, even if in circumscribed forms, in some religious thinking.)

Following up briefly on the points just discussed, Hampshire refuses the several views, of great prominence in philosophical and related literatures, that identify thinking, or at least thinking of value to human life, with reasoning, rationality, and deliberation. We have noted his conviction that, in fact, only a minority of human actions are preceded by deliberation and that those in which it is absent do not therefore necessarily contribute less to human well-being than those in which it is present. In respect to specifically moral conduct, he is yet more insistent. With reference to two thinkers he greatly admires and to whom he is otherwise much indebted, he objects that both Aristotle and Spinoza argued that "improvement of human life is to come from improved reasoning; and in their different ways both theories stress a contrast between reason on one side and desire and passion on the other. Slowly . . . I have come to disbelieve that the claims of morality can be understood in these terms. I have found reasons to disbelieve that reason, in its recognized forms, can have, and should have, the overriding role in making improvements which these two philosophers allot to it" (*M&C*: 1. See also *I&E*: 30–31. For qualifications of this view, see the following chapter.)

Thought and thinking are wider concepts than reason, reasoning, and deliberation. Particularly in public affairs and in science and mathematics, the latter have a distinctive importance and value. But in public affairs and in doing arithmetic as part of practical reasoning, they are neither always present nor necessary. When participating in politics, "[t]he prudent person [often] silently marshals and reviews arguments for and against alternative policies, and perhaps sometimes the arguments occur to him in some still identifiable and definite order." If so, we can say that he is reasoning. "But it need not be so, even with the most clear-thinking person, and often the arguments present themselves in no definitely assignable order. We do not expect the model of deliberation, derived from discussion in the council chamber, to be reproduced with unquestionable literalness in the inner forum [of the mind], any more than we expect our mental arithmetic to reproduce the successive moves of a calculating machine" (*I&E*: 52).

Sharpening the edge of the foregoing thoughts (especially the last among them), Hampshire derides as less than human "humanoids" who take the calculating machine as their ideal of rationality and attempt to "reproduce" its operations with "unquestionable literalness" in their own thinking and acting. If they lacked the dispositions and the power to tell stories and recall the past, "we should think of them as very superior robotics, an Alan Turing who had preserved no link with his school days at Sherborne, or a John von Neumann who had never reflected on his school in Budapest. Persons [?] who conspicuously enjoy and excel in reasoning, but who have no interest in any kind of story-telling or in recalling and recording their past [activities that usually involve thinking, but rarely reasoning in the sense Hampshire is discussing], tend to be considered monsters of rationality, and to be called inhuman" (Ibid.: 44).

The arresting thought that there are or could be "monsters" of rationality is developed in many places in Hampshire's writings, perhaps most expressively in chapter 7 of *Morality & Conflict*.

Broadening his attack on mechanical rationality to include overestimations of the power and duty of abstract reasoning regarding morality and other pervasive aspects of human affairs, he argues that Aristotle and Spinoza are by no means the only philosophers guilty of this mistake. Hume [?], Kant, the utilitarians, the deontologists, and ideal social contract theorists such as Rawls are all tarred with this brush (see pages 143–45). If we attempt, as these otherwise very different philosophers sought to do, to understand, assess, and prescribe to human affairs by engaging exclusively in "fully explicit and rational thinking," we will not find ourselves, "as the Enlightenment philosophers hoped, . . . unclothed in the sole light of reason . . . and guided by no considerations of another less rational kind. . . . [Rather,] they will find that they are disguising from themselves the moral [and other] considerations that explain much of their own conduct" (161).

The rational moralist can be expected to claim that this is what ought to be the case. On the views of those of this persuasion, it is the philosopher's task to use reason to struggle against sentiment and ordinary social influences. Whether a Kantian or a utilitarian, the philosopher, in particular the moral philosopher, properly issues statements as to what ought to be, not descriptions of the actual state of our "unreformed moralities," which are tainted by social custom and by inherited dispositions. Against such moralists, Hampshire says, "I am arguing . . . that reason both is, and ought to be, not the slave of the passions in practical matters, but the equal partner of the passions, when these are circumscribed as the reflective passions" (161–62), that is, by thinking but not exclusively by abstract reasoning or rationality. [5]

To repeat, these remarks are intended to circumscribe the role of reasoning and rationality, not to deny either that they are essential to important activities or their distinctive value in a wider variety of human undertakings. Before pursuing these points, however, attention must be given to conditions—further to those already discussed—and characteristics of thinking generally.

Thinking includes components such as forming and sustaining beliefs, framing intentions, adopting goals and ends, identifying means to try to enact the intentions and to try to achieve the goals and—usually—developing a more or less articulate conception of the good. All of these mental operations are performed in language and hence require the forms of thinking involved in more or less explicit awareness of and attention to the rules and conventions of language. There is, however, a condition necessary to these performances, namely some degree of awareness of the self as distinct, and hence some conception of more or less continuing self-identity.

a. Self-awareness, identity and singularity

For reasons discussed earlier, thinking occurs in the setting of identifiable objects to which the agent can refer. In their particularities, however, these objects change, come and go. But "[t]here is one continuing object about the existing and [main] identifying feature of which he is never in doubt and which he can always use as a fixed point of reference: himself. However uncertain he may be in referring to things in his environment, he can always identify himself as the man who is doing, or trying to do, so-and-so. He is aware of himself as the centre from which his perceptions radiate, and he is aware that, as he moves or is moved, his perspective changes. [For example, i]ntentional movement gives him his sense of being in the world, and prevents him from thinking of himself as a neutral point, outside the world, to which things or impressions are presented in a single natural order" (*T&A*: 68–69).

This thought is developed as follows: "The idea of a thinking observer who could form from his experience no notion of making a movement, or, more generally, of doing something, is one that can scarcely be entertained. . . . For instance he would have no reason to make any kind of identification of himself with his body, as 'his' body would only be for him one physical object among others. Yet his sense-organs are part of his body, and it must be presumed that he uses and directs them at will; or, if we suppose that he does not, 'observation' loses its sense" (69–70). (He notes that he is not "here concerned with the facts that might be disclosed by a psychologist studying exceptional cases of paralysis [severe mental illness, addiction?], but only with the necessary interconnection of the concept of action, observation and personality.")

Self-awareness involves, or rather presumes, some more or less explicit sense of one's more or less continuing identity and sometimes of his "singularity." One can identify with, and hence form parts of one's own conception of self as a participant in some way or form of life. But this identification cannot be total, cannot exclude respects in which I am the self that *I*, uniquely, am.

Hampshire develops this claim in important part by invoking the idea of memory. A distinguishing feature of humanity "is the habit of dwelling upon the past: of recalling the past and investigating it with motives [that may be] unconnected with prediction of the future." I may communicate the memories thus formed to others and thus share them with others. But "my memories are mine alone, the stuff of my inner life. . . . My memories, conscious or unconscious, preserve the continuity of my experience and they confer some unity and singularity on my life as a whole. Not even identical twins have the same memories, because of differences of perspective and of the accidents of location. Most of us have a multitude of memories which we know to be ours and no one else's" (*I&E*: 114–15).

It may well be thought that these remarks about personal identity are somewhat exaggerated. Agreement with them does not require that we fully endorse Hume's view that identities shift and fluctuate, sometimes rapidly and radically. Hampshire then draws a further distinction, between identity and singularity, a distinction that is at once a refinement of and perhaps a narrowing of the notion of identity. This notion of singularity, at least reminiscent of central notions in Nietzsche's thought, then becomes a salient part of what might be called his axiology. Here is the main passage: "A sense of one's own singularity is sometimes called a sense of identity. When a person thinks of himself as different from everyone else because he has had experiences which no one else has had, then it is probably better to say that he is thinking of his singularity. The identity of an individual includes his singularity . . . but the scope and emphasis of the concept is different, because it implies also the continuity of his existence, which justifies, for instance, his having one name applicable throughout his existence" (115).

It is evident from these sentences that, conceptually, the distinction is for the most part one of emphasis. This is in part because of the centrality of memory and hence a substantial degree of continuity to the concept of identity. Hampshire's general theory of value aside for now, the key to the difference between identity and singularity seems to be twofold. First, the former, but not the latter, allows of having largely the same memories and other components of identity with others, whereas singularity resides in there being at least some features of the self that are unique to it. Second, and this is a further respect in which singularity is narrower than identity, whereas identity imports continuing "existence," singularity allows of sharp breaks in the latter. "If a person seemed to alternate between existence and non-existence, his identity," as with Stevenson's Jekyll and Hyde, "would be in doubt, and he would be singular on each occasion" (Ibid.).

Introducing the idea of "individuality" that he develops in the immediate sequel and in other places, he argues that this notion includes both persons with an identity and persons who, in addition, manifest singularity. Because Jekyll and Hyde display singularity but lack identity, they do not count as examples of individuality. The importance of this distinction to Hampshire's thinking about the sort of persons we should try to be or to become emerges as the present discussion proceeds. To both anticipate and look back, the interplay that he promotes between identity and singularity aligns him closely with Nietzsche's argument that we need memories and other continuing attributes, but that the best memories, or at least the best habits, are those that are short-lived and that the most admirable individuals are those who are prepared to break decisively with many of the characteristics and commitments that they had previously developed and made.

In sum, identities and reflexivity or awareness of self is necessary to all thinking, and singularities in company with identities are essential to certain rare but especially admirable and valuable forms of thinking. These claims play further and vital roles in Hampshire's analyses and assessments of other of the usual components of thinking mentioned earlier, namely beliefs, intentions, ends or goals, conceptions of the good, and powers.

b. Beliefs and intentions

In an extended contrast between fearing something and believing it, Hampshire argues that "it is logically possible that Smith has no fears of any kind. . . . But it is not logically possible that a sane man should have no beliefs, as it is not logically possible that he should have no intentions. The only contingent matter to be discovered, is *what* a man's beliefs are and *what* his intentions are" (*FOI*: 78). Smith can recognize that he is fearful or anxious without being able to identify the object of his fear. But "it is impossible that one should have identified one's state . . . as one of believing, and yet not have identified definitely the proposition which is believed." Again, Smith can admit to being afraid and yet also admit that this is not an appropriate attitude on his part. "But he who allegedly has a belief, and at the same time confesses that the object of belief is utterly inappropriate as an object of belief, cancels the statement that he has this belief; strictly speaking, he has an idea, or a fantasy, an imagination . . . that the proposition is true, but not an attitude that can be dignified with the name 'belief,' as this word is used, at least in our culture" (Ibid.).

To say that a person believes something is to distinguish the believing "as an activity that satisfies a norm of order and directedness. To be counted as thought terminating in belief, the state and process must conform to *some* standard of correctness. A so-called belief, which was held in full conscious defiance of all the evidence, would scarcely count as a belief" albeit it might be regarded as a fantasy, a wish or possibly a kind of faith (79). Of course beliefs can be mistaken and are subject to correction by the believing person herself or by others who point out that the evidence is in fact against her. This much follows from the claim that to profess a belief is to be sincerely convinced, now, that the belief satisfies some standard of correctness. Thus, a) holding some beliefs is an unavoidable feature of all sane, adult persons; b) holding a belief necessarily involves some element of more or less conscious thinking; and, as will emerge, c) holding some beliefs is essential to other forms of thinking mentioned above, such as framing intentions and purposes, adopting courses of action chosen to enact the intentions and achieve the purposes, and forming conceptions of the good and of one's powers.[6]

For both backward- and forward-looking reasons, framing an intention involves thinking. The first is that a person's intentions "obviously arise out of his beliefs about his situation and environment, and they must alter as these alter" (*T&A*: 101). The second is that intentions, while formed in the present, point or are directed to the future. "My intention to do something is a settled belief about my future action, [albeit] a belief that illumines some part of the future, like a beam of light with a periphery of darkness, the periphery not being clearly marked" (123). As components of actions, intentions aim to alter the present state of affairs as I now believe it to be, to bring about some desired change in my situation. Thus intentions require the belief, or at least the expectation, that this action, the one that I know I now intend to take, will in fact or can be expected to bring about the desired change. Although formed in the present, the beliefs about my present circumstances and the possibility of changing them in a desired fashion are all but invariably formed by my thinking about the way things have been up to now. Similarly, my beliefs or expectations concerning the possibility of change are influenced by my estimation of the openness (or resistance) to change that are present in the features of my past and present environment. If my beliefs concerning these features change, my intentions will also change. "An intention involves . . . a definite and expressible expectation of an order of events in the future" (99), and it is a delusion to think that such expectations can be formed without reference to the past and present.

As noted, Hampshire argues that intentions can be formed in my mind "without conscious and controlled deliberation." This argument, however, does not contradict the claim that intending always involves thinking. Having formed the beliefs out of which an intention of mine arises and that are necessary to it, I may not, at the moment I form the intention, be focusing my attentions on those beliefs, may not be consciously subjecting them to scrutiny or drawing inferences from them. Thus the intention may be formed "silently," not only in the sense that I do not put it into language in order to mark it or communicate it to others, but also that it is—here and now—playing no role in the inner dialogue of my mind. If, whether in words or other actions, I make my intention known to others, they may challenge the beliefs out of which it arises and thereby challenge the appropriateness of my intention. And their doing so may lead me to question whether I should act, or rather attempt to continue to act, on the intention.

The statement that intentions sometimes form in my mind without conscious deliberation should be read along with two others. The first, which follows directly on the proposition now before us in *T&A*, runs as follows: "A man's present intentions and his beliefs . . . , taken together, constitute the present state of his consciousness" (101). Thus intentions, even if not now being consciously deliberated, are not to be regarded as pre- or subconscious events.

The second, which is further to the above discussion of self-awareness and identity, begins with a claim that is then sharply qualified as regards intentions here and now. There is, Hampshire argues, "a sense in which he [a sane and awake adult person] unfailingly knows what he is trying to do, in contrast with an observer, simply because it is *his* intention and not anyone else's. There is no question or possibility of his not knowing, since doing something with intention . . . entails knowing what one is doing; and intending to do something on some future occasion entails already knowing what one will do, or at least try to do, on that occasion" (102). The qualifier, familiar from the work of other students of intention, such as Wittgenstein and Anscombe, withdraws the verb "to know" from first person present tense statements or other expressions of intention. "There is therefore no need of the double, or reflexive, knowing which would be implied by the cumbrous phrase 'knowing what one intends.' To say 'I know now what I intend to do,' is a redundant way of saying 'I know now what I shall do,' and 'I know what my intention is in doing this' is an impossibly redundant way of saying 'I am doing this with intention or intentionally'" (102; readers will note, however, that Hampshire does frequently use the verb "to know" in discussing intentions).

If we permit ourselves some form of the verb "to know" we are simply repeating ourselves uselessly and misleadingly. But this is to affirm not deny that intentions are a vital part of consciousness.

It is, however, a distinctive part of consciousness, one that is signaled by the claim that my "knowledge" of my intentions is "direct" rather than derived or in any way inferred from anything other than the beliefs that give rise to it and inform decisions as to how to act on it. As with remembering, "intentions are sources of non-inferential knowledge. . . . I can only claim directly to remember a happening . . . which I in some way observed, and I can only claim to know, as a result of a decision or formed intention, what I shall myself try to do. Any other knowledge of the future . . . for which I claim certainty, must be justified as an inductive inference based upon some general proposition, which has been thoroughly tested and found to be true in all examined cases. The knowledge of the future, which is my own intention to act in a certain way, is in no way an inference" (128). For example, "I know directly whether I moved my arm or whether my arm moved of its own accord [or was moved by some other agent or force]. My knowledge is not derived from some perception of sensation" (54).

In making the points just discussed, Hampshire sometimes uses a distinction between deciding and discovering. Others can assist me in discovering what I want by calling attention to features of me or my circumstances of which I had not been aware, albeit their statements to me can be said to tell me what I want only if I "accept" them (105). This "acceptance" is "in many respects like a kind of decision," but is also partly the making of a discovery (105). By contrast, the "thought that accompanies and precedes action is inextricably connected with the processes of deciding and trying," that is, the process of deciding what my intentions are (106). I do not discover my intentions, I decide upon them, form or make them. And my decisions settle what I here and now intend to do, settle what I will try to do if nothing intervenes to change my intentions.

None of the foregoing denies that various mistakes are possible concerning my intentions. I cannot be mistaken as to what, here and now, my intentions are. But while there is no such thing as thinking apart from a language in which the thinking—including the forming of intentions—is done, it is only a usual not a necessary part of having an intention that I express it, in language, to myself and to others. If my command of a language were not in the background of the formation of my intentions, I could not identify them as such and certainly could not identify any one of them as *this* intention. And when I make these identifications I may make a variety of mistakes (120–21).

The most common mistake is simply to misdescribe my intention, to identify and classify it in ways that mislead others and perhaps myself concerning it. If "I intend to do something I infallibly know what I intend to do . . . although I am not infallible in putting into words what it is that I intend to do" (120). Just as the relation of words and statements to facts is elusive, so "the relation between words and actions is equally elusive. . . . [T]here are the same difficulties in dividing a human being's conduct into a set of nameable actions as there are in dividing the perceived world into a set of nameable facts" (121). "No sense can be given to the idea of an absolutely specific intention, any more than to an absolutely simple fact. As there are no atomic facts, so there are no atomic actions" (123).

Thus others may notice my mistake when I begin to enact the intention and it may become clear to them that my descriptions of it do not jibe with the actions I purport to take in its name. This is likely to engender puzzlement and lead them to ask me *what* I am doing or trying to do. If their questioning prompts me to think again I may either reformulate my description or give up the intention. But I may also notice, unaided, a discrepancy between what I am saying about myself and what I am in fact doing or trying to do. A clear case of both types of rethinking and restating is when I become convinced that what I have said I am doing or trying to do cannot be done, that the intention cannot be enacted because of a lack of power on my part or because my conception of what I am trying to do is so confused or incoherent that it is impossible to formulate an intelligible form of action that would enact the intention.

It is undeniable that such discrepancies between intentions and descriptions thereof are part of our experience of ourselves and of others. This cannot, however, be the ordinary or usual relation between the two. "A certain minimum of consistency and regularity is required in behavior, if that behaviour is to be counted as intentional action at all. There is here also the requirement of connectedness, of a trajectory of intention that fits a sequence of behavior into an intelligible whole, intelligible as having a direction, the direction of means towards an end" (146). "Some minimal consistency in the relation between statements of wants and ambitions and actual habits of performance is essential to the idea of intentional action" (147).

As his use of the term "idea" may indicate, Hampshire thinks of the immediately foregoing as conceptual points, points that will be understood and accepted by anyone with a minimally adequate command of the notions of intention, action, and related terms. As usual, however, these conceptual points have substantive not merely formal import. An example of the latter concerns lying and other insincere statements of belief and intention. These forms of speech are of course familiar to us. But the passages just quoted give part of the reason that such professions must be exceptional rather than usual or ordinary in the speech and other actions of this or that individual. "Intentions that were never put into practice would not count as genuine intentions, and beliefs which were never honestly expressed and which never guided action, would not count as beliefs. A man who with apparent sincerity professed intentions, which were never in fact translated into [further forms of] action, would finally be held not seriously or 'really' to intend that which he declared he had the intention to do, even if there was no suggestion of deceit" (159). Continuing to emphasize the conceptual as distinguishable from the moral or prudential, Hampshire continues this thought as follows: "He would be compelled, by mere respect for the meaning of words, to admit to himself that his so-called intentions were more properly described as vague velleities or idle hopes. . . . Under these conditions thought and belief would not differ from the charmed and habitual rehearsal of phrases, or the drifting of ideas through the mind" (Ibid.).

Of course the confirmed or even an occasional liar or hypocrite would not be "compelled" by the considerations Hampshire mentions. Such a person would know full well that she intended to break the usual—the expected by others—connection between her words and her deeds. Rather, having the intention to deceive, she would know that in "professing" her beliefs and intentions she was knowingly and deliberately violating the usual meanings of her words, doing so with the intention of deceiving those who heard or read her statements. Hampshire is of course aware of this. "I may make certain movements [or statements] that are ordinarily a sure sign that I am trying to achieve so-and-so, while in fact I have a quite different aim in view. For this reason I can pretend to be going to do something, or I can give the appearance of doing it, when in fact my intentions are exactly the opposite. Among the actions I can perform with an abnormal intention is the action of stating something—that is, I can lie" (137).

In his more explicitly moral and political writings, it becomes clear that Hampshire rejects Kant's unqualified condemnation of lying. He not only imagines but concretely describes circumstances in which lying is permissible, perhaps morally or politically mandatory. (See the following chapter for discussion of these views.) The arguments just considered, however, go some distance toward showing why such conduct can be successful only if it is exceptional in the activities of this or that person. When I lie, "I have not then meant something different" from the usual meanings of the words that I use (Ibid.). Rather, my lie succeeds only if others take my statement to mean what such statements ordinarily mean. If I lie repeatedly, others will notice the discrepancies between my words and my other deeds and will cease to credit my statements, thereby defeating my purpose in making them. This point can of course be generalized in ways that have substantial social and political import. Frequent and widespread lying and other forms of deception engender suspicion and erode the possibilities of mutually trusted communication on which anything approaching a decent or livable society and polity depend.[7]

c. Conceptions of the good and powers

In part because they connect importantly to conceptions of freedom, two further features of believing and intending should be noted. The first is the idea of a conception of the good, the second an understanding or mis-understanding of my "powers," of my ability to act on my beliefs and in-tentions.

Hampshire is unwavering in his rejection of teleological theories ac-cording to which some one conception of the good should play a domi-nant, a determining or overriding role in morality and perhaps, as in Aristotle as he reads him, in practical reasoning generally (which does not make him a deontologist in any usual sense). He nevertheless argues that "every [sane, adult, non-addicted] person has the potentiality of forming his own conception of the good. . . ." (*I&E*: 118). He acknowledges that not everyone realizes this potentiality; that some people "simply imitate others and drift indifferently and without commitment or passion throughout their lives" (Ibid.). But he argues that there is (no less than!) "one universal moral requirement that touches conceptions of the good: the higher-order requirement that every person should have formed through experience some conception of the good, which is *her* overriding concern, and which she is ready to defend" (117, italics mine). This conception may be articu-lated and defended in definite and closely considered terms, or it may do no more than "show itself" in the duties, obligations, and virtues that she accepts and admires. Again, the "overriding concern for the good may be simple, or it may be a complex set of distinct concerns, not all of which are closely related to each other. The [only] universal requirement . . . is that every adult person should have some authentic and defensible commit-ment, which engages her strongest feelings and which guides *her* actions" (Ibid.).

Together with my reasons for italicizing the pronoun, the phrase "guides her actions" helps to explain the connections between forming and acting on a conception of the good and other aspects of thinking and acting pre-viously discussed. We have seen that forming beliefs and especially framing intentions are end-oriented, end-seeking forms of thinking and acting. They aim at maintaining a state of affairs that the agent approves or at bringing about changes that the agent thinks she will value if achieved. These objectives of action vary from person to person and from time to time in the life of any one person. Many of them may have only loose con-nections with the agent's overall or most encompassing conception of the good. The conclusions of moral and other forms of practical reasoning cannot be logically inferred from or mechanically determined by any over-arching conception. But they can be "guided by" such a conception. And if the agent is convinced that there is a sharp conflict between this or that action or policy and the commitments that she regards as authentic to her and defensible by her, they may and should override the former.

I italicize the pronoun in these formulations because, developing further his idea of singularity, in discussing conceptions of the good Hampshire places great emphasis on his view that such conceptions are typically highly personal, distinctive of and to the person who forms and acts on them. He recognizes that in some cases overriding concerns have involved those who promote them "in legislating for humanity as a whole," in advancing what they regard as a "universal imperative" (116). It is clear, however, that this is not the stance that he thinks most readily defensible or that he prefers. In fact, there are many instances in which a person embracing such an ideal "will not be concerned, and will not argue, that all other people should share his overriding concern" (Ibid.). And even if he does so argue, as many Christians, utilitarians, and Kantians have been and now are wont to do, he will, and in most if not all cases should, "argue only that his conception of the good is defensible and coherent, not that it is mandatory" (117).

Thus the only universal requirement is the one already mentioned, a requirement that ordinarily does, and should, differentiate among persons rather than homogenize or even aggregate them. Aristotle, as well as the believers and thinkers just mentioned, "represent moral education as designed to produce the ideal specimen of humanity, having all or most of the excellencies that are peculiar to the species." Such philosophies introduce "the notions of completeness and of perfection, of the requirement that no essential virtue [be] missing in a complete life . . ." (115). An alternative aim "is to develop a single second-order disposition and ability: the ability of a person to work out for herself . . . a [more or less] specific picture of the best . . . way of life which is accessible to her and which, more than any other, engages her imagination and her emotions" (Ibid.).

Reminding the reader that he has criticized and rejected Aristotelian and related views earlier in this book (that is I&E, especially chapter 1), in a passage that follows directly on his discussion of singularity, he contrasts them with ideals that give pride of place to "a moral interest in individuality" (115). This emphasis "on the value of an individual life, as opposed to the life and survival of a species of animal or plant, is traceable to the presumed singularity of persons, each of whom possesses a character and style that is peculiarly theirs," an "individual essence [that] is destroyed when the individual is destroyed, and the world is to that degree impoverished. The loss is absolute, even when the person killed, or allowed to die, happened not to be an admirable human being" (117). There is, he goes on to say, "a reasonable argument behind . . . [this ideal], and this is the argument from singularity" (118).

The argument from singularity is both normative and descriptive/analytic. The "diversity in conceptions of the good is an irreducible diversity, not only because no sufficient reasons have been given, and could ever be given, for taking one end, such as the general happiness or the exercise of reason, as the single supreme end; but also because the capacity to develop idiosyncrasies of style and of imagination, and to form specific conceptions of the good, is the salient and peculiar capacity of human beings among other animals" (118).[8]

Before taking up the notion of powers, it will be well to pause to underline the affinities between those of Hampshire's views just discussed and ideas encountered in previous chapters. The conviction that reason and reasoning cannot themselves identify and give conclusive arguments for a particular conception of the good is prominent in Montaigne, Nietzsche, and Foucault, and Hampshire's emphasis on the role of passions, sentiments, and beliefs that may be little considered is also strongly reminiscent of them. The closest fit is with Nietzsche, both on the points just reiterated and as regards the emphasis on individuality understood as singularity. If it is unlikely that Nietzsche would give Hampshire's emphasis to the notion that every person has the potential to form and in part to live by an overarching conception of the good, the latter's acknowledgment that many people never realize this potential moves him close to Nietzsche in this regard. These and related similarities are further discussed later in this and the next chapter and in the Conclusion.

Powers and capabilities (*virtus* as Nietzsche often calls them) involve thinking, at least in that having them requires beliefs both about oneself and about the environment in which one attempts to act. They sometimes require physical strength, but to act effectively—and "powers" is a notion inseparable from the notions of efficacious and inefficacious action—the individual must accurately assess not only her own strength but the might and staying power of the obstacles and forces that must be overcome or resisted in order to achieve her objectives. In these respects judgments concerning one's powers require empirical as well as "direct" knowledge, "discoveries" as well as "decisions." The agent herself and observers of her "look . . . for causal explanations of h[er] power, or of h[er] lacking the power, to do something. 'Why was I unable [or able] at that moment to do so-and-so?' is typically a causal question; my powers to do certain things come and go . . . and I have every motive for discovering, if I can, the conditions on which their presence and their absence depend" (*FOI*: 16).

Of course such assessments require examination of resources less tangible than physical strength or available allies and weaponry: these include determination, courage, daring, cunning, and other qualities of character and mind that contribute to or diminish the prowess of the agent and the agent's adversaries. An agent and those who have known her for some time may arrive at these judgments by observing what she did and did not do on various occasions. This is because such judgments are akin to but not the same as discoveries. Rather, the concept of a power also involves direct knowledge. Occasionally using language reminiscent of Nietzsche, in discussing powers Hampshire sometimes employs the notion of will. The "concept of a power to do some specific thing is complementary to the notion of a will, or of wanting to do something: associated with the conception of an action, the *vouloir* and *pouvoir*, 'want' and 'can,' depend on each other for their sense. Whether someone lacks the power to do something is tested in actual performance, but only subject to the condition that the subject had the will to do the thing in question: whether someone lacks the will to do something may sometimes be revealed (in part, and only in part, and the lack is not conclusively established) in actual performance, but only subject to the condition that the power to do the thing in question exists. . . . I normally . . . decide, and know what I want to do, quite independently of observing my own patterns of behaviour; and I may authoritatively, though not infallibly, disclose my desires and interests to others, together with the conceptions and calculations that enter into them" (17).

Both the discoveries and the decisions involve thinking. Thoughtless persons may have considerable physical strength and other resources that might contribute to efficacy in action, but these attributes are rarely if ever sufficient to say that they possess powers. As we have seen, however, thinking is not a single process or activity and the species of this genus necessary to developing powers vary both within the agent's thinking and with the external demands that efficacy makes on the agent.

There are numerous complications that arise in applying the distinction between want and can, *vouloir* and *pouvoir*. Although the distinction is clear in the "normal" or "standard" cases with which Hampshire is primarily concerned, drawing it in particular cases "is notoriously difficult" (23–24). There are a number of reasons for this. The agent may want to perform this or that action, may have a will to do it, but the want or will may be too weak to carry her all the way to trying to do it. For example, her wants or desires may conflict with one another; she wants to do X but she also wants to do Y, and the latter want may prove to be stronger when it comes time to commit herself to one or the other. Or, as with Buridan's ass, the two may be of equal strength and the conflict between them may immobilize her. Again, the agent may be confused about her desires. She may be convinced that she wants to do X, but she hasn't thought through the ways in which doing X will interfere with doing Y or Z, or she may be mis-informed about the difficulties that would present themselves if she at-tempted X and/or the power she has to overcome those difficulties. When she encounters those difficulties she may give up the desire or make the at-tempt to X in no more than a half-hearted manner. In these and related cases, the agent's statement that she wants to do X will be true, but the want is not univocal or sufficiently strong to attempt the action. Yet again, the agent may be deceived about her desires or may attempt to deceive others concerning them.[9]

Further complications arise from the fact that, as with "thinking," the "notion of a power . . . is a very wide and general one. It includes the kind of power to do something which is an ability or skill, the power which is being in a position to do something, . . . a legal or customary power (e.g., to marry people if I am a priest), and many variations and combinations of these" (19). But Hampshire is confident, justifiably in my view, that his analysis of powers as normally involving shifting combinations of "want" and "can" must be the starting point for more or less radical conceptual re-visions. The bearing of this analysis, and the analyses of the other ideas and concepts considered above, on issues concerning freedom and unfreedom of action, discipline, and resistance are a central concern in the following chapter.

CHAPTER 6

Stuart Hampshire on Freedoms and Unfreedoms of Action
Freedom, Discipline, and Resistance

I. Freedom and Thinking

"Action" is a capacious but not an all-encompassing concept.[1] There are elements of and events in human life that should not be placed in this category. These include the movements and behaviors of those that are thoughtless and perhaps of those who "think" and move mechanically, for example "monsters of rationality." There are also events that occur in the mind and that may come to play a role in action but, because they themselves do not involve thinking or other components of action, such as believing and intending, should not be characterized as actions. These include beliefs, desires, and intentions that simply "occur," and they include imaginings prior to the moment at which they have been assessed as to whether it is appropriate to attempt to enact them. For reasons discussed in earlier chapters, on some conceptions of freedom these elements or features of human can be said to be free or unfree, but the conception of freedom and unfreedom now to be considered excludes them from such characterizations.

The announced "principal purpose" of *Thought and Action* is to "show the connection between knowledge of various degrees and freedom of various degrees" (133, and *T&An, Postscript*), an objective that is pursued at intervals throughout the book and perhaps more explicitly or directly in later works. Later in the same work Hampshire argues that "it is through the various degrees of self-consciousness in action, through more and more clear and explicit knowledge of what I am doing, that . . . I become comparatively free, free in the sense that my achievements either directly correspond to my intentions, or are attributable to my incompetence or powerlessness" in executing my intentions. "A man becomes more and more a free and responsible agent the more he at all times knows what he is doing, in every sense of this phrase, and the more he acts with a definite and clearly formed intention. He is in this sense less free the less his actual achievements, that which he directly brings into existence and changes by his activity, correspond to any clearly formed intentions of his own" (177).

It is clear that a number of these remarks refer to freedom of mind and speak to freedom of action primarily because freedom of the former is (on Hampshire's conceptualization) a condition of the latter. With qualifications discussed in Chapter 5, a person's mind is free if or to the extent that the beliefs she holds, the desires and intentions she forms, are recognizably her own, are part of her consciousness of self, as distinct from and opposed to having been caused by forces that are not part of her more or less self-conscious thinking. "A man is less free, in proportion as his interests and activities are adequately explained as the effects of external causes and of conditions which he has little or no power to change, even if these causes and conditions do not include the will of others. [Thus unfreedom can result even if the external causes do not involve human agency.] Insofar as there are genuine possibilities open to him, and he can be said to have decided to live as he does, he can be said to be self-directed and free." Crediting Spinoza and Kant with defining "the freedom of the individual in terms of their differing conceptions of an active mind," he says they have thereby "made explicit one element in the ordinary connotation of the word 'free.' . . . We ordinarily talk and act on the assumption, which we have built into the normal forms of speech, that many of our emotions and attitudes, desires and interests, were formed, and can be altered by our own thinking about the appropriateness and inappropriateness of their objects" (FOI, 93).

As these and previously quoted remarks indicate, a person's thinking can be, and for various purposes must be, influenced by past, present, or future events that the agent expects to occur. But it can be said that she enjoys freedom of mind only if or only to the extent that her identifications and assessments of those events are given by her own thinking.

The prominence of the arguments here briefly recapitulated makes it clear that Hampshire's conception of freedom of action cannot be understood without close attention to his analyses of freedom and unfreedom of mind. (That is why, if an explanation is necessary, extended attention is here given to his thinking concerning freedom of mind.) Phrases included in the foregoing passages, as well as much else, however, require us to recognize that freedom of action necessitates more than freedom of mind. A person can enjoy substantial degrees of freedom of mind and yet be prevented from acting on what undoubtedly are her beliefs, desires, intentions, and conception of the good. Consideration of the further requirements of freedom of action, the most important but not all of which are gathered under the rubric of "powers," lead to Hampshire's reflections concerning society, morality, and politics.

"If lack of will is excluded, lack of power is the only account that can be given of my not doing it, given that I made the attempt" (*FOI*, 24). For more than one reason, the last clause needs to be emphasized. I am sometimes deceived or confused about my own desires, but my making the attempt to act on them is sufficient evidence that, at the moment I made the attempt, they were the desires I was experiencing concerning how I should then act. If I later have second thoughts, I may regret the attempt or cease to continue to pursue the course of action that I had undertaken. Such second thoughts can be prompted by further self-examination, by encountering greater opposition or more formidable obstacles than I initially expected, or by various combinations of the two. In the first case, my attempt to act on a desire may itself convince me that desire X is less important to me than others that, at least here and now, I cannot satisfy if I attempt to satisfy desire X. More radically, the attempt may lead me to an awareness that X is incompatible with beliefs and values to which I am deeply committed, for example, beliefs and values that are central to my conception of the good.

In the second case, I have overestimated my powers and/or underestimated the powers of others, and of various institutions and arrangements, to resist my attempt to X or to raise to unacceptable levels the costs of continuing the attempt. Both cases involve further thinking on my part; the first, and sometimes in part the second, further self-examination, the second further investigation concerning the powers of other persons and of other sources of opposition to and obstacles in the path of my efforts. Of course, and this is the third case, the first two inducements to further thinking can interact and strengthen or weaken one another.

In these respects action, or at least successful action, typically—albeit not always—involves self-discipline. The qualifier is necessary because there are desires that simply "occur" to me and that prompt no uncertainty or ambivalence as to the appropriateness or propriety of my attempting to act on them. As noted earlier, in Hampshire's view only a minority of human actions are preceded by that form of self-discipline called deliberation. Various modes and degrees of self-discipline may have played a role in arriving at the beliefs and dispositions out of which the desires have arisen, but once those beliefs and dispositions have been formed, action on them can sometimes take place "effortlessly." Similarly, living in a society with a shared language and other conventions and institutions may have supplied its members with understandings and strong expectations as to how others will respond to many of their attempts, thus making further examination of likely reactions unnecessary.

We will not understand more or less stable, more or less "decent" (further discussion of the latter notion below) societies and polities unless we appreciate what might be called the matter of course character of a high percentage of the actions and interactions that take place in them. What is more—and more controversial—is Hampshire's repeatedly expressed view that to demand disciplined reflection and argumentation concerning *all* actions and interactions is not only to demand the impossible but to jeopardize some of the most estimable features of a society worthy of human life. As a part of his rejection of self-conscious and abstract reasoning as something required of all human beings, he argues that, as with the rules and conventions of language, there "is an advantage in [rules of conduct] being habitual, and in their being inbuilt, reliable dispositions." Introducing a notion that in other places he values very highly, he continues by saying "the less brooding on difficult cases the better for social ease and harmony" (*P&PM*, 29).

Both the descriptive/analytic and the normative articulations of these themes, however, coexist with others that are not contradictory to, but are in some tension with, those just discussed. On the first of these dimensions, there are few ideas that are more repeatedly and emphatically maintained in Hampshire's works than the idea that there is an irreducible diversity of human ends and goals and that conflicts among attempts to achieve them are not only common but ineliminable. In one of several manifestations of a dispositional (as distinct from an epistemological or otherwise programmatic) "sceptical nominalism" (*P&PM*, 40) that will require further discussion, Hampshire categorically rejects the possibility and the desirability of anything approaching an entire harmonization, by reasoning or any other method, of beliefs, desires, and intentions.

This thought bears directly on the mistaken idea that *all* human actions and attempts at action can be taken without disciplined self-examination and/or other-regarding inquiries and investigations. The likelihood is high that my attempts to X will be unacceptable to others who expect, rightly or wrongly, to be adversely affected by them. And while Hampshire forcefully champions those forms of discipline that foster and sustain a welcoming as well as a tolerant stance toward ideas, actions, and policies with which one sharply disagrees, he is convinced that such a stance will never entirely eliminate conflicts, including conflicts that will often be quite raw in character.

Faced with conflicting ideas and forces, the agent must assess their strength and her own powers to overcome them. And she must ask herself whether, if she is in some doubt as to her chances of prevailing or even if she is not, she wants to pay the price of engaging in the struggle that is likely to ensue. Further, if or to the extent that she is committed to values and virtues (or *virtus*) such as peaceful cooperation, fostering social diversity, or social and political justice, she must ask herself whether satisfying the desire or interest that she has formed warrants the costs to those values, both for herself and others, of continuing to pursue them. Consideration of these and related questions, sometimes called reflection on "second-order" beliefs and values, will ordinarily require forms of thinking that go beyond those that informed the "first-order" desires and interests that the agent initially developed. Thus encountering conflict is also very likely to goad the agent to further forms of discipline and capacities for resistance.

If the agent concludes that her desires and interests are sufficiently important to justify doing her part to engender and continue conflict, whether because pursuing them is compatible with or contributive to higher order values or otherwise, she must steel herself to marshal and find effective means of deploying her powers, thus to resist the forces she judges to be arrayed against her. And if she decides that the desires she has formed do not justify the costs that she expects will be incurred, by herself or others, in pursuing them, she must resist the temptation to do so and discipline herself to give priority to alternative objectives and courses of action. Needless to say, these requirements apply to those with whom the agent interacts as well as to herself, that is, they are requirements of all social, economic, and especially political life.

Leaving for a bit later the question of the appropriate substance or content of the beliefs and values that ought to discipline thought and action in the face of conflict, the issue arises as to the ways in which and the extent to which attention and responsiveness to the considerations just discussed is compatible with and perhaps contributive to freedom.

Relevant to answering these questions is an idea that Hampshire calls achieving "comparative autonomy." "It is the characteristic of men's thought that it is [or can be] reflexive and that the activity of thinking entails a process of stepping back, in order to attain greater objectivity, by making corrections for point of view. Active, conscious thought . . . naturally turns into self-consciousness, into thought about thought. This is the respect in which thoughtful creatures are, or may be, comparatively autonomous: comparatively, but in no absolute sense. Human beings act from the desires which their emotions engender, and which are constitutive elements of their emotions. Their passive emotions are the effects of external causes acting upon their drive to self-preservation and to power through their conceptions, usually inadequate, of the external objects that are affecting them" (*M&C*, 51).

Connecting with the "less's" and "more's" in passages already quoted concerning freedom, these remarks underline the point that both freedom of mind and freedom of action are matters of degree. The idea of "absolute" freedom of mind is a fantasy for the reasons just briefly summarized, and the idea of absolute freedom of action is a delusion of persons who imagine that their conduct is in no way affected by social and political circumstances. But both forms of autonomy, which are of course interdependent, are increased to the extent that the agent's thinking and attempted acting are disciplined by thought about thought and by more rather than less adequate conceptions of the powers of those with whom one must interact in order to pursue one's objectives. If we could imagine a human being totally incapable of either, we certainly could not describe them as autonomous; and if we could say that they enjoyed a degree of freedom—which we cannot say on Hampshire's conception of freedom—we would have to attribute their freedom, or their unfreedom, to good or bad luck.

It follows that in a large number of cases discipline is essential to achieving both freedom of mind and freedom of action. And in both dimensions or meanings of freedom, discipline is necessary because the agent must resist forces that, if not effectively combated, would diminish or eliminate both freedom and autonomy. In the first dimension, the agent must resist inclinations to act on passions and impulses that are not compatible with her considered beliefs and values. In the second, she must stand against external forces that oppose the actions she wants to take. Discipline and resistance are not necessary to *all* freedom of mind or to *all* freedom of action. A person may have the good fortune of repeatedly finding that intentions that simply "occur" to her congrue with such "higher order" thoughts, if any, that she has fashioned. Again, a person may be fortunate enough to live in a society and polity marked by a high degree of harmony or graced by a large number of fellow citizens with strong commitments to toleration or a well-developed appreciation for diversity and plurality. It is unlikely that such a person will contribute significantly to creating and sustaining a society and polity with these characteristics, and hence unlikely that she will contribute more than minimally to the conditions that make her own freedoms of action possible.

Recurring now to the distinctions among different conceptions of freedom introduced in previous chapters, it is clear from the foregoing that Hampshire rejects the notion of freedom as unobstructed movement. His insistence on the conceptual relationship between evidence of freedom of mind and freedom of action excludes this usage of "freedom" and "unfreedom." This is not to say that he does not, or could not, recognize the difference between obstructed and unobstructed movements, but presumably in identifying and describing events of these types he would employ language such as used in the present sentence. His emphasis on freedom of mind, and his occasional uses of the notion of autonomy itself, move him toward the idea that freedom, or perhaps comparatively full and especially valuable freedoms, should be understood as autonomous thinking and acting, not as mere freedom of action. But the elements in his thinking that are primarily responsible for this tendency coexist with others that would make it difficult for him to withhold the notions of freedom and unfreedom of action from forms of conduct that involve, minimally if at all, "thoughts about thoughts."

Lastly, there are reasons to think that he accords special value to what I above called freedoms4 and especially to regret the unfreedoms4 of persons whose attempts at action are shaped by higher-order reflections and deliberations. His repeated emphasis on the irreducible diversity of conceptions of good and other convictions resulting from second-order thinking, together with his equally strong emphasis on the likelihood of conflicts among such convictions, is perhaps reason to accord special privilege to freedoms in this sense. Higher-order thinking cannot eliminate conflicts, but it may provide the best hope of minimizing or ameliorating them. This is a particularly pronounced theme in his most specifically political thinking.

At the same time, however, closely related features of his thinking, and more generally the dispositional skepticism that inflects his reflections, provide decisive reasons for the conclusion that he would reject what in previous chapters was called freedoms5 and unfreedoms5. This last consideration is underlined in the following subsection, but it can be said now that the clearest formulations of and arguments for this conception of freedom and unfreedom overestimate the possibility of arriving at indisputable conceptions of the good and underestimate the likelihood that championing such a conception will breed and intensify conflict and will become tyrannical if they are insisted upon in the face of conflict.

It is appropriate to once again pause briefly here to underscore similarities on the foregoing points between Hampshire's thinking and the views of Montaigne, Nietzsche, and Foucault. Setting aside commonalities and differences regarding freedom of the mind, the most general of these similarities concerns the issue that has been central throughout these engagements. Hampshire is at one with the other theorists considered above in his conviction that discipline and the capacity for resistance it creates are essential to the most estimable forms of freedom of action and contributive to all or virtually all such freedoms. (If it is correct to say, as argued above, that consciousness of myself as acting in freedom depends on the belief that doing so requires that I think there are obstacles and forces that would hinder my desired actions if I do not successfully overcome or resist them, as a psychological or phenomenological matter the qualifier "virtually all" can be removed.) Of course there are differences among these thinkers as to the appropriate sources and characteristics of the necessary forms of discipline and resistance.

In much of his thinking Hampshire is close to Montaigne in his view that for many human beings much of the time the discipline will originate and take its character largely from the rules and conventions that are established and widely accepted in the agent's culture and society. In this respect, the terms discipline and resistance may be too strong. Having grown up in a way of life, and having internalized its language and the norms embedded in it, many agents will not experience its norms as restrictions and will not have any disposition to resist them. But this point can easily be overstated in respect to both Montaigne and Hampshire. For both, even the most thoroughly socialized or acculturated of persons will sometimes experience passions and impulses that prompt them to act against social and political conventions. If they are to remain members or citizens in good standing, they must discipline themselves to resist such inclinations. In his most Stoical moments, Montaigne's most frequent counsel is to sustain, even to welcome such impulses, but to keep them to herself or to express and give vent to them only when in company with her most intimate and trusted friends. But Montaigne shares Hampshire's view (more on this later) that all conventions are vulnerable to critical rethinking and that in any way of life some among them will be indefensible and must be combated.

Nietzsche and Foucault share the view that in fact, most, perhaps a preponderance of, human beings, "go with the flow" of social norms much of the time. Nietzsche not only accepts but sometimes welcomes the fact that a large number of Europeans have become "well-trained" and hence "reliable." Thus if he only rarely expresses admiration for those who are "enslaved" by custom and habit and have been reduced to herd-like behaviors, it is clear that he has a certain appreciation for the ways in which their presence permits and in some degree facilitates the more critical and adventuresome thinking and acting of the overpersons. Accordingly, he also thinks that even free spirits ought to "accept," meaning first and foremost not act to disrupt, the established understandings and arrangements that they regard as essential to civilized life. For the latter reason, and as indicated by his admiration for Montaigne, it can be said that there are recognizably Montaignian elements of Stoicism in his thinking about free-spiritedness. Which is to say that free spirits must discipline themselves to be polite to and magnanimous toward the members of the herd, to resist the temptation to manifest their disdain for them and to contain any inclination to impose their soaring ideals on them. They should cultivate and sustain a "pathos of distance" in their interactions with those mired in habit and conformism, but such interactions are unavoidable and the overperson should show her free-spiritedness in part by sustaining self-disciplines of the kinds just mentioned.

Nietzsche's critiques of the customary and conventional are of course more encompassing and—a few exceptions aside—more stridently expressed than Montaigne's. He never seriously entertains the possibility of a society consisting entirely of free spirits, but he does recognize, in passages reminiscent of Montaigne and certainly of Hampshire, that laws and rules, customs and conventions, rarely if ever fully determine the decisions and choices of human beings. The members of the herd are only animal-like, not animals; their capacities for critical thinking can be stimulated and enhanced by example and exhortation. It is arguable that the polemical and acerbic character of Nietzsche's writings have this objective as one of their purposes.

It is undeniable that Foucault accepts the view that discipline and resistance are essential to most if not all significant freedoms. It is sometimes argued that his emphasis on the pervasive and insidious character of power in human institutions and relations means that discipline always comes from others not from the self, that even the comparative autonomy of which Hampshire writes is an impossibility. Standing against this reading is his repeated insistence that power always engenders resistance, a resistance that cannot be effective, as he thinks it sometimes is, without discipline on the part of those who attempt to mount it. What is more, in the *History of Sexuality* and numerous essays and interviews, he strongly promotes the cultivation and maintenance of rigorous disciplinary regimens. If the fact that the slave Epictetus was for him an exemplary figure in this regard bespeaks a Stoical element in his thinking, it also indicates that this Stoicism is other- and social/political as well as self-regarding. In the remaining pages of this chapter it becomes evident that this is also true of Hampshire.

II. Skepticism and Individuality: Discipline and Freedom

To repeat, Hampshire's estimation of the value of a "sceptical nominalism" is not epistemological or otherwise grounded in the philosophical views commonly associated with skepticism. Certainly it is Pyrrhonic not dogmatic or Academic in character. But it does work an important influence on his thinking, particularly his thinking about morals and politics. It also plays a central role in his conception and vigorous promotion of notions such as individuality and singularity.

If we think of skepticism as a denial of the possibility of reaching warranted conclusions about ourselves and our world, it is evident from discussions thus far that there are numerous respects in which Hampshire is confident rather than skeptical concerning our prospects in these regards. The "immaterial" component of the dual aspect theory affirms or rather insists on the reality of various kinds of knowledge of self. Hampshire does caution against various high-flown expectations concerning knowledge of the material world, but he nowhere denies our capacity to arrive at valuable forms of such knowledge and repeatedly argues that the two kinds of knowing are, and can be shown to be, complementary one to the other. It is clear, moreover, that, especially in respect to moral, political, and in general practical thinking, he believes that dogmatic or unqualified skepticism (which he identifies with Hume and later empiricists) is unjustifiably limiting of possibilities in fact realizable by us, while various overly ambitious or inadequately cautious or circumscribed theories are unwarranted and often dangerous. (See especially *I&E*, Introduction and *passim*.) The more optimistic of his estimations of the likelihood of our achieving these objectives are underlined and assessed in the final section of this chapter. The more immediate task is to identify and evaluate his arguments for chastened—but not unduly pessimistic—expectations concerning practical reasoning generally and especially moral and political reasoning.

Some of these arguments have already made an appearance. Perhaps the most general of them concern both practical and theoretical reasoning. All reasoning begins with identifications, descriptions, and classifications, and there is no theoretical limit to the number and variety of these characterizations of ourselves and our world. I have "direct knowledge" of some aspects of myself and my thinking, but when I put this knowledge into language I can and not infrequently do make various errors. And, as with Nietzsche, my knowledge of the world external to me, including of persons other than myself, is always from one of a number of possible perspectives. Further, the convictions I form about the world and in some respects about myself are influenced by unconscious beliefs and intentions and by the "mood" I am in when I form them (*T&A*, 147–48). Science, and theoretical reasoning in general, properly aims to overcome these limitations and to arrive at laws independent of time and place. But practical reasoning always occurs in and takes some of its characteristics from a particular language and the way of life of which language is a necessary part. In addition, that vital human capacity called imagination operates in large measure independently of "facts" about myself and the world.

These features of human experience undergird Hampshire's arguments that there is an indeterminately large number of cogent and defensible moral and political programs, outlooks, and ideals, and that conflicts among them are inevitable. As emphasized below, these salient features of all human interactions do not entirely prevent us from arriving at convictions and devising arrangements which, if widely accepted in a society or polity, allow of agreements that confine diversity and diminish conflict. But it is neither possible nor desirable to entirely eliminate either.

For these and related reasons, "Moral theory, like other practical theories, is not a matter for conclusive and irresistible demonstration. The superiority of one moral theory to another is established by showing that it gives a more simple and more comprehensive, and less exception-ridden, account of the whole range of one's moral beliefs, and of the relation of one's moral beliefs to beliefs of other kinds, particularly philosophical beliefs" (*M&C*, 26). Again, "Moral theory cannot be rounded off and made completely tidy; partly because so much that is of value in a human life depends upon uncontrollable accident, partly because we still know so little about the determinants of behaviour and about human nature generally, partly because individuals vary so greatly in their dispositions and interests, partly because new ways of life should always be expected to arise in association with new knowledge and with new social forms" (*P&PM*, 53).

Hampshire makes clear that the views expressed in the preceding paragraph owe much to Aristotle. But the second passage just quoted ends on an un-Aristotelian note. There is no possibility of achieving a demonstrative and conclusive moral theory, but this has not stopped various thinkers and believers from pursuing this objective and from believing that their attempts had succeeded. Hence it has not stopped them from thinking that all those who reject their theories make identifiable and corrigible mistakes. In addition to their failure to appreciate the considerations just summarized, they make the further and often more consequential error of not realizing that "we expect [but also should hope for!] . . . leaps of the imagination, moments of insight, very rarely, and in unusual men, which will lead to transformations of experience and to new moral ambitions and to new enjoyments of living" (53).

Thus the discipline of a certain skepticism concerning the possibilities and desirabilities in practical theorizing helps to keep theorists in touch with the actualities of practical life and also helps them to stand against various forms of dogmatism which, if acted on, threaten freedom as well as some of the other estimable developments and potentialities that can be glimpsed in human affairs. These are not reasons for abandoning practical theorizing—which in any case is not a possibility (on this point see especially *T&An Postscript*)—but for continuing this ancient and honorable activity in a suitably chastened spirit.

Further advantages of this conception of practical thinking and theorizing are the subject of the pages that follow, but one among them deserves immediate notice. Hampshire never identifies himself directly or squarely with liberalism, but in several places extols beliefs, values, and practices commonly attributed to or strongly associated with most variants of that ideology. Recognition and "emotional acceptance" of the limits on human knowledge and theorizing fosters "a central virtue that leads to other virtues, and particularly to tolerance." More generally, "the virtues necessary to sustaining a liberal society naturally come from a philosophy which stresses the narrow limits of human knowledge and which stresses the fact that most human behaviour is governed by unconscious memories and by hatreds due to prejudice, and that it is not to be governed [entirely?] by rational calculation" (*M&C*, 65).

III. Morals, Politics, and Freedom: Justice and Individuality

Assuming that we recognize the value of a skeptical approach to practical thinking, how can we cultivate this disposition? And given that we do cultivate it, what conclusions, substantively speaking, can we nevertheless justifiably reach in our thinking and acting concerning the issues that present themselves in the practical domains of morals and politics?

Perhaps the general conclusion that comports most closely with a dispositional skepticism is that we ought to nurture our capacities to control our passions, impulses, and immediate inclinations, to restrain our proclivity to act on them by "stepping back" from them and subjecting them to check by our powers of thought. Anything "that I can be said to do is primarily identifiable as a change that I recognizably make in the common world of things, and that, corresponding to any such primarily identifiable action, there may be an arrested or inhibited form of it, when the identifiable change is not actually made" (*T&A*, 163). Some of the "second-order" thoughts that inhibit "first-order" impulses and inclinations stand in a "shadow-relation" to the latter. But to say this is in no way to diminish or deprecate such thinking. "A man to whom we attribute a rich inner life of belief and disbelief, of unexpressed doubt and self-questioning, must be a man of great powers of self-restraint, to whom the inhibition of action is [has become] natural. He has cut away the substance of human routines and chosen to live with their shadow. He does not shout but he exults inwardly; he does not weep, but he feels sad. He does not ask questions, but he doubts; he does not deny, but he disbelieves" (164).

Developing this "habit of inhibition" is of great importance to the possibility of a livable society and politics. It "replaces the substance of perceptible behaviour with its shadow in the mental life of thought and feeling," and it deserves to be called an important part of "the process of civilization." Manners create the inner life of the mind by placing barriers in front of the immediate and natural expressions of thought and feeling. The mental and inner life of men is the obverse of social restraint and convention" (164–65).

In later works this habit of inhibition reappears in the more public form of the readiness to engage in deliberations and negotiations with others, to give attention and weight to the views of those with whom one must interact in social, moral, and especially political life. Thus what is presented in the passages just quoted as a pronouncedly inner-directed, private, and in these respects Stoical virtue, loses much of its "shadowy" character and emerges into the brighter light of public discussion and exchange. This change in emphasis in no way demotes the importance of cultivating the inner aspects of the virtue. As the "obverse" of the restraints imposed by society and its conventions, among other contributions it makes is to preserve a domain or dimension of individuality and singularity. It should be added that where or to the extent there are little or no inner dispositions to inhibition among the members of a society or polity, the externally imposed constraints are likely either to be ineffective or to be experienced as coercive and heteronomizing. Inner-developed and impelled inhibitions are necessary to that "comparative autonomy" encountered earlier. These thoughts are of course closely akin to main elements in the thinking of Montaigne, Foucault, and especially Nietzsche.

As with the latter three thinkers, Hampshire is more than aware that the forms of reflection and deliberation involved in thinking about one's thinking are less prevalent than its value would lead us to hope. But the capacity for such thinking is present in all adult, sane, and undamaged human beings. Indeed this capacity, which along with imagination, enables us to invent and to be open to new ways of thinking and acting, "is one distinction of the species; it is one power that makes friends interesting to each other and that makes the species interesting to itself, and that makes its future interesting" (*M&C*, 28; *I&E*, 30). Much of the time most human beings passively accept beliefs and judgments that are widely accepted in their society. Along with such "passive attitudes," however, "There are indeed the active attitudes" and if only because of the diversity and frequency of conflict among received identifications and classifications of experience, these are attitudes or dispositions that "any conscious rational agent must sometimes have" (*FOI*, 80 *et seq.* 104–105).

Thus "seeing round" the array of considerations that bear upon my thinking and acting (*T&A*, 215–16), "stepping back" to assess my initial responses to them (*FOI*, 80 ff.), and "brooding" about what I should do now and into the future (*M&C*, 73) are always possible and sometimes necessary to form a belief or to frame and act on an intention. As noted earlier, Hampshire thinks that these "active" attitudes and reflections can be taken to excess. Too much brooding about what to think and do can paralyze the agent and/or disrupt the conventional arrangements on which human affairs depend for an essential modicum of stability and orderliness. But for those who have effectively cultivated these attitudes in themselves, this judgment is itself a thought about thinking, a thought about when, where, and why one should or should not step back and brood.

Whatever conclusion one reaches on the appropriateness of thinking about one's thinking, that conclusion will speak to the form that one's thinking should take, not to the issue of *what*, substantively speaking, one should think and do in respect to any of the issues that arise in day-to-day practical affairs. As with conceptions of the good—which may include the idea that a good life includes a developed and frequently enacted commitment to skeptically inflected second-order thinking—the modes of discipline and resistance thus far discussed may hold the agent back from immoderate or intemperate actions and may provide guidance as to *how* to go about deciding what would be the best or most defensible policy or course of action in this or that set of circumstances. The arguments for the possibility and desirability of cultivating these modes are at the theoretical level; as Aristotle teaches, theory can never take us all the way to warranted conclusions as to what to do here and now in practical affairs.

Hampshire nevertheless argues vigorously for certain general principles of thought and action. Indeed, he is convinced that there are modes of practical thinking and conduct that deserve universal acceptance and all but invariable implementation in all, or in all save the most absolutely evil, societies and polities. These principles, and the values that inform them and that the principles serve, come as close as human affairs permit to warranting the standing of moral and political imperatives. What are these principles and values, and what arguments can a skeptically inclined philosopher give for elevating them to this uniquely honored standing? Considering these questions takes us into the most substantive, and the most controversial, elements in Hampshire's moral and particularly his political thinking.

Notwithstanding expectations created by many of the views encountered thus far, Hampshire insists that he is not an unqualified conventionalist or relativist as regards morals and politics. He rejects those forms of universalism and imperativalism that he attributes to Kant, to Rawls, and to utilitarianism, and he also rejects Aristotelian perfectionism and natural law theories. But he argues that there are certain values that are and should be endorsed and honored by virtually all human beings and at least a few propositions that deserve close to universal and imperatival standing. His anti-relativism is not due to the respects in which he believes that we can arrive at warranted beliefs about the immaterial aspects of ourselves.

Rather, it is grounded in a combination of general judgments concerning the beliefs and values essential to human well-being and empirical generalizations concerning nearly exceptionless features of the conditions under which human beings must live their moral and political lives.

A summary statement of these anti-skeptical views, together with important qualifications of them, is presented in the *Postscript* of the new edition of *Thought and Action.* "The claim of the sceptic, in ancient Greece or now, is that all, or almost all, moral requirements are no more than the conventions of a particular society or of a group within a society. But it is not true that there are no moral [or political] requirements grounded in human nature, even though they are always modified by local conventions: for instance, the requirements of justice and a respect for law, of friendship, and of benevolence. Also the sceptic normally makes this false claim with the implication that because conventions are various, and not founded in unchanging human nature, they are not to be taken seriously by rational and enlightened men. The acceptance of this implication is a greater error, and the argument of [the original edition of] this book ought to have led to the exposure of this error. A moral requirement is not less binding, the necessity no less genuine, when the ultimate grounds for it are in a particular way of life. . . . As in the arts, so also in morality, the dispositions and needs of human nature emerge in the variety of conventions which prove to be adapted to them. An *entirely* universal morality, universal in its content, is as much a speculation or a dream as is a universal language, and for similar reasons. Morality, like language, serves to differentiate men and women, and to preserve their distinction and identity, at the same time that it also unites them in respect for their differences and in respect for the common requirements that arise from a common humanity" (*T&An*, 296–97, italics added).

Readers will recognize that Hampshire has more than a little sympathy for some of the views here attributed to the skeptic. Certainly he agrees that much of *what* is thought about morals and politics cannot be understood or assessed apart from the ways of life in which the thinking occurs; certainly he also agrees that there are important differences and rationally ineliminable conflicts among moral and political outlooks. But he draws back, holds himself back, from what he takes to be the indefensible and harmful inferences that ancient and modern skeptics have drawn from these true propositions.

Given the anti-naturalism that pervades so much of his thinking, it is not surprising that Hampshire is, at least initially, somewhat hesitant, even apologetic, concerning the "taint of naturalism" that is apparent in the remarks just quoted and particularly in the claim that certain normative propositions and principles can be grounded in features of human nature and general facts about the conditions under which human affairs are and must be conducted. He is of course aware that a number of "contemporary philosophers may find intellectually unacceptable and perhaps also morally repugnant" this appeal to "facts" in moral thinking. As he does in the closing sentences of the *Postscript*, when he broaches this idea he concedes more than a little to this form of skepticism. "From the existence of an established way of life, and from the fact that a certain set of facts support that way of life and are indispensable within it"—considerations that are prominent in his qualified universalism and imperativalism—"one certainly cannot derive an unconditional duty binding on anyone who enjoys that way of life to engage in those practices. One can derive only a qualified and conditional duty, a *prima facie* duty, to engage in those practices: conditional, first, upon overriding considerations of justice or utility, conditional, secondly, upon an evaluation of the way of life in question, taken as a whole, as comparatively respect-worthy and as not morally repellent and destructive" (*M&C*, 6–7).

These qualifications are themselves partly qualified in later discussions, but Hampshire first attempts to relieve his unease by explaining further what he does and does not mean by his appeals to nature. "The actual, well-established habits and institutions of normal men and women, revealed in their conduct and their language, are good evidence about human nature, that is, of common human aspirations, needs, and dispositions. The justification [such evidence provides for normative judgments], therefore, is by an appeal to human nature, as revealed in history, not to a human nature as studied by biologists and psychologists" (7). The moral and political philosophies to which he is most strongly opposed do not make this distinction; their proponents are convinced that it is possible to derive, or rather directly infer, values and principles from nature as such, a nature that not only can but must be known without reference to history and convention. But in a rare expression of admiration for Hume, he credits him with recognizing and placing his primary reliance on the notion of the "second nature" that develops among persons "living in a customary society, attached to the moral concerns that arise from comparatively local and temporary conditions" (Ibid.).

How does one reason or otherwise move in defense of—or against and beyond—established features of a way of life? As to the first, Hampshire distinguishes between two related modes of thinking and arguing. "In rational reflection one may justify an intuitively accepted and unconditional prohibition, as a common, expected feature of a recognisable way of life which on other grounds one values and finds admirable: or as a necessary preliminary condition of this way of life. There are rather precise grounds in experience and in history for the reasonable man to expect that certain virtues, which he admires and values, can only be attained at the cost of certain others, and that the virtues typical of several different ways of life cannot be freely combined, as he might well wish. Therefore a reasonable and reflective person will review the separate moral injunctions, which intuitively present themselves as having force and authority, as making a skeleton of an attainable, respect-worthy and preferred way of life. He will reject those that seem likely in practice to conflict with others that seem more closely a part of, or conditions of, the way of life that he values and admires, or that seem irrelevant to this way of life" (*P&PM*, 12).

Reasonings of these kinds may be conclusive for the agent whose reasonings they are, but he or she must remember that they are unlikely to be the only patterns or sets of more or less coherent reasons pertinent to the issues they address. Although taken as "absolute" by some agents, they "are not to be identified with Kant's categorical moral injunctions; for they are not to be picked out by the logical features of being universal in form. Nor are they prescriptions that must be affirmed, and that cannot be questioned or denied, just because they are principles of rationality, and because any contrary principles would involve a form of contradiction." Redirecting his fire to the utilitarians and perfectionists, he goes on to say that, for those who accept them they are or may be regarded as "judgments of unconditional necessity, in the sense [of unconditional] that they imply that what must be done is not necessary because it is a means to some independently valued end, but because the action is a necessary part of a way of life and [perhaps] ideal of conduct" (13).

As regards arguments *against* certain forms of conduct, there are prohibitions that take on a force stronger than that discussed thus far. There are "monstrous and brutal acts [that] are certainly vicious" at least in that "they undermine and corrupt" ways of life that are respect-worthy and deserving of admiration; "we can explain why they are, and what makes them so, provided that we do not insist upon either precision or certainty or simplicity in the explanation" (Ibid.). The possibility of arriving at and justifying such negative judgments is due to the fact that ways of life form more or less integrated or coherent ensembles of beliefs and values, institutions and practices, and those who understand and value such an ensemble, those who are able to give "thick descriptions" of it, can show that, and why, certain forms of conduct undermine and corrupt it. We cannot expect precision or simplicity in such reasonings because the "phrase 'way of life' is vague and is chosen for its vagueness. The unity of a single way of life, and the compatibility [or incompatibility] in practice of different habits and dispositions, are learnt from observation, direct experience, and from psychology and history; we know that [second] human nature naturally varies, and is deliberately variable, only within limits; and that not all . . . compatible achievements [even some that are theoretically compatible with it] are compatible [with it] in normal circumstances" (12).

To repeat and anticipate, Hampshire claims that yet stronger arguments, arguments to which there are no cogent responses, can be marshaled against actual or imagined and wished for ways of life that are *malum en se*, unqualifiedly and irredeemably evil. He also claims that there are values and corresponding virtues that should be accorded standing as "absolutes," values that require unqualified endorsement and virtues that demand persistent if not unswerving cultivation.

Briefly postponing the arguments for these controversial claims, I first put the discussion thus far in more concrete terms.

"Suppose," Hampshire suggests, "that there is a contrast and a tension between the definite and shared human powers, traceable to species-wide needs, and the . . . drive to diversity of human powers, traceable to individual needs" and other diversifying, disaggregating, and conflict-engendering features of human life. If so, which are the species-wide characteristics that ought to be accorded special value and standing? Here is Hampshire's usual list, several times repeated in his writings, of the "shared human potentialities" that every decent way of life ought to honor and cultivate: first among them is "the recognition of justice, which is necessary to all human associations" (*I&E*, 32). For reasons already discussed, he recognizes that substantive conceptions of justice vary somewhat from time to time and place to place, but he rejects the view that we do, can, or (especially) should share no more than a concept of justice and argues instead that there is single conception that ought to be preferred. The details of the, in reason, superior conception are discussed just below. In the passage now before us, the remainder of the list is as follows: "the obligations of love and friendship and of families and kinships; . . . the duties of benevolence, or at least of restraints against harm and destruction of life" (Ibid.); and in other places adds tolerance and measures to avoid or minimize "great evils of human experience" such as "imprisonment, enslavement, starvation, poverty, physical pain and torture, homelessness, friendlessness" (90).

Such moral judgments, "and specifically judgments about justice and fairness, are no less determinate and no less 'objective' than empirical judgments involving 'ought' and 'must' and related modal notions: no less determinate, in that they are equally susceptible of being true or false, or of being acceptable or unacceptable, and that they are equally founded on evidence and reasons; no less 'objective,' in that the apparent subject of a moral judgment (a person, a practice, an action, a state of mind) is also the real subject" (91). Judgments concerning justice and absolute evil aside, the content of obligations such as these will vary somewhat with differences among ways of life. But any but the "most primitive" or debased of societies will evolve and attempt to enforce morally and/or legally binding rules concerning family relations, duties of love, friendship, and benevolence. And every minimally decent society develops arrangements and adopts policies designed to mitigate if not eliminate the "great evils" he mentions.

In historical fact, conceptions of justice and their requirements have also varied importantly with time and place. It is therefore not surprising that the history of moral and political theorizing concerning justice is replete with sharply drawn disagreements. In one of the boldest aspects of his thinking, however, Hampshire proposes a minimal, primarily procedural, but quite definite conception, and argues that it is so clearly superior to the known alternatives that it not only ought but must be regarded as a fundament of every way of life. What is this conception and what are the arguments for it?

Conveniently, Hampshire provides an abbreviated statement of his answers to these questions. Because the several lengthier articulations of his thinking have already been considered, we can focus on the summary statement.

The minimal, procedural conception of justice "is trans-historical, being rooted in the indispensable institutions of civil society, within which people deliberate together, argue over practical issues, adjudicate between cases" (169). It is to be distinguished from more encompassing, and changing, conceptions of "substantial justice" that are grounded in conceptions of the good; its requirements concern *how*, that is the processes and procedures in and through which, disputes should be settled, not with the merits of the agreements arrived at or settlements reached. It "gets its sense from a minimum fairness in established procedures of settling conflicts . . . by argument and negotiation and by [at least] quasi-legal reasoning" (Ibid.) This conception of a minimum of "decent fairness, both in personal relations and [especially] in public affairs . . . is rooted" in two facts about human beings and their circumstances. The first of these facts, which at bottom is the reason why such a conception and practice is necessary in all human affairs, is the fact, fully familiar to his readers, that human beings have differing values and beliefs, desires, interests, and conceptions of the good. Their attempts to act on these self-understandings and commitments frequently result in conflicts among them, conflicts that, if not regularly contained or resolved in a more or less civil fashion, make a minimally decent and livable society impossible (or the result of nothing more reliable than good fortune). The second fact, which provides some reason for hope concerning human affairs, is that human beings have to some degree the [capacity to and] habit of balancing contrary arguments and of drawing conclusions from them. Minimum justice is the elaborate application of this habit to interpersonal relations, entailing rules of fair procedure" (Ibid.).

The model for this conception, derived from public/political affairs and one of numerous indications of its distinctly political character, is deliberations and negotiations in the "council chamber" and related types of assemblies. "This model of practical reason as deliberation," conceived by Aristotle and "as vivid and plausible as ever," provides an indispensable conception of how practical reasoning should be conducted and how decisions should be reached when there are competing and potentially conflicting interests and objectives. It has a "shadow" in the deliberations as to how to act that take place within an individual mind, but it is best understood by borrowing "the vocabulary . . . that describes the public and observable transactions of social life" (51). "Wherever and whenever human societies exist . . . issues of policy will be debated in some assembly of chosen persons. . . ." The participants in such assemblies are chosen in a great variety of ways, and the rules that govern debate among them are diverse and changing. But some version of the "institution of articulating and reviewing contrary opinions on policy is of necessity species-wide," (51–2) and the "essence" of their procedures is "that the pro and the contra should both be heard and evaluated, and that the procedure should not be cut off before all the arguments are in. The discussion of an issue of practical policy is both an adversary procedure, with two [or more] sides represented, and a judicial one, because in the end a Solomonic judgment will [one hopes!] normally be made, with the acceptance of some arguments and the dismissal of others" (53).

In assembly debates the "canons of rationality are . . . the canons of [procedural] fairness. If the full procedure of discussion . . . has not been followed, the final judgment is tainted with bias and unfairness" even if it seems to be substantively correct. A decision can be accepted as just and fair only if "the main relevant considerations have in fact been impartially weighed in the balance" (Ibid.).[2]

Habitual or otherwise effective commitments to public deliberation and negotiation, and hence minimal justice, evidently depend upon discipline and resistance. Agents must discipline themselves to "step back" from and resist not only their immediate impulses and inclinations but (sometimes) also their more or less considered conceptions of their own good. And they must discipline themselves to participate in good faith in the processes and procedures of bargaining, negotiating, and adjudicating. If, or to the extent that they do so, they contribute invaluably to the possibility of a minimally decent life for themselves and for those with whom they do and must live. And if or to the extent that they succeed in maintaining "a contrast between" their sentiments "and the observable manifestation[s]" of those sentiments in action, they will create for themselves "that sense of freedom which men take to be peculiar to themselves" (*M&C*, 78). If they are fortunate enough to live with others who do the same, they will enjoy freedoms of action as well as of mind.

These last thoughts strongly suggest that, while minimal in comparison with more encompassing and soaring conceptions of justice, primarily procedural justice is far from a negligible or inconsequential value. Where its requirements are respected and for the most part met, those degrees of cooperation and concord that sometimes result from less formalized interactions and less explicitly justified actions and policies can be substantially augmented. These desiderata, and the comparative autonomy of members of the society, can also be enhanced because the arrangements and practices in which the members interact, and the policies they adopt and follow, can be recognized by them as products of their own thinking and acting rather than of impositions upon them or mere strokes of good or bad fortune. By accepting and disciplining themselves to abide by the requirements of minimal justice, they take charge of their own lives and participate in shaping their own futures.

It therefore comes as no surprise that the "needed injunction, . . . the first commandment of a moralist, is the order actively to exercise the power of reflection, and to question immediate beliefs and sentiments" (*M&C*, 55). The human capacity to obey this command can easily be exaggerated—as it has been by numerous of the moral philosophers Hampshire most frequently criticizes—but the "power is always present in a sane and undamaged person" (Ibid.). Making effective use of this power is, finally, in the hands of individual human beings, but their resolve to do so can be strengthened by arguments and exhortations addressed to them by philosophers and by their fellow citizens. Above all, it can be strengthened by participation in a society and polity that honors procedural justice and cultivates the virtue of respecting its requirements.

This virtue is valuable in all the domains of practical life, but its greatest importance is in its original home, that is, politics, and the all but universal companion of politics, namely law. It is in politics and in courts of law that disagreements and the sharpest and most dangerous conflicts most frequently occur. If they do not initially arise in these domains, they are commonly referred or are impelled into them when they cannot be resolved or at least moderated in pre-political and pre-legal interactions. When they do so, they are often exacerbated by the well-known tendency of those in or seeking authority to employ violent and otherwise ruthless methods in their quest for power over others and to use these methods to enhance their own wealth and glory. In Hampshire's view, the shrewdest and most discerning reading of the history of politics, a reading that was powerfully reinforced by Nazism and Stalinism and that in his judgment remains highly pertinent today, was given by Machiavelli. (See *M&C*, 121–23; *I&E*, chapter 5, passim, and especially 161–68.)

There are no fully effective responses to, no entirely reliable means of coping with, these recurrent and often dismaying features of political life. Machiavelli's counsel was that force had to be met with force, cunning with cunning. In respect to "absolutely evil" regimes such as twentieth-century totalitarianisms, Hampshire accepts, ruefully, a qualified formulation of this dismal view and is prepared to endorse procedures and practices that are undeniably immoral and are to be condemned in all other circumstances. (As he indicates in the Introduction to *I&E*, his thinking concerning these unwelcome matters was heavily influenced by his experiences as a British intelligence agent during the Second World War.) But these extreme cases are not reason to sink into corrosive and self-perpetuating pessimism concerning politics generally. Hampshire could not be described as a political or any other kind of optimist, but he remains convinced that the worst evils can be combated and that human beings have the capacities necessary to create and sustain decent arrangements and relationships.

As regards politics and much else, primary—but not exclusive—reliance should be placed on the procedural conception and practice of justice. In political life, however, the demands of justice are particularly stringent: "[T]here is a greater requirement of explicitness of reasoning in public morality than in private. Partly because of the bias towards a consequential criterion" that is pervasive in part due to the influence of utilitarianism, "and partly because of representative roles in politics, there is a requirement that an agent in politics should be able to give an account of the reasons for his policies, both as a defence of the policies that he is following and as an explanation of his following them" (*P&PM*, 50. For slightly different reasons, the same is true of law; 29–31). This is partly a matter of political prudence, a condition of success as an agent pursuing a political agenda. The politician "normally needs an endorsement that his policies are right from his followers; and he needs to be understood by his followers, who will otherwise tend to distrust him if they do not know, or do not think that they know, how he thinks about substantial moral issues and what his calculations of consequences are" (Ibid.). But it is also a critically important element in political morality. Providing explicit and explicitly defended reasons for decisions and policies fosters trust and the kind of uncoerced acceptance that contains impulses to violent conflict and disorder and distinguishes a decent polity from a tyrannical regime. The arrogant refusal of American policy-makers to respect and make good-faith efforts to meet these requirements, their practice of a "naive and mechanical Machiavellianism" in conducting the American intervention in Vietnam, is one of many object lessons in this regard. Their disdain for these requirements, and hence for their fellow citizens, was importantly responsible for the "moral infamies" and ultimate failure of that intervention (51).

The same can be said, but much more must also be said, concerning the infamies perpetrated by and the ultimate failures of Nazism, Stalinism, and the other absolute evils that have disfigured public life in the twentieth century. The Nazis and Bolsheviks "repudiated justice" and its requirements. They took concern for those requirements as obstacles in their paths to what they regarded as world-historical aspirations and ideals. They knew that they could effectively pursue their objectives only if they won the support of substantial numbers of the members of their societies, but they disdained reasoning of all but the most crudely instrumental kind, both their own reasonings and the capacity for reasoning of their potential followers. They sought to secure and maintain the support they needed by promising unrealistic achievements, through propaganda, manipulation, and outright lying. And when they had won over enough of their subjects to allow them to deploy force and violence, they used these brutal methods to cow a yet larger number into submission. Those who would not submit, as well as some who might have been prepared to do so, were killed or otherwise reduced to political impotence.

If a politically significant number of Germans and Russians had been able effectively to demand respect for procedural justice, the Nazis and Bolsheviks might never have achieved the power necessary ruthlessly to compel the submission of the many who understood the at once hopelessly unrealistic and unbelievably horrendous character of their programs and policies. Thus one lesson to be drawn concerning incipient totalitarian movements, a lesson that Machiavelli, whose political thinking was grounded in experience not in "innocence," understood perfectly well, is that a populace confronted with individuals and groups who disdain justice must, in a timely way, discipline themselves to resist those movements. If they can do so only by partly suspending their own commitments to justice, justice may not be served in any other way. Ruthless injustice sometimes requires its staunchest adherents to soil their hands with the filth of injustice. This is one reason why justice is a "near-universal" not a fully universal requirement of political morality.

Reflection on the experience of totalitarianism is also one way to learn the lesson that justice is an essential but by itself insufficient good and virtue. The disdain—revulsion might be a better word—of the fanatical totalitarians for justice was accompanied and reinforced by their unqualified rejection of numerous other moral and political values and virtues. Doing justice is in large part a matter of striking a fair "balance" among competing claims. But "there is also unmixed evil" in the form of claims or proposals that deserve no hearing or weighing. "The Nazis tried to establish a way of life which entirely discarded justice and gentleness, among many other generally recognized virtues, and they deliberately made the claim 'anything goes' under these headings." This claim "is a sign of evil, because it calls for the destruction of the human world of customary moral claims precariously established within the setting of natural human interests. An uncritical Machiavellianism, or an uncritical consequentialism such as Lenin's . . . may extend [this claim] . . . across several of the virtues, draining past ways of life of their value, without a compensating vision of new virtues in a new way of life" (*M&C*, 156).

In addition to repudiating justice, the Nazis "dismissed considerations of utility and benevolence; they also undermined most of the moral conventions of their society," including those concerning family, love, and friendship. "There is a kind of moral dizziness that goes with such destruction of conventional restraints and of normal decencies in social relations." Something like this vertigo can be experienced even without the sweeping challenges presented by fanatics. Thoughtful persons will recognize that most of these decencies are conventional, have been different in earlier societies, and are now different in many places. With the exception, however, of the (in)decencies promoted, perhaps successfully, by evil regimes, the recognized "contingency of the rules does not detract from their stringency: on the contrary, a consciousness of the contingency . . . tends [should tend] to reinforce the shared sense that the rule must not be broken . . . except for an overriding consideration; to break it is to undermine morality generally (Ibid.).

Thus, in a reasonably stable and decent society, moral and political thinking and acting require a complex and often difficult-to-sustain combination of understandings and commitments.

The moral and political agent must understand the value, even the necessity, of some number of well-settled principles and rules while at the same time not investing them with a standing to which in reason they are not and cannot be entitled. Thus such an agent must act to sustain, or at least not deliberately to disrupt, established principles and rules while at the same time remaining open to the possibility that they ought to be modified and perhaps replaced. This is why moral and political life are not easy and it is why the first commandment of the moralist is to be thoughtful.

It is also why both moral and political stability and moral and political improvement depend on the presence of some considerable number of persons, always in limited supply, who are affirmatively responsive to the moralist's command. "People will behave more reasonably, and the social order will be improved, if and only if at least a ruling minority of persons are converted from egocentricity to detachment in their thought about themselves and about their relations to external things and persons. The conversion depends upon their realizing that their innate drive to increase their power and liberty requires disciplined thought, and an assertion of independence; this is a necessary but not a sufficient condition of the conversion," but, if or to the extent that it is satisfied, a person "begins to enjoy the exercise and to feel the power of understanding, which is a positive pleasure" (*M&C*, 51). The enjoyment of this pleasure is likely to supplement and reinforce the commitment to disciplined thinking, thereby increasing the likelihood that its benefits will continue to be available to the individual and through her to her fellow citizens.

Returning briefly to Hampshire's analysis of totalitarianisms, it is necessary to enter a qualification of, and an addition to, the foregoing discussion of justice. The qualification concerns the phrase "at least a ruling minority of persons." If we take "ruling" to mean doing so effectively, the phrase and the thought that informs it may be acceptable, at least to its author. But it must be remembered that in a more or less stable and orderly polity, ruling can be effective for long only if those who are ruled trust their rulers because they understand the reasons for the rules and commands that the rulers adopt and issue. This of course requires that the rulers present those reasons to the ruled as well as to themselves and one another. But it also presupposes that the ruled are capable of understanding and are willing to discipline themselves to act on the reasons the rulers provide. The qualification is yet more urgent in respect to polities threatened or already dominated by totalitarian fanatics. We know that a considerable minority of Germans and Russians were capable of and actively committed to the kind of disciplined thinking that Hampshire promotes. But they were not, or soon ceased to be, a "ruling minority." They could have sustained, or regained, this standing only if a substantially larger number of their fellow citizens had also disciplined themselves to demand respect for the requirements of justice. In the event, this further condition was not adequately satisfied and totalitarianism prevailed for a disastrous length of time.

The necessary addition underlines the point, applicable to all societies and polities, that primarily procedural justice is the first and fundamental feature of a decent society and polity but not more than that. There must also be widespread acceptance of and disciplined commitment to other near-universal values, goods, and virtues, and principles and rules that embody and require respect for them. These include other items on Hampshire's lists: tolerance; welcoming acceptance of diversity; understanding of and readiness to abide by rules governing family relationships and relations of love and friendship; willingness to support arrangements and policies that diminish the great evils discussed earlier; an at least minimal commitment to benevolence. If we had not otherwise appreciated these further moral and political necessities, reflection concerning the enormities produced by Nazism and Stalinism, which destroyed them as well as justice, is a good way to learn to do so.

The thoughts and arguments discussed in the last pages concern both internal and external, both personal and interpersonal, aspects of moral and political thought and action. Those that remain to be considered do the same, but the emphasis shifts somewhat to the former of these and related pairs. To the extent that he focuses on justice as the single most essential requirement of morals and politics, Hampshire repeatedly underlines his view that doing justice requires—albeit does not exclusively require—procedural rationality and reasoning. In the council chamber, and yet more pronouncedly in courts of law and other legal venues and circumstances (see especially *M&C*, 29–30), arriving at a result that is and can be seen to be just demands listening attentively, the careful weighing of interests and claims, and the striking of a fair, which primarily means an explicitly defended, balance among the latter. These procedures, strongly akin to those followed by scientists and mathematicians but in a more heightened form than in much practical reasoning, involve careful identification of the facts relevant to a decision, generalizing cautiously concerning them, gathering principles and precedents that have been employed in previous cases of a similar character, and reasoning as logically as possible from these considerations to a conclusion.

The most meticulous use of these rational procedures will rarely if ever yield an indisputable decision, will rarely if ever be fully syllogistic in character. Legal reasoning and judging sometimes approximate this and related models. Students and theorists of jurisprudence have emphasized that legal reasoning at its best "exhibits the familiar, circular pattern of general principles being used to guide decisions in particular complex cases and particular cases being used to modify general principles and to suggest new ones" (29). Unlike Kant, however, few among them claim that the conclusion of such reasoning "is a necessary one" (28). Rather, "legal reasoning recognizes the unpredictable variety of circumstances which leave a margin of indeterminacy, an area for judicial discretion, when laws and legal principles are interpreted and applied. Imperfect fit between general principles and particular cases is assumed in the working of legal systems" (29).

For these reasons, and because conflict among principles can never be fully eliminated, what is properly called the "craft" of legal reasoning makes further demands on the reasoning abilities of those who practice it. In addition to the ability to see differences as well as similarities among cases, they must have "some flair and a natural feeling for the subject matter" and the ability "to find the right move without the guidance of principle" (30).

And they must have a "feeling," which will always be partly intuitive but that can be cultivated and refined by "stepping back" from particular cases to try to understand how alternative possible decisions, and the principles that would or might inform them, fit together with one another and cohere or fail to cohere with the larger way of life of which the legal system is one part. As seen above, this stepping back or seeing round involves reasoning, but it also calls upon a "power" that should be distinguished from the powers essential to and characteristic of public reasoning, that is, the power of imagination.

It follows that we must reject unrealistic notions of a possible and desirable "mechanical jurisprudence," as in some theorists of legal positivism and their deeply confused American progeny who promote an "original intent" constitutional practice. Even when these absurdities have been dismissed, however, the "resemblance"—which should not be denied— "between the practical reasoning of lawyers about the law and practical reasoning on matters of moral [and political] concern is imperfect" (29). Among several differences—all of which are of degree—between the two, the one to be emphasized at this juncture is "that imagination will not be called for in legal argument as [frequently] as . . . in moral [and political] contexts" (30). Hampshire does not elaborate on this remark, but it is plausible to think that the difference is due to the fact that much legal reasoning concerns conflicts that have already been somewhat narrowed by the process of bringing them within the confines of the legal system. Ordinarily a lawyer can advise a client that she "has a case" only if laws or judicial precedents are already in place that are pertinent to the claims the client wants adjudicated. The same is also true of prosecutors who can indict an accused if and only if an argument can be made that the accused has violated an existing law. By contrast, issues and conflicts concerning their resolution ordinarily come before councils and legislatures because there is no established law that speaks to them—"there ought to be a law"—or because parties to the conflict want the law changed. Of course these sorting and sifting processes also operate in public life generally and also in the more private or personal domains of moral interaction. It is difficult to assign moral praise, and more particularly moral blame, if there are no already available rules or conventions to which appeal can be made to justify the judgment.

To repeat, these differences are ordinarily matters of degree. But in both law and more especially in morals and politics the differences are sometimes large enough to be described as differences in kind. Particularly in systems that distinguish between constitutional or other "basic laws" and ordinary legislative enactments, judges, legislators, and those who advise and appeal to them are sometimes in a situation akin to that of the moral reformer who campaigns for large-scale additions to, or changes in, widely accepted principles and rules. In such circumstances the judge, the legislator, and the moralist will almost certainly begin from beliefs and values that already have some standing, but will necessarily go beyond them. This "going beyond" involves the invention or creation of at least partly new legal or moral principles, perhaps new ideals, and new laws and norms that express and embody the principles and ideals. Doing so requires supplementing conceptual thinking and intentional acting with "imagination," perhaps even supplanting the former by the latter.

Many of Hampshire's discussions of imagination associate this mental power or activity with aesthetics and the arts. "Human creativeness in art prevents the recognized varieties of feeling, and established conceptions of the mind, from ever hardening into a final patterns. There are always surprises, the identification of new attitudes and states of mind through freely invented works of art that seem an exact expression of them for the first time" (*T&A*, 246). Although mistakenly characterized by empiricists as no more than expressions of subjectivity, artistic creations are of great importance to practical life. "Any closed morality, . . . left to itself, is always threatened with this unpredicted shock and disturbance, which suddenly illuminates another possibility of human feeling and desire through the invention of a new form of expression. Without these unexpected achievements we should be left to acquiesce in some much narrower and more static conceptions of possible human attainment and of possible discrimination. They add another dimension, that of the unpredictable and uncontrolled sources of change in our perceptions and attitudes, and in our idea of men's normal powers. It is characteristic of any considerable work of art that its interest cannot be exhausted in any plain statement of the artist's intention. He always does more than he could previously have said that he was doing. . . . The idea of original art is the idea of an achievement that goes beyond any previous intention, and that must always be to some degree unexpected even by its maker" (246–47).

As already noted, these remarks also apply to important aspects of legal thinking and practice and to moral thinking concerning that most legal-like of moral requirements, namely justice, that makes the strongest demands on explicit rationality and reasoning. The near universality of the requirements of justice, and the demands that must be met to satisfy those requirements, is reason against viewing them as "artificial" in character and standing. "In so far as artificiality is taken to imply, or is associated with, the imagination and imaginative invention, the principles of justice must be represented as not artificial, just because they are intended to be principles solely [or primarily] defensible by rational argument" (*M&C*,

131). There "are some definite and comparatively clear restraints, argumentatively and rationally defensible, upon what is counted as just and fair. With justice the notion of imagination seems out of place, and reason, and reasonable considerations are alone in place, as in the establishment of law" (130–31).

These last sentences are of course exaggerations of Hampshire's usual view. Immediately before writing them he had again emphasized that the difference between justice and other virtues "is only a difference of degree." For example, "Aristotle's chapters on justice . . . bear about as close a resemblance to a representative modern treatise on justice such as Rawls', as Aristotle's chapters on love and friendship bear to some later treatise on that subject, for example, that of Montaigne or Stendhal" (130). The differences, however, are neither unimportant nor entirely to the advantage of justice. Justice "is to be contrasted with love and friendship because the prescriptions that express these [latter] virtues may be justified . . . by appeals to imagination as much as to reason. New forms and varieties of love and friendship are brought into existence and are recognized as new forms, and are recognized even as new kinds of love and friendship." These recognitions, as with new forms of visual and other arts, may be slow in coming and are "not defensible by rational considerations without any appeals to imagination: one has to envisage," as Montaigne did regarding La Böetie, "a particular person or persons in a particular situation and to invent or to recognize a form of behaviour that seems to be right in the peculiar circumstances. There is not the same requirement of convergence just because reasonable argument is less in place in such cases. . . . There is no obvious requirement that everyone at all times should love and be friendly in the same way . . ." (131).

We have seen that the same is true of conceptions of the good. It is also true of duties of kinship, of benevolence, and of the duty to participate in or at least to be supportive of policies aimed at diminishing great evils such as poverty and homelessness. Any more or less decent society and polity will evolve conventions and rules that give specificity to these and related duties such as tolerance and a welcoming attitude toward plurality, but the rules and conventions will vary with time and place and must be adapted to changing circumstances. Doing so requires reason and rationality, but it also demands imagination.

There is no need to underline Hampshire's high estimation of the values and virtues just mentioned. They are not likely to be sustained or effective in the absence of justice, but it is equally true that justice will not be respected or effective for long in their absence. When we have recognized and appreciated the importance of the distinctions he makes among differing meanings and kinds of reasoning, we must also recognize and accord high value to powers of the mind that are not to be assimilated to powers of reason and reasoning. This conclusion is as valid and as important in practical affairs as it is in aesthetics. Or rather it is valid and important in both because, finally, the distinction between aesthetics and practical matters such as morals and politics cannot be fully sustained.

"Prominent among the essential potentialities of the human soul . . . is this capacity for linguistic, cultural, and moral diversity, for imaginative invention, which is to be ranked alongside the power of the intellect. . . . 'Alongside' seems the appropriate word, because there is no good reason for exalting the power of intellectual understanding over the power of imaginative invention as being the 'higher' power, or as more evidently distinctive of human beings" (*I&E*, 30–31). All human beings have, at least potentially, this power; a number of the reasons why it is important for them to develop and use it were emphasized in the foregoing paragraphs. But there is an additional reason, one that further blurs the distinction between aesthetics and morals and politics. In a previously quoted remark that brings Hampshire close to Nietzsche, Hampshire says that moral and political theory cannot be "rounded off" in part because "we expect . . . leaps of the imagination, moments of insight, very rarely, and in unusual men, which will lead to transformations of experience and to new moral ambitions and ways of living" (*P&PM*, 53). The import, both positive and negative, of "leaps of the imagination" and "moments of insight" is available from discussions above. What is to be made of "very rarely" and "unusual men?" To answer this question we must return to the notion of "singularity" and more particularly to its value-laden companion "individuality."

Hampshire's emphasis on the actuality and the value of plurality, or diversity as he usually describes it, is a central theme in his thinking. Of course in fact it is usually confined or contained in various ways, and enthusiasm for it is possible only if this is the case. It is confined by language and convention, and it should be circumscribed by principles and rules of justice and the other prudential and moral norms repeatedly emphasized above. When, where, and to the extent that such limitations are well established and regularly respected, an abundant diversity of beliefs and values, dispositions, orientations and sensibilities, desires and interests, not only make notable contributions to the quality and enjoyment of human affairs but are essential to a society in which even moderately or occasionally thoughtful human beings are able to find pleasure and satisfaction.

Hampshire's pluralism, however, reaches well beyond the most familiar versions of both descriptive and prescriptive theories and doctrines whose proponents adopt that name or are so designated by students of social and political theory. In addition to arguments already discussed, the distinctive feature of his view is articulated in the following statement: "It is an error and a distortion to grade human beings on some universal scale of human virtue as more or less admirable, more or less praiseworthy, as if they were pointed by God or nature towards some single target. . . . The exercise of imagination in pursuit of the private good calls for more than toleration: it calls for the encouragement of individuality as an absolute value" (*I&E*, 130).

Several comments are appropriate concerning this audacious declaration. The first, which needs no more than to be mentioned once again, is that Hampshire is far from championing what is often scornfully called an "atomistic individualism." In addition to his forceful promotion of values and virtues that ought to be widely if not universally cultivated and respected, he clearly thinks that most human beings have the identities and commitments that they do in large measure owing to the ways of life into which they are raised and within the languages, conventions, and rules of which they do much of their thinking and acting. As is evident from the last words of the passage just quoted, this is true of thinking and acting that includes a strong desire to achieve and sustain a recognizable individuality. Rare and unusual persons may succeed in cultivating distinctive, even singular, characteristics against the grain of cultures and societies that actively disapprove and discourage expressions of them, but they are far more likely to develop in cultures in which they are valued and welcomed rather than disapproved or feared and oppressed.

As is perhaps indicated by the words "pursuit of the private good," the absolute good that is individuality is first and foremost a good for the persons who achieve it. That is, it is a good and a virtue (or *virtu*) which, unlike benevolence and other primarily other-regarding goods and virtues (especially as promoted by utilitarianisms and Kantianisms), should be more than merely tolerated even if achieving it does not redound to the benefit of other persons or satisfy allegedly universal requirements of reason. When its pursuit is disciplined by the primarily other-regarding considerations reiterated just above, it adds qualities such as zest and delight to the life of the individual, qualities that can be experienced and enjoyed in no other way. And it does so in ways that may well arouse *ressentiment* in others but that do no other harms to them.

For these reasons, a person's cultivation of her own individuality is a good, not a duty owed to others. As with conceptions of the good generally—and conceptions of the good that feature individuality are among those that Hampshire most admires—it is to be expected and indeed to be hoped that the substance of conceptions of individuality will vary importantly from person to person. It is arguable that I owe it to others to welcome and to encourage their cultivation of their several individualities, but I have no duty, certainly no "perfect duty," to them to cultivate my own. If there is a duty of the first kind, it is grounded first and foremost in what ought to be my respect for their freedom to pursue their own good as they see it so long as they do so in ways that meet the requirements of justice and other near-universal conditions of a decent society.

But there is a further argument that strongly supports a welcoming and otherwise encouraging stance toward individualities. This further argument, elements of which have been encountered earlier but that deserve emphasis here, may support a firm policy or strong commitment to maintaining such a stance rather than a strict duty to do so; it nevertheless merits the strong standing that Hampshire accords to it. The considerations that urge its acceptance were first encountered in discussions of the role of imagination in art and in aesthetic domains generally, and of the unique and uniquely valuable contributions that works of art make to the quality of human experience. It was then seen that strongly analogous imaginative performances are also invaluable in law, in politics and in numerous other aspects and domains of social and cultural life. There is evidence that some artists, judges, and politicians have thought that, given evidence that they had the requisite powers of imagination, they had a duty to use them to provide these great benefits to humankind. To the decidedly limited extent to which this latter thought can be regarded as cogent, it will always gravitate toward the suspect notion of a duty to oneself. But there is nothing suspect about the idea that the beneficiaries of the "leaps of imagination" and "moments of insight" of rare and unusual persons, from the "transformations of experience" and the "new enjoyments of living," that they sometimes engender, ought to encourage and welcome the presence of such persons among us.

IV. Concluding Thoughts Concerning Hampshire

An overall assessment of the positions and arguments considered in this and the previous chapter, and their relations with those of other thinkers considered earlier, is attempted in the general Conclusion to follow. The comments presented here are limited to a few of the views that are distinctive to Hampshire as I have construed salient features of his several works.

Chapter 5 is as long as it is for two related reasons. The first is that, with something of an exception of Nietzsche (especially the Nietzsche of several sections of the collection entitled *Will to Power*), Hampshire gives closer and more sustained attention to issues in the philosophy of mind than the other theorists examined in the present work. Because he regards these issues as vital to the theory of action, the distinctive aspects of his thinking concerning the latter cannot be adequately understood or assessed apart from his views concerning thinking, believing, intending, and related concepts central to the philosophy of mind.

I said above that I have no more than minor disagreements with his treatments of these concepts. A few of those disagreements are briefly mentioned in comments inserted, often in brackets, in the course of a primarily expository presentation. I have neither the space nor the competence to elaborate significantly upon them and the reasons for considering them minor, but two issues, both of which concern the "dual aspect" theory and hence the distinction and the relations between the immaterial and the material, warrant some further discussion.

Although insisting on the distinction, Hampshire says candidly that, as of his writing, available knowledge concerning the conditioning, limiting, and influencing effects of the material on the immaterial, for example of the brain and other organs and bodily processes on thinking, is inadequate to draw the distinction with clarity of detail. It is my layman's understanding that in recent years knowledge of this interaction has improved. The development of various scanning and other investigative techniques allow neuroscientists to specify which segments of the brain and other components of the central nervous system are primarily operative in respect to differing forms of perception, emotion, and thinking. As general laws concerning these mind-body interactions are identified, it becomes possible to think about aspects of thinking by thinking in detail about the material conditions necessary to or enabling of them. These techniques also make it possible to explain with some precision why it is that some of the individuals that Hampshire calls "damaged" are unable to sustain certain lines of thought, to perceive certain classes of objects, and to experience or control certain emotions. As to both, but especially to the latter, it is arguable that continuing work in the philosophy of mind should enlarge or otherwise amend "the usual European concept of a person" that Hampshire says he is "presupposing" in his investigations and reflections (*I&E*, 120).

The foregoing, however, are not telling criticisms of his dual aspect theory. This is in part because Hampshire not only acknowledges and encourages the development of an enlarged body of knowledge of the body and other of the material conditions of thinking and acting, but is explicit that improvements of this kind would be directly relevant to work in the philosophy of mind and hence of moral and political philosophy. Recall that one of the reasons that "moral theory cannot be rounded off and made completely tidy" is that "we still know so little about the determinants of behaviour and about human nature generally" (*P&PM*, 53). More important, Hampshire gives an eloquent and convincing defense of the general lines of his theory. As valuable as advancements in such knowledge have been, are, and are likely to be, no such discoveries will or could abolish the distinction between "first" and "second" nature and none among them will or could entirely relieve human beings of the responsibility to reflect upon and to decide *what ought to be* thought about morals and politics. If a "taint of naturalism" is and will always be an appropriate, even an essential, part of moral, political, and other aspects of practical reasoning, the conclusions of such reasoning can never be directly inferred from or entirely defended by appeal to it.

More difficult questions should be considered concerning the thesis that agents have "direct" knowledge of certain of their mental states, in particular their own intentions. At bottom, the problem here arises because Hampshire insists that forming intentions is part of thinking *and* that all thinking is in language. What then is the status of the "knowing" that is my knowledge that I now intend to X but have yet to state to myself or to others what my intention is, that is, have not identified, in language, *what* I intend to do? The thesis allows that, if or when I so identify X, I may make mistakes that are subject to correction. Prior to or apart from doing so, however, I cannot be mistaken concerning my intentions. We have seen that Hampshire sometimes argues that "to know" and the several grammatical forms of the verb are misleadingly redundant concerning first person present tense intentions, a claim that might be taken as recognition that there is a difficulty here. As noted, however, he is not consistent in upholding this further claim. More important, to the extent that he is consistent on this point, the question I am trying to raise recurs rather than is answered. What is the status of the mental state that we, and he, are strongly tempted to classify in epistemic terms?

Should we analogize "it" to those states of, shall we say as yet amorphous "self-awarenesses," that he discusses under the heading of imaginings? This is a tempting response. Although as yet unarticulated and usually if not always not yet articulable, an agent who imagines a something she as yet knows not quite what, is aware that something is brewing or churning in her mind. It is also tempting because it manifests Hampshire's welcome conviction that the human mind is a richer and more fecund place than can be *fully* captured in language and other already established categories and conventions. The immense value that he attaches to this human potential is clear from previous discussions, and emphasizing this feature of his thinking underlines similarities between him and Nietzsche's musings concerning the pre- or extra-conscious. (Also the acknowledged influences on him of Merleau-Ponty. On the latter point see *T&An*, 277–78.) But if the analogy helps to put the issue before us in a welcome perspective, it does not fully resolve it.

As with intentions, imaginings are somethings, not anythings or nothings. In order to say that a person is imaginative, or is engaged in imagining, there must be evidence that she has been or is doing more than letting her mind drift, aimlessly as it were. Perhaps the usual, but by no means the only, such evidence is that her imaginings eventuate in some outcome or product, a work of art, an idea or ideal that, if only with the passage of time, can be recognized by herself and perhaps by others as responsive to some difficulty or dissatisfaction that has troubled her or with which she has been wrestling. Of course many imaginings yield no tangible product or result. They are identified as such by the efforts expended; the concentration of attention, the experimenting with ideas, impulses, inclinations, and the like. These criteria of the established uses of "imagination" and its cognates can be satisfied in many ways, but in the absence of any evidence pertinent to those criteria the concepts have no applicability.

The same is true of intentions. If there are no "atomic" or fully specific intentions, it is nevertheless the case that to say or otherwise show to myself or other persons that I have formed an intention is to identify my mental state in a particular way and to distinguish it from other such states. The concept of an intention may range more widely and freely than, say, concepts such as fearing and believing, may be a member of a larger and more diverse family of loosely resembling terms, but if there were no criteria for its use it would not be a concept; it would be no more than a noise, a scribble, or an empty gesture. Hampshire agrees with this proposition as regards intentions that are expressed in language, but there is no reason to deny it as regards intentions that are formed with minimal reflection and that are never articulated to others. The concept of having an intention does and must include the notion of being mistaken not only about *what* intention I have but also about *that* it is an *intention* that I have.

Turning briefly to positions and arguments primarily discussed in the present chapter, there is reason to question or at least to qualify one of the most pronounced features of Hampshire's theory of justice and its relation to other goods, values, and virtues. The objections are not to his argument that justice is essential to so much as a minimally decent society. His insistence that there are and should be an irreducible diversity of conceptions of the good, and that it is not only highly likely but desirable that there should be competition and conflicts among them, are among the most convincing and attractive features of his moral and political thinking. Moreover, they constitute a persuasive argument not only for regarding justice as essential but also against soaring and encompassing conceptions of justice that tie the concept of justice to a particular conception of the good. Such conceptions, even comparatively modest ones such as that of Rawls which restricts itself to a "thin" theory featuring no more than a short list of "primary goods," introduce into thinking about justice the very issues and problems that justice is distinctively capable of resolving or at least containing.

It was noted earlier that Hampshire's attempt to limit justice to primarily procedural considerations sometimes imparts an overly formalistic or mechanical quality to his proposals as to how to think under this rubric. There is no objection to his emphasis on listening attentively to competing claims and arguments, particularly when that admonition is qualified by the recognition that there are some views that do not merit so much as a hearing. If there is an objectionable feature to this aspect of his thinking, it enters when he employs notions such as weighing and striking balances among conflicting claims. What is the "scale" on which all such claims are to be "weighed" and a "balance" struck among them? This familiar metaphor is serviceable when thinking about conflicts among interests, objectives, and proposals all of which—and perhaps all of the champions of which—have recognizable or at least arguable merits. And it conveys as well as any alternative figure of speech much of what actually occurs in conflict resolution and policy making in a tolerably decent but pluralistic society and polity.

The difficulty with the metaphor is abbreviated in the phrase "recognizable or at least arguable merits." We do routinely speak of weighing the merits of arguments and proposals, but here the criteria are and must almost always be qualitative not merely quantitative. Just assuming that we know what we are talking about if we say that the merits of two or more competing proposals are of equal weight, we might conclude that there is no pertinent difference between them and hence to "divide" the outcome as equally as possible between them. A gets X, part of what she wants, and B gets Y, also part of what she wants. There is no denying that thinking of this kind occurs in assemblies and even in courts of law, and it may even be said to represent a small part of what is meant by the phrase "equality before the law." But the metaphor of weighing quantities of merit strains credibility to or rather beyond its limit. Deciding that two proposals or claims have equal merit is already a judgment concerning their qualitative characteristics, and this is yet more obvious when some proposals or claims are judged to be entirely without merit. (Readers of Chapter Three will recognize the similarities between my argument and arguments of Montaigne on the same subject.)

These thoughts, of course, are at no great distance from considerations that have great prominence in Hampshire's theory. He insists that respect for goods and virtues other than justice are essential to a decent society. He is convincing in his rejection of fully universalizing theories of these goods, but this is to say that differing conceptions of them will regularly be in play in moral and especially political conflicts. One can agree that the primarily procedural requirements of justice should contain and otherwise discipline the conduct of such disputes and hence can also agree that there are advantages to keeping the conceptual distance between justice and other values as clear as possible. But the very fact that numerous disputes must be settled makes it clear that in many if not all cases there will be an interaction between the requirements of justice and those of the other goods and values that he recognizes. Justice should not be *equated*, conceptually, with utility, benevolence, or friendship, but there are few if any cases in which justice can be done without consideration of the demands of the latter and related goods and values.[3]

The last of these concluding remarks concerns a feature of Hampshire's conceptualization of freedom of action. As briefly noted earlier, while insisting that freedom of action requires elements of agency such as believing and intending, not mere movement, he allows that a person's freedom can be inhibited or prevented by obstacles or forces not knowingly or intentionally placed or left by other human agents. For example, a person can be made unfree by forces of nature. In this one respect he adopts a conception of freedom articulated by Hobbes and further developed by proponents of "pure negative freedom." It is of course undeniable that freedom of movement (freedom1) is frequently restricted or prevented by such forces, and persons experiencing such restrictions may describe themselves as unfree. But the distinction between freedom of movement and of action (between freedom1 and freedoms2–3) is important to the normative theory of freedom. I may *regret* the fact that my way has been blocked by a flood or an avalanche, but I can *resent*—in any but a figurative sense—the restriction on my movement only if I have reason to think that human agents could and should have prevented it. The unfreedoms as well as the freedoms that matter to us are *inter homines*.

Conclusion

Some of the results anticipated in the Introduction have been confirmed but the reasoning in support of them has been rendered more complex by the engagements conducted in Chapters Two through Six. The one un- qualified proposition that has been confirmed is negative in character, namely that there is no categorical, invariable, conflict between freedom on the one hand and discipline on the other. That is, there is no argument, either conceptual or empirical, to the conclusion that discipline is every- where and always incompatible with freedom. Neither critical examina- tion of the meaning(s) of "freedom" and of "discipline," nor critical assessments of lived experience that occurs under these rubrics, supports this conclusion. Insofar as I was previously disposed to embrace this con- clusion I was mistaken.

A number of further generalizations concerning these relationships have emerged as well supported by both conceptual and empirical consid- erations. As we have seen, however, all of them are subject to important exceptions and qualifications. The most significant of these further gener- alizations are the following:

On the conception of freedom accepted and promoted here, that is, freedom of action and autonomy or a robust independence, forms of disci- pline—and the capacity for resistance that they create and help to sus- tain—that are in some meaningful sense adopted and maintained by the agent herself are more compatible with and contributive to her freedoms than those that are adopted and imposed on her by other agents and agen- cies. As emphasized at intervals throughout the book, "meaningful" here does not require that the forms of discipline and resistance be imagined, in- vented, and constructed, out of whole cloth as it were, by the agent herself. Less demanding criteria are discussed below, but it should be noted that there is abundant reason to think that there have been forms of discipline and resistance that, in their particulars, meet something close to this stringent test. Montaigne's notion of enacting himself by writing essays is a plausible example, as is Nietzsche's conceptions-cum-ideals of self-overcoming and free-spiritedness. There are numerous examples in the arts, one of many being Schoenberg's invention of the twelve-tone system of musical notation and the self-discipline he exercised in resisting established notational forms and in making his compositions meet its requirements. A plausible and more specifically political example is the development of the theory and practice of various forms of civil disobedience by Thoreau, Gandhi, King, and others. Of course one can find anticipations of these highly self-disciplined practices and activities in previous artistic and political thinking and activity; of course their development cannot be understood apart from the fact that those who developed them were closely familiar with and were reacting against the practices that were then authoritative. Their self-created and maintained novelty, however, is their most striking feature and is reason enough to think that forms of discipline and resistance that are self-adopted and maintained in this stringent sense best exemplify ways in which discipline and resistance not only contribute to freedom but are a necessary condition of certain forms of it. It should of course be added that their enjoyment of a substantial measure of freedom in more mundane senses contributes invaluably to the ability of their creators to invent and act on their singularities.

To repeat, the notion "self-adopted and maintained in a meaningful sense" does not require satisfaction of the stringent requirements just discussed. As Foucault insists, most of the disciplinary regimens that he discusses, including those that he most admires, have developed over time in a society or culture and are adopted by individuals and groups largely in forms that have become customary or at least widely familiar to members of the society or participants in the culture. Individuals and subgroups may or may not introduce variations in the regimens as generally practiced, but even if they do not do so it can often and meaningfully be said that they choose to adopt and follow them. There are of course many cases in which the sense in which they are chosen and self-adopted is so weak as to be meaningless. Foucault (and Nietzsche) seem to think this is the case with many Christian monastic institutions where, if there is choice at all, it is often the once and for all choice to enter the order and commit oneself to unquestioning obedience to all of its rules and requirements. Even this element of decision or choice is absent in the case of persons who are forcibly committed to highly disciplinary institutions such as prisons and asylums or conscripted against their will to military service. He also gives us reason to think that it is largely absent in not a few families, schools, and workplaces. He of course insists that resistance is always possible in such circumstances and, or rather also, argues forcefully that the severe disciplines that such institutions attempt to impose incite or elicit resistance and that, to varying degrees, resistance is often at least partially successful. But if it can be said that those who resist choose to do so and hence choose to discipline themselves sufficiently to achieve some degree of freedom—hence that even here discipline and some freedom are compatible—it cannot be said that they choose the disciplines that they resist. In such cases, the disciplines imposed on them conflict sharply with their freedom.

In most empirical instances, the freedom-discipline/resistance relationship is somewhere between radically innovative and strongly autonomous disciplinary regimens on the one hand and regimens that have substantial approval in a society or culture but are affirmed and maintained—internalized as Hampshire says—by individuals and groups for whom or which the society or culture constitutes a "way of life." As we have seen, all of the thinkers discussed here hold this view, albeit their evaluations of instances of "comparative autonomy" differ somewhat. According to widely accepted readings of Foucault and especially Nietzsche, these writers are skeptical concerning claims that any very substantial number of the members of the societies they studied deserve to be characterized as more than minimally autonomous and they, again especially Nietzsche, strongly promote more robust forms of creative independence. We have, however, encountered salient elements in their thinking that require qualification of such interpretations, and we have also found prominent instances of "Nietzsche-like" views in the supposedly conservative outlook of Montaigne and certainly in Hampshire's ringing endorsement of individuality—including singularity—as an "absolute good." (I return briefly to this theme by way of ending this chapter.)

As should be clear from the foregoing summary remarks, any further generalizations concerning the relationships that have been my central concern are and must be primarily empirical and will be subject to important qualifications. As many social and political scientists and historians have attempted to do, one can investigate and attempt to generalize concerning the social, political, and cultural conditions that are or have been either conducive to or diminishing of the possibility and the desirability of various freedom-enhancing institutions, practices, beliefs, and values. With something of an exception for Foucault, none of the writers engaged here are properly characterized as conducting empirical investigations in a "scientific" spirit, and doing so is not among the objectives of this study. Nevertheless, a number of broad empirical generalizations concerning the conditions of freedom and unfreedom are advanced by them.

Without rehearsing particulars discussed in previous chapters, it can be said that all four thinkers think, correctly in my view, that societies and polities that are highly pluralistic and fluctuating internally, and cultures that welcome and celebrate an abundant plurality and frequent competition and change, are most conducive to and supportive of the freedoms of their members. And in part because all of them accord great value to freedom, they strongly favor societies, polities, and cultures that have these characteristics.

Of course each of them argues that there must be commonalities in thinking and acting, hence all of them promote a pluralism that is limited by some number of values, beliefs and conventions, institutions and practices that are widely shared and for the most part respected. Perhaps because the times and places in which he lived were marked by mutually destructive discord and conflict, Montaigne puts greater emphasis on the indispensability of moral and political commonalities than the other three, although as Hampshire turns his reflections to the totalitarianisms of his time, his thinking moves in Montaigne's direction in this regard. All four thinkers, however, fear and despise what are now sometimes called communitarian societies and polities; human communities characterized by homogeneity and, more often than not, unthinking conformity. For them, such societies and certainly such polities are enemies not only of freedom but of the human spirit.

These generalizations bear directly on concepts that have been prominent in the foregoing reflections, concepts such as persons, individuals, and selves. As might be expected, the conceptions of persons or selves that figure in these pages importantly mirror the conception of societies, polities, and cultures just summarized. That is, selves are figured as complex not unified or strongly integrated entities. They present to themselves and to others a variety of characteristics, many of which frequently change and some of which are regularly in tension and sometimes in conflict one with the others. These complexities and dissonances, consisting of differing and often contending impulses and inclinations, beliefs, intentions, and purposes, must in some degree be controlled, and discipline of some and resistance to others must be maintained; they are not to be suppressed or eliminated because they are sources of the energy and vitality necessary to action, especially action in the face of obstacles and dangers. Just as pluralistic societies and polities require conventions and agreements, institutions and practices that maintain a degree of predictability, stability, and order in interactions among their members, so individuals must sustain a degree of continuing identity sufficient to allow them to conceive of their perceptions, dispositions, and actions as their own and to differentiate *themselves* and their experiences from others. As Hampshire in particular emphasizes, some degree of more or less continuing *self*-awareness is a condition necessary to agency and action and most if not all of the components thereof.

The qualifier "a degree of" in the foregoing sentences must be underlined. As regards pluralistic societies and polities, it is a mistake to think that order and stability are or could be maintained by some ominipotent, some "sovereign," agent, agents, or agencies. Something called sovereignty is commonly attributed to, even said to be a defining feature of, a polity, but as pluralist political thinkers have without exception insisted, locating the bearer or bearers thereof is notoriously difficult. And if a sovereign agent or agency can sometimes be identified for certain purposes, for example, relationships with other polities and as regards "courts" of last resort for purposes of the resolution of some conflicts internal to the polity, the idea that its writ could reach to, and could be effective concerning, every or even a substantial proportion of life in the polity is a (dangerous) fantasy. At a minimum, it must be said that the reach and certainly the efficacy of its writ are continuously dependent on widespread acceptance of its authority.

Much the same must be said of the analogous notion of a "higher" (highest?) Self that controls and directs all other aspects of the self's thinking and acting. In company with the theorists considered here (and of course numerous others), I have found distinctions such as between lower and higher order, better and worse, desires, volitions, and the like to be useful in thinking about the components of thinking and acting and about the selves who think and act. Making use of such distinctions, however, neither must nor should involve positing some continuing "Master" or Sovereign self that draws the distinctions and employs them to ride herd over all other aspects and characteristics of the self of which it is supposedly the master. That partial and often changing characteristic called an identity consists of, is produced and maintained—to the extent that it is produced and maintained—by the continuing interactions among the diverse elements and forces that operate within it.

Nietzsche's remarks about the "will," one of the frequently proposed candidates for the standing and role of "Master" of the self, are pertinent here. "[I]n every willing there is first of all a multiplicity of feelings: the feeling of a condition to get *away* from, the feeling of a condition to get to; . . . furthermore, an accompanying muscular feeling which, from a sort of habit, begins a game of its own as soon as we 'will'. . . . In the first place, feeling—many different kinds of feeling—is to be recognized as an ingredient in willing. Secondly, there is thinking: in every act of the will there is a thought which gives commands—and we must not imagine that we can separate this thought out of 'willing' and still have something like the will left. Thirdly, the will is not merely a complex of feeling and thinking but above all it is a passion—the passion of commanding. . . . But now let us note the oddest thing about the will, this manifold something for which

people have only one word: because we . . . are simultaneously the com
manders *and* the obeyers, and, as obeyers know the feelings of forcing,
crowding, pressing, resisting, and moving . . . ; on the other hand, we are
in the habit of glossing over this duality with the help of the synthetic concept 'I' " (*Beyond Good and Evil*, 20–22).

This sense of a Self that is in command of its parts, in addition to being
thought by many to be essential to the notion of personal identity, is for
many a source of pleasure. The conception of the sovereign will "adds the
pleasurable feeling of the executing, [of] successful instruments, the sub-
servient 'lower wills or 'lower souls' (for our body is nothing but a social
structure of many souls) to his pleasurable feeling as Commander. L'effet
c'est moi—the same thing happens here that happens in any well constructed
community" (Ibid., 22). Whatever pleasures this sense of a Self that controls the self may afford, and however essential it has been thought to be to
a cogent conception of the self and its identity, we must not reify or sublime (as Wittgenstein liked to say about the urge to treat as singular concepts that stand for no more than "family resemblances") the notion of *the*
Master or Commander that makes the self what it distinctively is.[1]

It might be thought that an emphasis on the complex, fluctuating, and
often internally dissonant character of selves is at odds with the notions,
prominent in all of the thinkers engaged here and in my appreciations of
and appropriations from them, of selves, persons or individuals who are
distinctive to the point of singularity. If there is a tension here, it is not between the idea or, or rather the ideal, of a singular self and the understanding of selves as diverse and changeable.

Montaigne and Nietzsche, Foucault and Hampshire (and Ryle) all insist
on the latter while at the same time strongly valuing and promoting the
former. Singular selves are works in progress in a stronger more continuing
sense than the works of art with which they are sometimes, in important
part appropriately, compared. To use Nietzsche's language, they emerge,
they are created by or out of, the continuing interactions among the feelings that well up in the individual and the thoughts (of course including
the memories) that the individual forms in the course of her lived experience. In this generic respect the creation of a singular self is no different
from the processes by which any and every person develops and sustains
an identity. It is plausible to say that singular individuals have greater powers of imagination than do most other persons, and this may be partly explained by noting that they experience their feelings more intensely and
form their thoughts more self-consciously than do others, and that for this
reason their feelings and thoughts enter into and stimulate their powers of
imagination more forcefully than do the feelings and thoughts of those
from whom they are distinguishable. As argued earlier, imaginativeness is

sometimes identified by processual or procedural criteria as partly distinct from assessments of the "products" of their imaginings. We may say, for example, that individuals are distinctive not because their feelings and thoughts are, substantively speaking, notably different from the feelings and thoughts of numerous other people, but because their feelings are stronger and their beliefs and values more critically formed and more emphatically expressed. For reasons discussed at intervals above, persons who are distinctive in these ways make highly valuable contributions to cultural, social, and especially political life (perhaps particularly to life in a liberal polity).

As developed and promoted by the thinkers here considered, however, it is first and foremost by their fruits that individuals are known to be bearers of individuality and singularity. Whether admirable or otherwise, their feelings and thoughts, and hence their actions, differ from and are commonly at variance with those around them. As with creative artists, they engender new feelings in their fellow human beings and they give the latter things to think about and thoughts to think about them that would not have entered their minds. Having resisted and partly freed themselves from the received, the conventional, and the authoritative, they are themselves free in a distinctive sense and their feeling, thinking, and acting sometimes enlarges and enhances the freedom of others. As with great works of art, the works of art, namely themselves, that they create are gifts to humankind that are beyond all price. Any society or polity that can be called liberal will treasure their presence.

Notes

Chapter 1
Introduction

1. See Flathman, 1987, 1989, 1992, 1998. I do not reiterate the reasoning for these views in the present work. It is my hope and expectation, however, that the following arguments for altered views will make clear the respects in which I am here disputing positions that I previously embraced. Readers left uncertain in this regard can consult the books cited in this note.

2. "Songez que la soumission n'engage a rien pour l'avenir, et que la discipline imposée n'est rien non plus quant on a le bon esprit de se l'imposer soi-même." Augustine to Dominique, Eugene Fromentin, *Dominique*. [Think, dream, that submission makes no engagements for the future, and that discipline imposed is nothing as much as (nothing more than) the good spirit (mind) imposes on itself.]

3. See Flathman, 1998, esp. chs. 4–5 for an elaboration of these considerations. There and more particularly later in this work I explore the Montaignian (but also Foucauldian) notion that resistance to established expectations is itself an option that is always in some sense at my disposal.

4. See Benn and Weinstein in Flathman, ed., 1973.

5. In this regard, cf. Harry G. Frankfurt, 1988. There is a question here as to how real or immediate the disciplining or otherwise constraining forces must be in order that thinking and talking concerning freedom be meaningful or significant (as distinct from true or false). Because, for Montaigne as well as for Foucault and Hobbes, we are never, or virtually never, in circumstances in which no such forces are operative, there is an important sense in which the conceptual point becomes trivial; i.e., the conditions necessary and sufficient to felicitous uses of "freedom" are always and everywhere satisfied. But this is clearly an exaggeration. We look first and foremost to the agent's own assessment of her situation. We can expect that there will be circumstances in which she perceives no immediate or serious obstacles to her desired or intended actions and hence neither thinks nor talks in

the language of freedom. But her perceptions in this regard are in principle corrigible in both directions. She may imagine constraints that do not exist, just as she may be unaware of forces that are in fact controlling, impeding, or directing her thought and action. Despite what I just said about them, Montaigne, Foucault, and Hobbes are aware of and responsive to these possibilities. Looking ahead, it is plausible to say that for Montaigne a main objective of self-discipline, or more generally being at once against and for the self, is to arrive at a condition or state of the self such that one makes realistic, that is, accurate, assessments of the forces to which one is and is not subject and hence—although he never puts the matter this way—makes perspicuous or felicitous uses of the language of freedom. (I am indebted to comments by Peter Digeser on these and related points.)

Chapter 2
Discipline, Freedom, and Resistance

1. Foucault, Michel, 1977.
2. This thematic is also explored, often brilliantly, in Judith Butler, 1997
3. Conducted in 1981, first published in 1982, consulted here in Michel Foucault, 1997.
4. I have not found a place at which Foucault explicitly or formally explicates the concept of "domination" as distinct from various forms of discipline, influence, and control that are (presumably) *less* determinative in their impact on those subjected to them. The most familiar uses of the term (in both French and English), as well as his most frequent employments of it, strongly suggest that he reserves it to circumstances in which power relations leave their subjects—whether objectively as a matter of what any observer would judge to be the realistic alternatives open to the subjects, or subjectively as regards the subjects' assessments of the possibilities at their disposal—with a minimum of practicable choices. As we see below, however, powers that deserve to be called dominant do not and perhaps cannot reduce choices to one. Resistance is *always* possible. Thus "domination" seems to occupy a position toward one end of a continuum of concepts that Foucault uses to identify and assess situations or relationships in which some number of persons are "subject" to the power of other persons or more or less institutionalized arrangements and relationships. Resistance is a possibility all along the continuum, but it is more difficult and less likely to be mounted, or mounted effectively, toward the domination end. These complexities will become important in considering his thoughts concerning "reflective" freedom as a feature of the employment of "techniques of the self" that are chosen but not invented by this or that agent or agency.
5. In another place he makes the point in the following slightly different terms: "Let's say . . . that through studying madness and psychiatry, crime and punishment, I have tried to show how we have indirectly constituted ourselves through the exclusion of some others: criminals, mad people, and so on. And now my present work deals with the question: How did we directly constitute our identity through some ethical techniques of the self which developed through antiquity

down to now?" Foucault, 1988, 146. As the title of his lecture indicates, however, in this presentation Foucault focuses his concern on the specifically political technologies used to form or produce individuals with the characteristics desired by the political agents and agencies who or which discipline them.

6. It is less clear that this would be true of a situation entirely lacking in relations of domination.

7. *If* the views sketched in the last two sentences were Foucault's (there is evidence for and against this reading and I will not attempt to sort the matter out), I disagree with him. As indicated above, it is plausible to think that talk of agency and freedom are meaningful—both literally and in the sense of playing a meaningful, a significant, role in our discourse—only where there is some sort of resistance against or obstacles to action. But I agree with Hobbes that, at least conceptually, the resistance or obstacles can come from non- or extra-human sources. This is not the conceptualization adopted in this work, but the reasons for rejecting it will be developed in later chapters.

8. Foucault's studies of these techniques, in *The History of Sexuality* and in various preparatory and surrounding courses and lectures, essays and interviews, focused on the Greco-Roman world and involved a combination of "archeological"—concerned with the "form" or "codified" elements of practice—and "genealogical"—concerned with the "substance" of practice—approaches and methods. (As already noted, he also gives, intermittently, attention to the beliefs and practices of early Christianity, for the most part presenting the latter as involving more domination than their Greek and especially their Roman counterparts. But the details of his studies of the Christian experience, which were to form the fourth volume of *The History of Sexuality*, remain available only in fragmentary forms.)

9. Perhaps in part as justification for his focus on ancient materials, Foucault remarks that, aside from some primarily "academic" attention to and valorization of self-making in the Renaissance and the phenomenon of "dandyism" in the nineteenth and twentieth centuries (1997, 271), in "our [modern] societies, at a time that is difficult to pinpoint, the care of the self became somewhat suspect. Starting at a certain point, being concerned with oneself was readily denounced as a form of self-love, a form of selfishness or self-interest in contradiction with the interest to be shown in others and of the self-sacrifice required." (All this happened, he goes on to say, "during Christianity; however, I am not simply saying that Christianity is [solely] responsible for it," 284.) Given his view that in the Greco-Roman world "the care of the self was the mode in which individual freedom . . . was reflected as an ethics" (Ibid.), this contrast between ancients and moderns is clearly to the advantage of the former. As an empirical but also an axiological matter, however, these remarks and this periodization, while not without foundation, seem contestable. They of course reflect his concentration on "practical" works, that is works explicitly devoted to how to go about caring for the self as distinct from theoretical works concerned with, say, whether, and if so why, the self is a proper object of care. Foucault would be the last to deny that

"modern" theorists, for example Nietzsche and Heidegger, concerned themselves with the latter questions.

But is it accurate to say that care of the self became suspect in modern societies? At the theoretical level just mentioned, the modern obsession with autonomy, authenticity, and independence, with individual rights, entitlements, and equal concern and respect in Kant and the later Kantians, with self-overcoming and free-spiritedness à la Nietzsche, with self-enactment and self-disclosure à la Oakeshott and Arendt, with *bon* as opposed to *mauvaise foi chez* Sartre and other existentialists, these concerns seem rather to be pervasive. (Anyone disposed to dispute this claim might do worse than to consult the by now large and intensely felt literatures produced by communitarians and republicans, literatures that incessantly lament the dominance of these themes and concerns in "modern" and "postmodern" societies.) Are "modern" societies lacking in "practical" treatises or homilectics akin to those Foucault examined in the Greco-Roman world? Leaving aside the difficulties with the distinction between "theoretical" and "practical," mere mention of such household names as Dale Carnegie and Abigail van Buren—and their innumerable and widely read and followed imitators—puts this view in serious question. *Souci de soi*, rather, would seem to be a, if not the, preoccupation of "modern" women and men.

Needless to say, the foregoing observations in no way diminish the value of Foucault's investigations of *Aphrodisia, Chresis,* and *Enkrateia,* of Dietetics, Economics, and Erotics, among the Greeks and Romans. If they lead us to wonder about his characterizations of modernity and his corresponding choice of research strategies, they perform the more important service of inciting us—as may well have been his intention—to bring the results of his investigations to bear on our own thinking about *epimeleia houtou,* that is, about the relationships between discipline and freedom.

10. "I don't think the word *trapped* [in, by, power relations] is a correct one. It is a struggle, but what I mean by *power relations* is the fact that we are in a strategic situation toward each other. For instance, being homosexuals, we are in a struggle with the government, and government is in a struggle with us. When we deal with the government, the struggle, of course, is not symmetrical, the power situation is not the same; but we are in this struggle, and the continuation of this situation can influence the behavior or nonbehavior of the other. So we are not trapped. We are always in this kind of situation. It means that we always have possibilities, there are always possibilities of changing the situation. We cannot jump outside the situation, and there is no point where you are free from all power relations. But you can always change it. So what I've said does not mean that we are always trapped, but that we are always free—well, anyway, there is always the possibility of changing" (1997, 167). "So I think that *resistance* is the main word, *the key word,* in this dynamic" (Ibid.).

11. Surprising particularly when compared with the "prose" of Nietzsche's anti-Christian and anti-asceticism diatribes in, say, *The Anti-Christ.* (Foucault thought that Nietzsche gave Christianity "too much credit" for the rise of self-

abnegating asceticisms. See 1997, 276.) As Jane Bennett and Peter Digeser have suggested to me, it is arguable that Foucault's own characterizations of Christianity are one-sided and polemical. This is clearly true in the sense that he ignores aspects of Christian belief and practice that differ importantly from those he foregrounds and criticizes. For the purposes of this essay, however, I simply accept and work with his characterizations and critiques of Christian doctrine and practice. I do the same as regards his discussions of Greco-Roman materials.

12. See esp. Michel Foucault, 1990.
13. Michel Foucault, 1990, 80.
14. Ibid., 73, 77.
15. Ibid., 78–9.
16. Ibid., 81–82.
17. Ibid., 92, 97–8, 101, 106.
18. Michel Foucault, 1988, 238–39. Appropriately, given the primary concerns of his book, the passage foregrounds the mastery of sexual desires. This, however, is a salient but by no means an exclusive focus of attention.
19. These remarks have obvious bearing on the frequently discussed question of the freedom to alienate one's freedom by, for example, voluntarily entering into indentured servitude or other forms of temporary or permanent slavery. There are both similarities and differences between the two types of case. On the similarity side, just as it is undeniable that substantial numbers of women and men have chosen to submit themselves unqualifiedly to the more or less embracing authority of monastic institutions and other radical forms of religiously inspired self-renunciation discussed by Foucault, so there are indisputable instances of persons voluntarily submitting themselves to various (secular) forms of servitude. In both types of case, the person in question transfers all or very large parts of what previously had been her freedoms of choice and of action to some person or persons who henceforth will have authority and (presumably) power over her. The two most commonly emphasized differences concern the circumstances under which the submissions/alienations typically occur and the possibility of self-elected cancellation of or exit from the submission. As to the first, in most known or readily imagined cases of submission to slavery, both the person herself and we others (perhaps excepting the master or masters) would regret the circumstances that convince her to choose self-enslavement as her best option. By contrast, there are well-attested instances of individuals electing a monastic life with a profound sense of gratitude for its availability and of exhilaration over the prospects they believe it opens to them. It is important, however, to recognize a continuum not only of possibilities but actualities in these regards. It is not easy to credit the idea of "happy slaves," but it is undeniable that there have been large numbers of persons who have on balance welcomed the possibility of some form of servitude as providing an escape from what they judged to be yet worse life circumstances. In the other direction, it would be naive to think that the monastic life has been not only freely but enthusiastically chosen by all those who have lived it. "Get thee to a convent" is itself a highly resonant phrase and we know that

many members of monastic communities were destined, by others, for this form of life. As regards exit, the indentured servant may have assurances that her servitude will end at a specified time and the chattel slave may have some hope of manumission. Moreover, from, say, a Hobbesian point of view, if there is a contracted obligation to remain in servitude or submission, it ends whenever she who undertook it judges it safe(r) and otherwise to her advantage to terminate it. Of course some of these qualifying conditions also apply to submissions to monastic authority and discipline, but those who enter such arrangements out of an inculcated faith in a dogma and with the expectation that doing so will bring them salvation or some other transcendent good have reasons to sustain their commitment that slaves are far less likely to have—reasons of which, we are told, they are frequently reminded by their superiors.

All of these deeply disciplining and often powerfully dominating (in Foucault's sense) institutions and practices are of course obnoxious from the perspective of liberal individuality, and it is as indefensible as it has been, and remains, common, for them to be supported and enforced by law and general opinion. But I know of no cogent grounds on which to deny that numerous human beings have entered into them freely and with the expectation that by doing so they will enhance their well-being, including enlarging their freedom as they have come to conceive of it. There are very good general reasons for thinking that these forms of discipline are antagonistic to human freedom and we should follow or rather go beyond Foucault in giving eloquent expression to them. But, to repeat, freedom is first and foremost a condition of individuals and their actions, and when it is their own freedoms that are at issue, it is moraline paternalism to deny them the right to use those freedoms as they see fit or to condemn or disdain them for doing so.

20. I can care for others by caring for myself at least in the sense that by taking good care of myself I diminish as much as is in my power the need for others to care for me. Somewhat more affirmatively, to the extent that I have taken good care of myself I enhance my capacities to care for others who need to be cared for. Yet more affirmatively, by taking good care of myself I may make myself into a person whose presence is, in various ways, valuable to others, whom others can care for in the sense of liking or even loving.

21. In my judgment, this view is faithful to or consonant with the thinking of Nietzsche. I will not defend this judgment here, but I address this aspect of the relationship between Foucault and Nietzsche in Chapter Four.

22. Although in a different register, Foucault's hostility toward Descartes is consonant with his rejection of Sartre and his own identification with Nietzsche. The "extraordinary thing in Descartes's texts is that he succeeded in substituting a subject as founder of practices of knowledge for a subject constituted through practices of the self." Whereas the great preponderance of his intellectual predecessors—most emphatically the Stoics—believed that a condition of gaining access to the truth was "work on the self" in the context of a culture and its norms, "Descartes . . . broke with this [conviction] when he said 'To accede to truth, it

suffices that I be *any* subject that can see what is evident.' Evidence is substituted for ascesis at the point where the relationship to the self intersects the relationship to others and the world. . . . [For Descartes] [i]t suffices that the relationship to the self reveals to me the obvious truth of what I see for me to apprehend the truth definitively. . . . With Descartes, direct evidence is enough. After Descartes, we have a nonascetic subject of knowledge" (1997, 278–9). In this perspective, Foucault follows Nietzsche in reviving, against Descartes and followers of his such as Kant, the idea and ideal of the "ascetic" self, that is the self who seeks truth and "self-overcoming" or "free-spiritedness" in important part through work on the self itself.

23.   I find persuasive Jane Bennett's suggestion to me that "care for the self" has, fundamentally or most generally, the objective of making and sustaining the self as a "subject" in the second of the two senses discussed earlier. With rare if any exceptions, selves can become subjects in this sense only when situated in a culture, society, and polity. At the same time, this very situatedness threatens to destroy their "subjectivity" (to reduce them to ciphers, to members of the mob or herd). Hence they must at once submit to and resist the disciplines to which they are subjected.

24.   Note that if we assimilated them, reduced them, conceptually, one to the other, not only the subtlety but the coherence of Foucault's elaborations/reflections would disappear.

25.   From at least Thoreau forward, doctrines concerning civil disobedience, particularly those according to which resisting injustice is a cultural duty, constitute a powerful expression of this idea/ideal.

26.   Nevertheless, throughout Volume III of *The History of Sexuality* he underlines the centrality, for the Romans of the first and second centuries, of "individualism" understood as primarily concerned with "the intensity of the relations to self, that is, of the forms in which one is called upon to take oneself as an object of knowledge and a field of action, so as to transform, correct and purify oneself." For Epictetus, care of the self is "a privilege-duty, a gift-obligation that ensures our freedom while forcing us to take ourselves as the object of all our diligence" (1988, 47). In their particulars, the privilege and gift, the duty and the obligation, may come to us through the medium of our history and our culture; but ultimately or fundamentally (ontologically?) the privilege/gift is ours by nature—is due to the fact that by nature we, all of us, are rational beings. And if the "duty/obligation" is owed to anyone, it is owed by me to myself, by you to yourself. Thus my reading/appropriation may be tendentious but it is not without grounding in the texts I have mainly consulted.

Chapter 3
The Self Against and for Itself: I

1.   *The Complete Essays of Montaigne*, Book III, Essay 13, 820–21. Translated by Donald M. Frame. Second Edition. (Stanford: Stanford University Press, 1958.) Hereafter in this chapter "F" followed by Book, Essay, and page number. Where it

seems pertinent to do so, I also give references to and sometimes quotations from the French. For this purpose I have used Michel de Montaigne, *Les Essais*, Edition de Pierre Villey, Trois Livres, avec Appendices, Sources, Index. Deuxieme Edition. (Paris: Quadrige/Presses Universitaires de France, 1992). Hereafter in this chapter "V", followed by the Livre and page number. In the Villey edition, the passages quoted above are from III, 1072, and it is perhaps worth noting that the phrase Frame translates as "so sick for freedom" reads "Je Si affady après la liberté" which Villey's note modernizes as "Je suis Si avide de" (Ibid.).

2. I have not found a citation, by name, of Sextus in the *Essays*. Villey speaks of those parts of "Apologie de Raymond Sebond" (II, 12) that "s'inspire directment de Sextus Empiricus et qui contient les declarations pyrrhoniennes les plus fermes" (V, 436) [are directly inspired by Sextus Empiricus and that contain the firmest declarations of pyrrhonian thinking] and later says that "Montaigne a etudie Sextus Empiricus . . . environ de 1576" (612) [Montaigne studied Sextus Empiricus around 1576]. In any case, it is impossible to deny the similarities between Montaigne's formulations in "Raymond Sebond" and those of Sextus. I argue below, however, that these similarities should not be viewed as an "attitude passagere" (Ibid., 437) [a no more than passing attitude or tendency] but rather as a continuing and quite central dimension of Montaigne's thinking about freedom.

3. Sextus Empiricus, *Outlines of Pyrrhonism*, Book I, Ch. III. Because of its ready availability, I for the most part quote from Philip Hallie's selections from Sextus's works as presented in Sextus Empiricus, *Selections from the Major Writings on Scepticism. Man & God*, ed., Phillip P. Hallie, Sanford C. Etheridge, trans. (Indianapolis: Hackett Publishing Co., 1985). Hereafter Sextus, "H." Where it is pertinent, I also give citations and sometimes quotations from the complete Loeb edition translated by R. G. Bury (Cambridge, Mass.: Harvard University Press, 1933). Hereafter Sextus, "B." In the passage referred to above, Hallie gives "discipline" (32) and Bury "school" (Vol. I, 5).

4. If we distinguish between capacity on the one hand and enablement or empowerment on the other, we might say that all or nearly all human beings are born with or naturally acquire the capacity for skepticism, but only those who practice the appropriate forms of self-discipline develop the ability or the power sufficient to it.

5. Is there, to follow but perhaps to parody Harry Frankfurt (1988), a yet higher self that monitors the activities of the skeptical self, preventing it from excesses that would reduce the questing, asserting self to a nullity? And a further self that . . . ?

6. Cf. Nietzsche's thought that "truth is a woman who has reason for not letting us see her reasons." *The Gay Science*, 38. (New York: Vintage Books, 1974.)

7. "We do not escape philosophy by stressing immoderately the sharpness of pain [or need, or death] and the weakness of man. For we force her to fall back on these unanswerable replies [no skepticism here!]: If it is bad to live in need, at least there is no need to live in need. No one suffers long except by his own fault. He who has not the courage to suffer either death or life, who neither resists nor

flees, what can we do with him" (F, I, 14, 47). "And death is not the remedy for just one malady, but the remedy for all ills. It is a very sure haven, which is never to be feared, and often to be sought. It comes to the same thing whether man gives himself his death or suffers, whether he runs to meet his day or awaits it. . . . [But] The most voluntary death is the fairest. Life depends on the will of others; death, on our own" (F, II, 3, 252).

8. Cf. Sextus, H, esp. 62–4: Sextus, B, Vol.1, esp. 67, 69. Sextus generalizes the argument in saying "we ourselves are party to the disagreement" (H, 49, 56, 58: B, esp. 37, 59, 67) and yet further with his somewhat sardonic view that reason is (as Hallie characterizes Sextus's position 34, n. 1) a "rogue"; is itself undisciplined and yet aspires to discipline other parts of the soul and the body. Montaigne characterized reason as a "two handled jug" (F, II, 12, 438) and "a two-edged and dangerous sword . . . [and] a many-sided stick" (F, II, 17, 497). For later expressions of these views by Montaigne, see esp. III, 8, 13, and III, 13, 815–16.

9. For a brief but pungent summary of this tradition, see Hallie's Introduction, H, 5–9.

10. As regards the second "head," Bury translates "constraint of the passions" rather than "compulsion of the feelings," but I take him to intend Sextus's meaning to be not that we constrain the passions but rather that they constrain or compel us. B, I, 17.

11. The French is "C'est Folie de Rapporter le Vray et le Faux à Nostre Suffisance." Villey explains "Suffisance" as "Faculté de juger" (V, 178, n. 1). As Villey underlines, although there is reason to date the original composition of the essay to 1572, it contains numerous additions that do little or nothing to qualify its main original assertions.

12. F, III, 13, 821, emphasis added. Note that this passage immediately precedes the remarks about the authority of and obedience to law quoted just above.

13. III, 13, 831. The sentence ends "unless to those, if any there are, to which bondage and slavery is useful" (Ibid.). "If any there are" seems to express the skepticism pervasive in the opening pages of this essay. However this may be, the apparent suggestion that a kind of bondage or slavery might be useful must be read with and against Montaigne's general condemnation of all forms of servitude and also those of his thoughts pungently expressed in "Of the Useful and the Honorable." "We poorly argue the honor and beauty of an action from its utility, and we commit a fallacy in thinking that everyone is obliged to perform—and that it is honorable for everyone to perform—an action merely because it is useful" (F, III, I, 610). I return to the distinction between the honorable and the useful below.

14. Cf. Proust: "L'habitude! Amenageuse habile mais bien lente et qui commence par laisser souffrir notre esprit pendant des semaines dans une installation provisoire; mais que malgré tout est bien heureux de trouver, car sans l'habitude et reduit a ses seuls moyens il serait impuissant à nous rendre un logis habitable." (*Du Côté de chez Swann.*) I will not attempt a translation of this beautiful passage, but I take it to express an understanding very close to the one I attributed to

Montaigne above. As we will see with Montaigne, as at other places, Proust significantly qualifies the idea.

15. Cf. II, 10, "Of Books:" "For faults often escape our eyes; but infirmity of judgment consists in not being able to perceive them when another reveals them to us. Knowledge and truth can lodge in us without judgment, and judgment also without them. Indeed the recognition of ignorance is one of the fairest and surest testimonies of judgment that I find" (F, 297).

16. See esp. II, 7. Friendship in the highest sense is an exception which I discuss below.

17. In his introductory remarks concerning this essay ("Of the Useful and the Honorable"; "De l'Utile et de l'Honneste"), Villey comments on the ways in which it at once associates Montaigne with and differentiates him from Machiavelli and the "mirror of princes" literature more generally. See V, 789–90. Briefly, Montaigne acknowledges, recognizes, not only the unavoidability but the excusability of actions that are "utile" but not "honneste" but he wants to distance himself from the former, to leave them to others less scrupulous than he. Is this no better than a squeamish aversion to "dirty hands"? Or, does Montaigne think that in the longer human term there can be useful actions only if there are persons who are "honest"? The latter. Elsewhere Montaigne comments, almost always disparagingly, on the unavoidable predicaments of kings and others who hold public office (I, 42, esp. 194–6) and on his hatred of sycophancy and the courtier mentality so often associated with office and office holders. See I, 13. His own stance toward those in positions of authority is nicely expressed in "Of the Art of Discussion" and earlier in his essay on "The Education of Children": "What I myself adore in kings is the crowd of their adorers. All deference and submission is due to them, except that of the understanding. My reason is not trained to bend and bow, it is my knees" (III, 8, 714). The teacher will see to it that his pupil is a "very loyal, very affectionate, and very courageous servant of his prince; but he will cool in him any desire to attach himself to that prince otherwise than by sense of public duty. Besides several other disadvantages which impair our freedom by these private obligations, the judgment of a man who is hired and bought is either less whole and less free, or tainted with imprudence and ingratitude. A courtier can have neither the right nor the will to speak and think otherwise than favorably of the master who among so many thousands of other subjects has chosen him to train and raise up with his own hand. This favor and advantage corrupt his freedom, not without some reason, and dazzle him" (I, 26, 114).

18. It also demeans and diminishes virtue itself. Thinkers such as Aristotle, Carneades, and Cicero, who give "glory the first rank among external goods" promote a view "so false that I am vexed that it could ever have entered the head of a man who had the honor of bearing the name of philosopher." If this view were correct, "we should be virtuous only in public; and there would be no point in keeping under rule and order the operations of the soul, where lies the seat of virtue, except in so far as they should come to the knowledge of others" (470).

19. Montaigne's dismissive reference to that part of his life that "lies in the knowledge [of him] of his friends" clearly concerns friendship in the casual sense of neighbors and acquaintances, not the deep relationship that he had with La Boétie and that he celebrates in I, 28, "Of Friendship." In the friendship he speaks of there "our souls mingle and blend with each other so completely that they efface the seam that joined them, and cannot find it again" (139); there is a "complete fusion of the wills" and the relationship becomes "that of one soul in two bodies" (141), thereby obviating the self-other distinction on which the passage quoted above depends. Friendship in this profound and indeed mysterious sense is extremely rare and Montaigne thinks that no person can have more than one such friend.

20. The workability of this practical ethic, of course, depends on the good fortune of living in a time and a place in which there are no significant conflicts or dissonances among the customs, conventions, and laws to which one is expected to conform. In assessing Montaigne's endorsement of such a practical ethic, we must bear in mind not only his explicit qualifications to and of it, but the background circumstance that he lived in a time and a place riven with disagreement and conflict.

21. Even the counsels of moderation advanced by the philosophers "are in my opinion still a bit rigorous" (681).

22. Oddly, given the passages thus far quoted, the essay ends by arguing that sexual relations are for the young, virile, and beautiful, and that the elderly, both men and women, should abstain from acting on what he admits are their continuing physical desires. He is "ashamed to find myself amid this green and ardent youth, 'Whose member firmer stands, in its undaunted pride/ Than a young tree upon a mountainside' " Horace (682).

23. In a familiar sense of "Epicurean," in the essays just discussed we could characterize Montaigne as taking an Epicurean turn. (Needless to say, this would not be the sense in which Montaigne himself invoked Epicurus when praising the concealed life.) I am of course by no means the first to suggest that in his later essays Montaigne's thought went in an Epicurean direction; the sequencing schema Stoic then Skeptic then Epicurean, is a familiar feature of Montaignian commentary. I have myself employed these stylizations because I believe they usefully characterize recurrent features of Montaigne's thinking. As already indicated in part, however, I reject the notion of a clearly delineable sequencing. Stoical elements remain in the latest essays and amendments, there is skepticism from beginning to end, and while the "Epicurean" tendencies are most pronounced in the later writings, they are discernible as early as the first versions of "That to Philosophize is to Learn to Die" (I, 20).

25. The distinction between natural and artificial, Montaigne insists, should not be confused with that between thoughtless and thoughtful, mindless and reflective. "[L]est it be thought that all this is done through a simple and servile bondage to usage and through the pressure of the authority of their ancient customs, with-

out reasoning or judgment, and because their minds are so stupid that they cannot take any other course," he gives examples of "their capacity" for nuanced and discriminating performances (158). He has in mind a knowing, we might say a canny, simplicity.

Chapter 4
The Self Against and for Itself: II

1. Cf. Wittgenstein on ostensive definition: "an ostensive definition can be variously interpreted in *every* case" (Ludwig Wittgenstein, *Philosophical Investigations*, I, 28: 14).

2. Cf. Balzac: "Il exist des pensées auxquelles nous obeissons sans les connaitre: elles sont en nous a notre insu. Quoique cette reflexion puisse paraitre plus paradoxale que vrai, chaque personne de bonne foi en trouvera mille preuves dans sa vie." (*La Femme de Trente Ans.*) Not quite Nietzsche's thought, but resonant with my remarks in the paragraph above.

3. It might be thought that the latter three are less attentive than is Nietzsche to the respects in which control and discipline emanate from and are, in part, imposed on the individual by society and culture. But this would be a mistake in all three cases. A substantial part of Epictetus's thinking is concerned with slavery and his attempts to cope with it. Montaigne's awareness of and even his readiness to go along, at least outwardly, with custom and convention are if anything more pervasive and emphatic than Nietzsche's. And Foucault repeatedly underscores the respects in which the regimens recommended by Epictetus are rarely invented by individuals but come to them via their participation in cultural conventions and practices.

4. Bill Connolly has suggested to me that the concept of "autonomy" does not adequately capture or express those of Nietzsche's thoughts presently under discussion. Although I think it works well as regards the ideas and forces that Nietzsche opposes, I agree that it does not convey the sense of exuberance and abundance that Nietzsche associates with the free spirit.

5. The following remarks draw on Flathman, 1987.

Chapter 5
Stuart Hampshire on Freedoms and Unfreedoms of Mind and of Action

1. The present chapter is organized as follows:
Freedoms and Unfreedoms of Mind
Thought and thinking
  1. Conditions of and limitations on the mind and on thinking
  2. Operations and capacities of thinking; its relations to action
    a. Self-awareness, identity and singularity
    b. Beliefs and intentions
    c. Conceptions of the good and powers

2. On mind versus brain see Ibid.: 3, 5, 7 and *passim; Freedom of the Individual*, esp. 17, 62–63 (hereafter *FOI*); *Morality and Conflict*, 48, 56, 59–63 (hereafter *M&C; Innocence and Experience*, 36 (hereafter *I&E*). On behaviorism and "scientific" linguistic, social scientific, and historical reductionisms and unwarranted generalizations, see *Thought and Action*, 174–81 (hereafter *T&A*) or *Thought and Action: A New Edition with Original Postscript* (hereafter *T&An*); *FOI*, 27–28, 52, 93, 112; *Public and Private Morality*, 3–5, 40 (hereafter *P&PM*); *M&C*, 2, 6–7, 28, 48, 56–63, 80–81, 142, 160; *I&E*, 179.

3. *T&A*, 31–2, 18, 19. As readers of Montaigne, Foucault, and especially Nietzsche will recognize, these views are closely congruent with views of the thinkers just mentioned. (The same should be said of the passages concerning corporeality discussed just above.) The passages just considered, however, underline Hampshire's view that an at least minimally functioning body is a necessary condition of and places limitations on thought and thinking. No particular thought or pattern of thinking can be sufficiently explained by reference to the material world, but the possibility of thought cannot be fully explained without such reference. It is in part in this sense that he advances "a kind of materialism" (*FOM*, last essay).

4. This seems to be his view, closely similar to Hannah Arendt's assessment of Eichmann, of many Nazis, and followers of Stalin. See *FOM*, 66–68, 70–77. There may also be human beings who are entirely incapable of thinking, but it is doubtful that Hampshire would regard them as persons.

5. It should also noted that in places Hampshire seems to endorse something like Nietzsche's thought that there are reasons that reason does not know. See, e.g., *FOM*, 16. For references to Nietzsche that might suggest this comparison, see 1–2 and *I&E*, 156–57.

6. Some of these statements in FOI may evidence a change of mind on Hampshire's part. In *T&A* he says that "Intentions, like beliefs, are not always and necessarily the outcome of a process of thought or of a datable act of decision. They may, like beliefs, effortlessly form themselves in my mind without conscious and controlled deliberation. . . . Any human mind is the locus of unquestioned and silently formed intentions and of unquestioned and silently formed beliefs" (101). As to beliefs, the passages in question might be reconciled by saying that beliefs are subject to challenge, and when challenged the person who holds them must either give up the belief or try to show that it does satisfy some standard of correctness. In any case, the position taken in *FOI* predominates in Hampshire's texts.

7. As anticipated by the phrase "the drifting of ideas through the mind," Hampshire goes on to bring these thoughts to bear on controversies concerning so-called private languages and Cartesian notions of *thinking* as opposed to imagining, dreaming, wishing as occurring exclusively or primarily within the private place that is the mind. See esp. 157–64.

8. The theme of irreducible diversity is developed at length and with great emphasis on ineliminable conflicts among conceptions of the good in *M&C*, esp. ch. 7. On diversity and its value he says that having "the power to invent ways to think about

differently characterized alternatives, and to weight good and bad features of situations and of actions and ways of life on different scales, is one distinction of the species; it is one power that makes friends interesting to each other and that makes the species interesting to itself, and that makes its future interesting. The single criterion and single aim theories discard the peculiar interest of the species, and the interest of its future, as perpetually open to unforeseen alternatives through continuous thought. The single criterion arrests development, both historical and personal" (*I&E*, 28). The emphasis on "powers" in this and related passages leads directly to the next concept to be discussed. And because power in most of his discussion of it concerns overcoming and resisting obstacles to and forces opposing desired and intended actions, it is also directly pertinent to later discussions of discipline and resistance and their significance for freedom.

9. In radical formulations of this last possibility, Sartre and numerous others have argued that there are cases in which "failing to do something, because of an alleged inability, are to be counted as cases of lack of will to do it." These arguments propose "a thorough-going conceptual revision" and have a "systematic and metaphysical basis" which Hampshire says he is omitting, presumably because he is focusing on what he takes to be the best established uses of the concepts in question.

Chapter 6
Stuart Hampshire on Freedoms and Unfreedoms of Action

1. The present chapter is organized as follows:
I. Freedom and Thinking
II. Skepticism and Individuality: Discipline and Freedom
III. Morals, Politics and Freedom: Justice and Individuality
IV. Concluding Thoughts Concerning Hampshire (This section addresses issues discussed in both Chapters 5 and 6.)

2. The phrase "main relevant considerations" signals a qualification that Hampshire enters in the notion that justice should be *purely*, exclusively, procedural. "[J]ustice and fairness are always *in part* procedural notions; a decision . . . can be accepted as completely just and fair only if the reasoning that supports it has been adequate . . . (Ibid., italics added). I take "adequate" to refer to the quality of the reasons presented, not merely to the fact that they have been voiced and heard. This reading is supported by a previous sentence: "The notion of rationality in practical issues, as Aristotle knew, does not allow the evaluation of the reasons for a decision to be cleanly separated from the evaluation of the decision itself" (Ibid.). The reasons themselves must be evaluated, not merely counted. This is of course also implied by the idea that the assembly will "dismiss" some of the arguments presented to it. I return to this qualification below, but it can be said at once that it is a welcome amendment to the sometimes overly formal or even mechanical character of Hampshire's conception of justice.

3. The significance of these points, perhaps particularly the difficulties with the figure of "weighing," is heightened if individuality, including singularity, is regarded as a high-order value. As Hampshire rightly insists, individualities are commensurable and hence can be weighed on the same scale, only in the formal sense that they are all individualities. Substantively speaking it is of their essence that they are incommensurable. I return to this point in the Conclusion.

Conclusion

1. Cf. Gilbert Ryle: "I hope to refute the doctrine that there exists a Faculty, immaterial Organ, or Ministry, corresponding to what it describes as 'volitions.' I must however make it clear from the start that this refutation will not invalidate the distinctions which we all quite properly draw between voluntary and involuntary actions and between strong-willed and weak-willed persons. It will, on the contrary, make clearer what is meant [and not meant] by 'voluntary' and 'involuntary,' by 'strong-willed' and 'weak-willed' by emancipating these ideas from bondage to an absurd hypothesis" (*The Concept of Mind*, 63).

Bibliography of Works Cited

Balzac, Honoré de. *La femme de trente ans.*

Butler, Judith. 1997. *Excitable Speech* (New York: Routledge).

Cavell, Stanley. 1979. *The Claim of Reason* (London: Oxford University Press).

Empiricus, Sextus. 1933. *Outlines of Pyrrhonism.* Trans. R. G. Bury (Cambridge, Mass.: Harvard University Press).

————. 1985. *Selections from the Major Writings on Scepticism. Man & God.* Trans. Sanford C. Etheridge, ed. Phillip P. Hallie (Indianapolis: Hackett Publishing Co.)

Flathman, Richard E. Ed. 1973. *Concepts in Social and Political Philosophy* (New York: Macmillan).

————. 1987. *The Philosophy and Politics of Freedom* (Chicago: University of Chicago Press).

————. 1989. *Toward a Liberalism* (Ithaca: Cornell University Press).

————. 1992. *Willful Liberalism* (Ithaca: Cornell University Press).

————. 1993. *Thomas Hobbes: Skepticism, Individuality and Chastened Politics* (Newbury Park, Calif.: Sage Publications).

————. 1998. *Reflections of a Would-Be Anarchist* (Minneapolis: University of Minnesota Press).

Foucault, Michel. 1977. *Discipline and Punish* (New York: Pantheon).

————. *The History of Sexuality.* Vol. I, 1978, *The Will to Truth*, Robert Hurley, trans. (New York: Pantheon Books); Vol. II, 1990, *The Use of Pleasure*, trans. Robert Hurley (New York: Vintage Books); Vol III, 1988, *The Care of the Self*, trans. Robert Hurley (New York: Vintage Books).

————. 1988. "The Political Technology of Individuals." In *Technologies of the Self: Seminar with Michel Foucault.* Edited by Luther H. Martin et al. (Amherst: The University of Massachusetts Press).

————. 1997. *Ethics, Subjectivity and Truth. The Essential Works of Michel Foucault, 1954–1984*, Vol. One. Paul Rabinow, ed. Translated by Robert Hurley and others (New York: The New Press).

Frankfurt, Harry G. 1988. *The Importance of What We Care About* (Cambridge: Cambridge University Press).

Fromentin, Eugene. 1994. *Dominique* (Paris: Bookking International, 1994).

Hampshire, Stuart. 1965. *Freedom of the Individual* (New York: Harper & Row).

———. 1971. *Freedom of Mind* (Princeton: Princeton University Press).

———. 1989. *Innocence and Experience* (Cambridge, Mass.: Harvard University Press).

———. 1983. *Morality and Conflict* (Cambridge, Mass.: Harvard University Press).

———. with Ronald Dworkin, Thomas Nagel, T. M. Scanlon, and Bernard Williams, eds. 1978. *Public & Private Morality* (Cambridge: Cambridge University Press).

———. 1962. *Spinoza* (Harmondsworth, UK: Penguin Books).

———. 1959. *Thought & Action* (New York: The Viking Press).

———. 1982. *Thought & Action*, A New Edition with Original Postscript (Notre Dame, Ind.: University of Notre Dame Press).

Montaigne, Michel de. 1958. *The Complete Essays of Montaigne.* Translated by Donald M. Frame. (Stanford: Stanford University Press).

———. 1992. *Les Essais.* Edition de Pierre Villey. Trois livres, avec Appendices, Sources, Index. Deuxième Edition (Paris: Quadrige/Presses Universitaires de France, 1992).

Nietzsche, Friedrich. 1968. *The Anti-Christ.* Trans. R. J. Hollingdale (Harmondsworth, UK: Penguin Books).

———. 1955. *Beyond Good and Evil.* Trans. Marianne Cowan (Chicago: Henry Regenry).

———. 1956. *The Birth of Tragedy.* Trans. Francis Golffing (Garden City, N.Y.: Doubleday Anchor).

———. 1982. *Daybreak.* Trans. R. J. Hollingdale (New York: Cambridge University Press).

———. 1979. *Ecce Homo.* Trans. R. J. Hollingdale (London: Penguin Books).

———. 1974. *The Gay Science.* Trans. Walter Kaufmann (New York: Vintage Books).

———. 1956. *The Genealogy of Morals.* Trans. Francis Golffing (Garden City, N.Y.: Doubleday.

———. 1966. *Human, All Too Human.* Trans. R. J. Hollingdale (Cambridge: Cambridge University Press).

———. 1979. *Philosophy and Truth.* Selections from Nietzsche's Notebooks of the early 1870's. Edited and Translated by Daniel Breazeale (Atlantic Highlands, N.J.: Humanities Press International).

———. 1957. *Thus Spake Zarathustra.* Trans. Marianne Cowan (Chicago: Gateway Editions).

———. 1968. *Twilight of the Idols.* Trans. R. J. Hollingdale (Harmondsworth: Penguin Books).

———. 1967. *Will to Power.* Trans. Walter Kaufmann and R. J. Hollingdale (New York: Vintage Books).

Proust, Marcel. *Du côté de chez Swann.*

Ryle, Gilbert. 1949. *The Concept of Mind* (New York: Barnes & Noble).

Wittgenstein, Ludwig. 1953. *Philosophical Investigations.* Trans. G. E. M. Anscombe (New York: The Macmillan Company).

Index

"*À Demain les Affaires*" (Montaigne), 44

akrasia, 19

Alcibiades, 30

Anscombe, G. E. M., 116

Anti-Christ, The (Nietzsche), 79

aphrodism, 19

"Apology for Raymond Sebond" (Montaigne), 38, 40, 42–43, 45

Arcesilaus, 57

Arendt, Hannah, 18

Aristippus, 57

Aristotle, 58, 59, 61, 138, 153

askeses, 15, 16

ataraxia, 40

Benn-Weinstein argument, 2

Berlin, Isaiah, 54

Beyond Good and Evil (Nietzsche), 168

Bolsheviks, 147

Cahn, Sammy, 28, 29

Care of the Self, The (Foucault), 34, 81

Cato, 41, 55, 61

Cavell, Stanley, 48

chresis, 19

Christianity
    Foucault's review of practices in, 15–22, 24–25, 27, 34, 164, 174–75*n*11
    Nietzsche remarks on, 83–84, 91, 93, 164

Chrysippus, 57

Cicero, 55, 58

civil disobedience, 154

Cleanthes, 42

communitarian societies, 166

constraint, 3

criminality, 11

Crispin, 52

Daybreak (Nietzsche), 76, 80

delinquency, 11

de lui-même, 20

democracy, 85–86, 97

Derrida, Jacques, 50

Descartes, 31, 33, 176–77*n*22

"Dietetics" (Montaigne), 60

Diogenes, 57
Discipline and Punish (Foucault), 11, 12
Discourses, 81

Ecce Homo (Nietzsche), 87
Empiricus, Sextus, 3, 38–40, 41, 43, 178*n*3, 179*n*8
enkrateia, 16, 19, 20, 21, 25
Epictetus, 29, 34, 41, 80, 81, 82, 182*n*3
Epicureans, 30, 32, 34
Epicurus, 42, 57–58, 181*n*23
epimelia houtou, 19, 25, 26, 27
erotic relations, 28–29
erotics, 19
Essays (Montaigne), 51, 54, 81
"European Nihilism" (Nietzsche), 78
existential thesis, 7

felicity, 19
Ficino, 59
Flathman, Richard, 77, 86, 88
fortuna, 18
Foucault, Michel, 3, 4, 6
    on ancient Greek and Roman practices, 13, 14, 15, 16–17, 19, 22–31, 33–34, 173–74*n*9
    on "*assujettissement*," 12, 14
    on Christian beliefs and practices, 15–22, 24–25, 27, 34, 164, 174–75*n*11
    on concept of domination, 12, 172*n*4
    on ethics and freedom, 14–15, 20–21
    on freedom and discipline of self, 25, 164, 175–76*n*19
    on "local resistance," 11, 13
    on "moderation" of the self, 20
    on "problematization" of human interactions, 12
    on "resistance" to power, 33–34

    on "self-preoccupation," 30
    on techniques of the self, 12–14, 172–73*n*5, 173–74*n*9
    on "total power" and freedom, 32
Frame, Donald M., 44, 47, 177–78*n*1
Freedom of Mind (Hampshire), 102, 104, 114, 122, 126–27, 137
Freedom of the Individual (Hampshire), 105, 183*n*2
"freedoms2," 8
"freedoms3," 8

Gay Science, The (Nietzsche), 31, 66, 69, 75, 77, 78, 82
Genealogy of Morals, The (Nietzsche), 73, 76, 77, 83

Hallie, Philip, 39
Hampshire, Stuart, 3–6
    on beliefs and intentions, 114–20
    on conceptions of good and powers, 120–24
    conditions of and limitations on the mind and thinking, 103–8
    on freedom and thinking, 125–33, 166
    on the freedoms and unfreedoms of action, 125–61
    on the freedoms and unfreedoms of mind, 102–24
    on a minimally decent society, 7
    on morals, politics, and freedom, 136–56, 184*n*2
    on self-awareness, identity, and singularity, 112–14, 166
    shared views with other thinkers, 133–34
    on skepticism and individuality, 133–36, 165
    on thought and thinking, 103–24
Hebrero, Leon, 59
hermeneutics, 21

History of Sexuality, The (Foucault), 22, 133, 177*n*26
Hobbes, Thomas, 3, 19, 46, 50, 54, 61
Human, All Too Human (Nietzsche), 65, 66, 84, 97
Hume, David, 25, 111

Innocence and Experience (Hampshire), 105, 109, 110–11, 113, 120–21, 134, 137, 142, 146, 154, 155, 157, 183*n*2
"It Is Folly to Measure the True and False by Our Own Capacity" (Montaigne), 49

James, William, 89
je, 25

Kant, Immanuel, 50, 107, 111, 119, 126, 138, 141, 150

La Böetie, E., 153
Les Essais (Montaigne), 37
le soi pour lui-même, 56
"Let Business Wait Till Tomorrow" (Montaigne), 44
liberal ideology, 5
Lucretius, 43
lui-même, 20
Luther, Martin, 65
Lycurgus, 61

Machiavelli, Niccolò, 146–48
Marcus Aurelius, 81
mauvaise foi, 55
Merleau-Ponty, M., 158
Metrocles, 42
Metrodorus, 42, 57
moi, 20, 25
Montaigne, Michel de, 3, 4, 5
  on the appetites of the body, 60, 181*n*22
  on customs and habits, 50–53, 55–56, 166
  on developing skeptical abilities, 40–53, 165
  essays of, 37–64
  on external submission and inner life, 53–56, 59
  on man living appropriately, 62–64
  as Mayor of Bordeaux, 56
  "negative" understanding of freedom by, 38, 39–40
  on the self and itself, 7
  on the self for itself, 57–61
  on suspension of mind and spirit, 39–40, 178*n*4–5
  as a "virtue theorist," 44
Morality and Conflict (Hampshire), 104–6, 108, 110–11, 130, 135–37, 140, 145–46, 148–50, 152, 183*n*2

Nazism, 146, 147–48, 150
negative freedom, 8
Nicocles, 30
Nietzsche, Friedrich, 3, 4, 5–6
  on Christian practices, 24–25, 83–84, 91, 93, 164
  on cognition and conation, 66–72, 89–90
  on control, resistance, and freedom, 82–89
  on discipline and control, 72–82, 90–91, 92–94, 164
  on faith and the faithful, 75–76
  on freedom and free-spiritedness, 66, 89–91, 92
  on ideals of autonomy and freedom, 98–99
  on nationalism and democracy, 84–86, 97

Nietzsche, Friedrich *(continued)*
  on the nature of freedom, 95–96
  on passion and reason, 66–72
  on "pathos of distance," 56
  on the practice of creativity, 30–31, 165
  on seeking knowledge, 67–68
  on the self and itself, 7–8, 168

Oakeshott, Michael, 50
"Of Ancient Customs" (Montaigne), 51
"Of Cannibals" (Montaigne), 60
"Of Custom, and Not Easily Changing an Accepted Law" (Montaigne), 51, 54
"Of Democritus and Heraclitus" (Montaigne), 45, 54
"Of Experience" (Montaigne), 37, 45, 50, 51
"Of Glory" (Montaigne), 57
"Of Husbanding the Will" (Montaigne), 42, 56
"Of Moderation," 59
"Of Physiognomy" (Montaigne), 45
"Of Prayers" (Montaigne), 40
"Of Presumption" (Montaigne), 49
"Of Some Verses of Virgil" (Montaigne), 59
"Of the Affection of Fathers for Their Children" (Montaigne), 53
"Of Vanity" (Montaigne), 45
"Of Virtue" (Montaigne), 41–42
"On Experience" (Montaigne), 60
"On Truth and Lies in a Non-Moral Sense" (Nietzsche), 89
Outlines of Pyrrhonism (Sextus), 38, 39, 178n3

peut-être même un trahison, 20
Philosophy and Truth (Nietzsche), 89
Plato, 61
Plutarch, 51

polity, 21, 169
positive freedom, 8
Propertius, 59
Public & Private Morality (Hampshire), 105–7, 128, 135, 141, 146, 154, 157, 183n
Pyrrho, 42, 46–48

Rawls, John, 111, 138, 153, 159
reflechi, 19
Reflections of a Would-Be Anarchist (Flathman), 50
regret/remorse, 18, 19
Rousseau, Jean-Jacques, 61
Ryle, Gilbert, 168, 185n1

Sartre, Jean-Paul, 30–31, 33
savoir-faire, 18
Schoenberg, A., 164
self, 7, 12–14, 172–73n5, 173–74n9
self-knowing, 29, 168
Seneca, 29–30, 34, 41, 42, 45, 81
Sextus, Empiricus, 47–48
singularity, 6
"Social Triumph of the Sexual Will, The" (Foucault), 12
Socrates, 41, 52, 54, 61, 62
souci de soi, 15, 25
sovereignty, 167
Spinoza, Baruch, 126
Stalinism, 146, 147, 150
Stoics, 29, 30, 32, 34, 41, 42, 47, 81

Taylor, Charles, 2
tehknes, 15, 17, 29
Thought & Action (Hampshire), 103, 104, 106, 108, 112, 115, 116, 134, 136, 137, 152, 183n2
Thought & Action, Postscript (Hampshire), 125, 135, 139, 140, 158
Thus Spake Zarathustra (Nietzsche), 69, 79, 86–87

une deception, 20
unfreedom, 18

Vietnam, 147
Villey, Pierre, 40, 177–78*n*1
virtus, 18

"We Taste Nothing Pure"
    (Montaigne), 44

"Will to Power as Knowledge"
    (Nietzsche), 66
Will to Power (Nietzsche), 5, 65–67,
    78, 79, 80, 82, 87, 89, 156,
    167–68
Wittgenstein, Ludwig, 116
Wittgensteinian theory, 2

Zarathustra, 72